1992

POPULAR CULTURE, SCHOOLING, AND EVERYDAY LIFE

Critical Studies in Education Series

BETWEEN CAPITALISM & DEMOCRACY
Educational Policy & the Crisis of the Welfare State
H. Svi Shapiro

BROKEN PROMISES
Reading Instruction in Twentieth-Century America
Patrick Shannon

CRITICAL PEDAGOGY & CULTURAL POWER
David Livingstone & Contributors

EDUCATION & THE AMERICAN DREAM
Conservatives, Liberals & Radicals Debate the Future of Education
Harvey Holtz & Contributors

EDUCATION UNDER SIEGE
The Conservative, Liberal & Radical Debate Over Schooling
Stanley Aronowitz & Henry A. Giroux

LITERACY
Reading the Word & the World
Paulo Freire & Donaldo Macedo

THE MORAL & SPIRITUAL CRISIS IN EDUCATION
A Curriculum for Justice & Compassion in Education
David E. Purpel

THE POLITICS OF EDUCATION
Culture, Power & Liberation, with a Dialogue on Contemporary Issues
Paulo Freire

TEACHERS AS INTELLECTUALS
Toward a Critical Pedagogy of Learning
Henry A. Giroux

WOMEN TEACHING FOR CHANGE
Gender, Class & Power
Kathleen Weiler

POPULAR CULTURE, SCHOOLING & EVERYDAY LIFE
Henry A. Giroux, Roger I. Simon & Contributors

POPULAR CULTURE, SCHOOLING,
AND
EVERYDAY LIFE

Henry A. Giroux
Roger I. Simon
& Contributors

FOREWORD *by* **Henry A. Giroux & Paulo Freire**

CRITICAL STUDIES IN EDUCATION

BERGIN & GARVEY
New York • Westport, Connecticut • London

This book is dedicated to Emma Goldman, Antonio Gramsci, Raymond Williams, Toni Morrison, and Adrienne Rich—who in their own terms have recognized culture as a terrain of pedagogical and political struggle.

Library of Congress Cataloging-in-Publication Data

Popular culture, schooling, and everyday life / Henry A. Giroux, Roger I.
  Simon & contributors: foreword by Paulo Freire.
      p.   cm.
    Bibliography:
    Includes index.
    ISBN 0-89789-187-2 (alk. paper)
    ISBN 0-89789-186-4 (pbk. : alk. paper)
    1. Education—Social aspects—United States.   2. United States—
Popular culture.   3. Students—United States.   4. Education—United
States—Curricula.   I. Giroux, Henry A.   II. Simon, Roger I.
    LC89.P66   1989
    370.19—dc20   89-35822

Library of Congress Catalog Card Number: 89-35822
ISBN: 0-89789-187-2
       0-89789-186-4 (pbk.)

First published in 1989

Bergin & Garvey, One Madison Avenue, New York, NY 10010
An imprint of Greenwood Publishing Group, Inc.

Printed in the United States of America

Published simultaneously in Canada by Ontario Institute for Studies in
Education Press, Toronto.

10 9 8 7 6 5 4 3 2

PHOTO CREDITS   *Dirty Dancing* stills, cover and page 206, courtesy of
Vestron Pictures, Inc. © copyright 1987 Great American Films Joint
Venture; page 112, courtesy Warner Records; page 136, Todd Kaplan
photograph, courtesy Jon Landau Management; page 177, courtesy Eric
Lieber Productions.

CONTENTS

PEDAGOGY, POPULAR CULTURE, AND PUBLIC LIFE: AN INTRODUCTION

Paulo Freire and Henry A. Giroux

♦ Like Klee's angel in the painting "Angelus Novus," modernity has faith in human agency even as it recognizes that the past was often built on human suffering. In the best Enlightenment tradition, reason offers the hope that men and women can address and change, when necessary, the world in which they live. The task of modernity, with its faith in reason and emancipation, is perhaps then to renew a sense of urgency in a postmodern world, the world where difference, contingency, and power increasingly challenge the boundaries of nationalism, sexism, racism, and class oppression.

In this world new challenges present themselves not only to educators but to everyone for whom contingency and loss of certainty do not necessarily mean the inevitable triumph of nihilism and despair but rather a state of possibility in which destiny and hope can be snatched from the weakening grasp of the totalitarianism exhibited by nation-states on both the Left and the Right. In this world that no longer has firm boundaries, not only is reason in crisis, at the same time pedagogical and ideological conditions exist for fashioning forms of struggle defined in a radically different conception of politics. For educators this is as much a pedagogical issue as it is a political one. At best, it points to the importance of rewriting the relationship among knowledge, power, and desire. It points as well to the necessity of redefining the importance of difference while at the same time seeking articulations among subordinate groups and historically privileged groups committed to social transformations that deepen the possibility for radical democracy and human survival. It also points to the need to develop a language of educational reform that can be analyzed as part of a much wider debate over the crisis of public philosophy that has emerged in this country and elsewhere over the last decade. In this case, the language of educational reform, leadership, and pedagogical practice must be linked to a public philosophy that extends the most dynamic and democratic possibilities of public life.

At stake here is the recognition that the issue of purpose and meaning is central to creating a language of reform that returns the notion of educational theory and practice to the realm of public discourse. *At its best*, the language of educational theory should embody a public philosophy dedicated to returning schools to their primary task: to be places of critical education in the service of creating a public sphere of citizens who are able to exercise power over their own lives, and especially over the conditions of knowledge production and acquisition. This is a language linked to the imperatives of a practical hope, one that views the relationship between leadership and schooling as part of the wider struggle to create the lived experience of empowerment for the vast majority.

At its worst, the language of educational theory and practice is organized around a claim to authority that is primarily procedural and technical. This is a language that not only defines leadership in terms profoundly antiutopian but also is incapable of referencing what administrators and teachers actually do in terms of the underlying principles and values that structure their beliefs and work. This is a language that ignores its own partiality, that refuses to engage the ideological assumptions that underlie its vision of the future, and that appears unable to understand its own complicity with those social relations that subjugate, infantilize, and corrupt. It is a language that in its quest for control, certainty, and objectivity cannot link leadership to notions of solidarity, community, or public life. It is a language that reduces administrators, teachers, and students to clerks and bad theorists, that removes schools from their most vital connections to public life, and that more often than not defines teaching in instrumental rather than enabling terms. It deskills teachers and disempowers students while purporting to empower them.

In opposition to this view, various contributors to this book argue for a theory of popular culture that embodies a language of both critique and possibility, a language that not only frees educators from certain ways of defining public philosophy, leadership, and pedagogy but that also sheds light on some of the most pressing problems confronting schools and society, while simultaneously providing a vision capable of animating a democratic and popular public culture. The authors in this book argue that the language of schooling and everyday life has to provide teachers and students with the skills they will need to locate themselves in history, find their own voices, and establish the convictions and compassion necessary for exercising civic courage, taking risks, and furthering the habits, customs, and social relations essential to democratic public forms.

Central to this text is the assumption that a critical pedagogy must not only link itself to the demands and purposes of a radical democracy, it must also engage the conditions for the production of knowledge that is both relevant and emancipatory. It must incorporate aspects of popular culture as a serious educational discourse into the school curriculum, and it must bring into the discourse of school policy and pedagogical planning the voices of those who have been marginalized and excluded. This means, in part, engaging schools not merely as instructional sites, but also as cultural sites, as social forms that introduce students to particular ways of life and in doing so often marginalize and exclude the voices, histories, and experiences of those groups who by virtue of their class, race, ethnicity, and gender are not part of the dominant classes. At the very least this means recognizing that schools are about somebody's story, and that story if it is to expand its possibilities for educating students to be critical rather than merely good citizens must recognize the multiple narratives and histories that make pluralistic societies. Educational programs need to provide students with an understanding of how knowledge and power come together in *various* educational spheres to both enable and silence the voices of different students. At issue here is a notion of diversity that takes up not the easy and sometimes sloppy demands of liberal pluralism but engages the power-sensitive relations that articulate between and among different social and cultural groups. This means that educators need to educate students to view schools as places that not only produce subjects but also subjectivities and that learning is not merely about the acquisition of knowledge but also about the production of social practices which provide students with a sense of place, identity, worth, and value. In other words, educators need a theory of pedagogy and popular culture that alerts them to overcome the ways schooling makes some students voiceless, the ways teachers and students are often reduced to technicians, the ways particular forms of authority subvert the ethical force and possibilities of educational leadership and learning.

Overall, this text does more than provide analyses of the relationship between popular culture and critical pedagogy or of the need to reclaim the language of democracy, critical citizenship, and learning for empowerment. Each of the authors in this book, implicitly or explicitly, also points to the need to redefine the role of educational leaders as engaged and transformative public intellectuals. At issue here is a view of leadership in which educators undertake the language of social criticism, display moral courage, and connect rather than distance themselves from the most pressing problems and opportunities of the times. To be engaged in this sense means not only to address through one's theory and practice these problems but also to steep oneself as an educator in the language of the everyday, the discourses of the communities that our students are produced within, and to engage difference as part of the broader discourse of justice, equality, and community. What is being presented in various ways throughout this book is a view of theory and pedagogical practice that offers the promise of reforming schools as part of a wider revitalization of public life. But this is a notion of public life which recognizes the polyphonic and contradictory voices that constitute the diverse strands of dialogue over various versions of the common good. This is a notion of public life and democracy developed around a shared conception of social justice, one which extends the democratic principles of liberty, equality, freedom to the widest possible set of social practices and relations. Central to this notion of public life, pedagogy, and popular culture are questions regarding the relationship between power and knowledge, learning and empowerment, and authority and human dignity. All of these questions are understood in this book as part of a wider political discourse that organizes the energies of a moral vision that raises issues about how educational leaders can work for the construction of subject positions in which the interplay between ethics, politics, and education function as part of the reconstruction of social imagination in the service of human freedom. This book offers a valuable way of rethinking the relationship among critical pedagogy cultural diversity, and public life, through a particular conception of critical literacy, and it is to that issue that we now turn.

One of the most important educational projects over the next decade will be the development of a critical literacy that incorporates the politics of cultural diversity with a view of politics that recognizes the importance of democratic public life. This suggests not only acknowledging in school curricula the diverse voices, experiences, histories, and community traditions that increasingly characterize many countries, it also means finding a language that articulates within and between these differences the shared political ends of a democratic society. In this case, critical literacy would mean restoring for students those knowledges and skills that create solidarity with respect to principles such as freedom, equality, and justice, without denying the importance of diverse individual rights and cultural traditions. This means, in part, recognizing the inadequacy of curriculum programs and calls for cultural literacy that merely affirm and express the interests and values of an Anglo, white, middle and upper-class segment of the population. In this case, prevailing views of the curriculum as espoused by E. D. Hirsch and Allan Bloom must be rejected either for being at odds with a literacy of cultural diversity or for being resistant to viewing schools as sites for educating students to be critical citizens willing to struggle for a vital, democratic society.

At stake here is the need to reclaim a cultural literacy for each and every person as part of a democratic idea of citizenship that dignifies and critically engages the different voices of students from both dominant and subordinate groups in ways that help them to redefine schools as part of the communities and neighborhoods they serve. This is not an argument against providing students with access to what some have called the "Great Books" or a romantic celebration of popular culture, but rather a call for situating any debate about what constitutes meaningful knowledge in relationship to considerations that expand rather than limit the potentialities that various students have to be literate not only in the language of their community, but also in the languages of the state and the larger world. The notion of critical literacy that permeates the various chapters of this book is fashioned around specific questions of purpose and meaning and not around debates that merely justify one canon over another. For example, both radical and conservative educators often talk about the notion of the canon as if all that matters is that it contain the appropriate ideological knowledge and skills. Knowledge becomes something to be transmitted rather than questioned for its potential to help students critically assess the role they might take up as engaged and democratic citizens living in a world of increasing cultural diversity and conflict. Literacy in this case is reduced to appropriating the specific content of a given canon. In our minds, there is more at stake here than simply a debate over the content of course syllabi.

Throughout this book, it is suggested that critical literacy be constructed and experienced within social relations that legitimate popular culture, cultural diversity, and dialogue as crucial elements in the debate about citizenship and cultural/social justice. Equally important, critical literacy is conceived of as a pedagogy that educates students to govern, that provides them with the history, knowledge, and skills they will need in order to effectively assert their role as citizens capable of exercising moral responsibility through forms of public leadership. This suggests, more specifically, linking the notion of cultural literacy not only to what people learn, but also to how they learn. It suggests a notion of literacy that corresponds with an understanding of the books, ideas, values, and social practices that have played and continue to play an important role in shaping this country's history. On the other hand, it means affirming those histories, traditions, stories, and everyday events that have been denied their rightful place as important legacies in the struggle for democracy and cultural justice. If the question of literacy is linked to questions of purpose and meaning that take seriously the imperatives of educating students for critical citizenship in a mass society, it will have to be concerned with the issue of how students actually become self-reflective about the spheres of popular culture as part of the very process of learning. To be literate is not simply to know something; it also means knowing how to participate reflectively in the very act of producing knowledge. It also means learning the limits and partialness of specific languages, cultures, and experiences in terms of both the positive and the negative impacts they have had and might have in contributing to the construction of a democratic state.

In effect, the various authors in this book are arguing, with respect to their diverse positions on popular culture, for a notion of critical literacy that shapes the development of school curricula around a plurality of democratic demands and traditions, that is attentive to critical knowledges that create webs of possibility within shared conversations, and that encourages pedagogical practices that allow students to see the standpoint of others while simultaneously recognizing the partial nature of all discourses, including their own.

By situating learning within contexts that blur the distinction between high and popular culture, by rewriting the boundaries of the so-called disciplines, by linking learning to the revitalization of public life, and by urging educators to become engaged public intellectuals, this book attempts to redefine both the notion of pedagogy and the terrain of popular culture as part of a wider struggle for democracy.

Finally, it is worth repeating that this book represents an important attempt to bring together certain elements of the discourse of modernism and postmodernism. In effect, the various contributors are arguing that talk about popular culture, daily life, and reason must be simultaneously about the discourse of an engaged plurality and about critical citizenship. This is a discourse that breathes life into the notions of democracy and the everyday by stressing a view of lived community that is not at odds with the issues of justice, liberty, and the good life. The modernist concern with enlightened subjects, coupled with the postmodernist emphasis on the particular, the heterogeneous, and the multiple, points to educating students for a type of citizenship that does not separate abstract rights from the realm of the everyday and does not define community as the legitimating and unifying practice of a one-dimensional historical and cultural narrative. The postmodern emphasis on refusing forms of knowledge and pedagogy wrapped in the legitimating claims of universal reason, its refusal of narratives that disclaim their own partiality, and its opposition to all analyses that treat culture as an artifact rather than a social and historical construction provide the pedagogical grounds for radicalizing the emancipatory possibilities of teaching and learning. What is at work in this text is a discourse that represents a political as well as a pedagogical project, one that demands that educators combine a democratic public philosophy and pedagogy with a cultural politics that enables and extends the possibilities for a society and world where the act of communicating and living extends rather than restricts the creation of critical democracy.

Chapter 1

POPULAR CULTURE AS A PEDAGOGY OF PLEASURE AND MEANING

Henry A. Giroux and Roger I. Simon

◆ In the past decade radical educators have begun to take seriously the issue of student experience as a central component in developing a theory of schooling and cultural politics.[1] The way in which student experience is produced, organized, and legitimated in schools has become an increasingly important theoretical consideration for understanding how schools produce and authorize particular forms of meaning and implement teaching practices consistent with the ideological principles of the dominant society. Rather than focusing exclusively on how schools reproduce the dominant social order through social and cultural reproduction or how students contest the dominant logic through various forms of resistance, radical educators have attempted more recently to analyze the terrain of schooling as a struggle over particular ways of life. In this view the process of being schooled cannot be fully conceptualized within the limiting parameters of the reproduction/resistance model. Instead, being schooled is analyzed as part of a complex and often contradictory set of ideological and material processes through which the transformation of experience takes place. ·Schooling is understood as part of the production and legitimation of social forms and subjectivities as they are organized within relations of power and meaning that either enable or limit human capacities for self-and social empowerment.[2]

Although the theoretical service that this position has provided cannot be overstated, radical educational theorists have nonetheless almost completely ignored the importance of popular culture both for developing a more critical understanding of student experience and for examining pedagogy in a critical and theoretically expanded fashion. The irony of this position is that, even though radical educators have argued for the importance of student experience as a central component for developing a critical pedagogy, they have generally failed to consider how such experience is shaped by the terrain of popular culture. Similarly, they have been reluctant to question why popular culture has not been a serious object of study either in the present school curriculum or in the curriculum reforms put forth by critically minded liberal educators. This lacuna can be partly explained by the fact that radical educators often legitimate in their work a theory of pedagogy in which the ideological correctness of one's political position appears to be the primary determining factor in assessing the production of knowledge and exchange that occurs between teachers and students. Guided by a concern with producing knowledge that is ideologically correct, radical theorists have revealed little or no understanding of how a teacher can be both politically correct and pedagogically wrong. Nor can there be found any concerted attempts to analyze how relations of pedagogy and relations of power are inextricably tied not only to what people know but how they come to know it in a particular way within the constraints of specific social forms.[3]

We argue that the lack of an adequate conception of critical pedagogical practice is in part responsible for the absence of an adequate politics of popular culture. Within critical educational theories the issue of pedagogy is usually treated in one of two ways: as a method whose status is defined by its functional relation to particular forms of knowledge or as a process of ideological deconstruction of a text. In the first approach, close attention is given to the knowledge chosen for use in a particular class. Often the ways in which students actually engage such knowledge is taken for granted. It is assumed that if one has access to an ideologically correct comprehension of that which is to be understood, the only serious question that needs to be raised about pedagogy is one of procedural technique, that is, should one use a seminar, lecture, or some other teaching style?[4] In the second approach, pedagogy is reduced to a concern with and analysis of the political interests which structure particular forms of knowledge, ways of knowing, and methods of teaching. For example, specific styles of teaching might be analyzed according to whether or not they embody sexist, racist, and class-specific interests, serve to silence students, or promote practices which deskill and disempower teachers.[5] In both approaches, what is often ignored is the notion of pedagogy as a cultural production and exchange that addresses how knowledge is produced, mediated, refused, and re-presented within relations of power both in and outside of schooling.

In our view the issue of critical pedagogy demands an attentiveness to how students actively construct the categories of meaning that prefigure their production of and response to classroom knowledge. By ignoring the cultural and social forms that are authorized by youth and simultaneously empower or disempower them, educators risk complicitly silencing and negating their students. This is unwittingly accomplished by refusing to recognize the importance of those sites and social practices outside of schools that actively shape student experiences and through which students often define and construct their sense of identity, politics, and culture. The issue at stake is not one of relevance but of empowerment. We are not concerned with simply motivating students to learn, but rather establishing conditions of learning that enable them to locate themselves in history and to interrogate the adequacy of that location as both a pedagogical and political question.[6]

Educators who refuse to acknowledge popular culture as a significant basis of knowledge often devalue students by refusing to work with the knowledge that students actually have and so eliminate the possibility of developing a pedagogy that links school knowledge to the differing subject relations that help to constitute their everyday lives. A more critical pedagogy demands that pedagogical relations be seen as relations of power structured primarily through dominant but always negotiated and contested forms of consent.

The basis for a critical pedagogy cannot be developed merely around the inclusion of particular forms of knowledge that have been suppressed or ignored by the dominant culture, nor can it center only on providing students with more empowering interpretions of the social and material world. Such a pedagogy also must attend to ways in which students make both affective and semantic investments as part of their attempts to regulate and give meaning to their lives.[7] This is an important insight that both makes problematic and provides a corrective to the traditional ways in which radical educators have explained how dominant meanings and values work. The value of including popular culture in the development of a critical pedagogy is that it provides the opportunity to further our understanding of how students make investments in particular social forms and practices. In other words, the study of popular culture offers the possibility of understanding how a politics of pleasure addresses students in a way that shapes and sometimes secures the often-contradictory relations they have to both schooling and the politics of everyday life. If one of the central concerns of a critical pedagogy is to understand how student identities, cultures, and experiences provide the basis for learning, we need to grasp the totality of elements that organize such subjectivities.

We shall particularly emphasize that, while the production of meaning provides one important element in the production of subjectivity, it is not enough. The production of meaning is also tied to emotional investments and the production of pleasure. In our view, the production of meaning and the production of pleasure are mutually constitutive of who students are, the view they have of themselves, and how they construct a particular version of their future.

In what follows, we first want to argue that critical educators need to retheorize the importance of popular culture as a central category for both understanding and developing a theory and practice of critical pedagogy. In developing this position we examine some conservative and radical views of popular culture and then analyze the pedagogical practices implicit in these positions. Second, we will attempt to develop the basic elements that constitute a theory of popular culture, one that would support a critical pedagogical practice. Third, we will analyze a particular Hollywood film as a popular form, treating it as an exemplary text in order to demonstrate how the formation of identities takes place through attachments and investments which are as much a question of affect and pleasure as they are of ideology and rationality. Finally, we will discuss the implications of this analysis for the practice of a critical pedagogy.

RADICAL AND CONSERVATIVE APPROACHES TO POPULAR CULTURE

Historically the concept popular culture has not fared well as part of the discourse of the Left or of the Right.[8] For the Left, two positions have held center stage in different instances of Marxist theory. In the first, popular culture lacks the possibility for creative, productive, or authentic forms of expressison. In this view, popular culture simply represents a view of ideology and cultural forms imposed by the culture industry on the masses in order to integrate them into the existing social order. Within this discourse, popular culture becomes commodified and produces people in the image of its own logic, a logic characterized by standardization, uniformity, and passivity. The structuring principle at work in this view of popular culture is one of total dominance and utter resignation. People become synonymous with cultural dupes, incapable of either mediating, resisting, or rejecting the imperatives of the dominant culture.

The paradigmatic example of this position comes from Theodor Adorno and Max Horkheimer, two major theorists of the Frankfurt School.[9] For Adorno and Horkheimer, popular culture is equated with mass culture. This is seen as a form of psychoanalysis in reverse; instead of curing socially induced neuroses, mass culture produces them. Similarly, popular forms such as television, radio, jazz, or syndicated astrology columns are nothing more than ideological shorthand for those social relations that reproduced the social system as a whole. For Adorno, in particular, popular culture is simply mass culture whose effects have no redeeming political possibilities. The people or "masses" lack any culture through which they can offer either resistance or an alternative vision of the world. Adorno is clear on this issue:

The total effect of the culture industry is one of anti-enlightenment, in which, as Horkheimer and I have noted, enlightenment, that is the progressive technical domination of nature, becomes mass deception and is turned into a means for fettering consciousness. It impedes the development of autonomous, independent individuals who judge and decide consciously for themselves.... If the masses have been unjustly reviled from above as masses, the culture industry is not among the least responsible for making them into masses and then despising them, while obstructing the emancipation for which human beings [might be] ripe.[10]

Adorno's remarks summarize one of the paradoxical theses of the Frankfurt School theorists. Reason is not only in eclipse in the modern age, it is also the source of crisis and decline. Progress has come to mean the reification, rationalization, and standardization of thought itself, and the culture industry plays a key role in transforming culture and reason into their opposite. Within this perspective, the distinction between high culture and mass/popular culture is preserved. In this case, high culture becomes a transcendent sphere, one of the few arenas left in which autonomy, creativity, and opposition can be thought and practiced. While arguing that mass culture is an expression of the slide into barbarism, Frankfurt theorists such as Adorno and Horkheimer fall back upon a unfortunate legitimation of high culture in which particular versions of art, music, literature, and the philosophic tradition become a utopian refuge for resisting the new barbarism.[11]

The elitism that informs this view degenerates into a politics and a pedagogy characteristic of their conservative counterpart, which also subscribes to such a distinction. In the conservative case, the refuge of political insight and engagement is no longer open to those contemptuously labeled as "the people." In this perspective, popular culture has little to do with complex and contradictory notions of consent and opposition, which necessitate exploring the pedagogical principles that structure how people negotiate, mediate, affirm, or reject particular aspects of the terrain of the popular. Instead, the popular collapses into an unproblematic sphere of domination where critical thought and action remain a distant memory of the past.

The second view of popular culture predominant in Marxist theory is developed mostly in the work of historians and sociologists who focus on various aspects of "peoples' history" or the practices of subcultural groups. In this view, popular culture becomes a version of folk culture and its contemporary variant, that is, as an object of historical analysis, working-class culture is excavated as an unsullied expression of popular resistance. Within this form of analysis the political and the pedagogical emerge as an attempt to reconstruct a "radical and...popular tradition in order that 'the people' might learn from and take heart from the struggles of their forebears," or it appears as an attempt to construct "'the people' as the supporters of [a] 'great culture' so that they might eventually be led to appropriate that culture as their own."[12]

A similar and more contemporary version of this discourse opposes the high or dominant culture to the alternative culture of the working class or various subcultural groups. This is the culture of authenticity, one which is allegedly uncontaminated by the logic and practices of the culture industry or the impositions of a dominant way of life. At work here is a romantic view of popular experience that somehow manages to escape from the relations and contradictions at work in the larger society. This view falls prey to an essentialist reading of popular culture. It deeply underestimates the most central feature of cultural power in the twentieth century. In failing to acknowledge popular culture as one sphere in a complex field of domination and subordination, this view ignores the necessity of providing an understanding of how power produces different levels of cultural relations, experiences, and values that articulate the multilayered ideologies and social practices of any society.[13]

Both of these traditions on the Left have played a powerful role in defining popular culture within a theoretical framework that helps to explain why the people have not risen up against the inequities and injustices of capitalism. Ironically, the Right has not ignored the underlying logic of this position and, in fact, has appropriated it for its own ideological interests. As Patrick Brantlinger points out, the category of popular culture has been "just as useful for helping to explain and condemn the failures of egalitarian schools and mass cultural institutions such as television and the press to educate 'the masses' to political responsibilty."[14] Conservative critics such as Arnold Toynbee, José Ortega y Gasset, Ezra Pound, and T. S. Eliot have viewed popular culture as a threat to the very existence of civilization as well as an expression of the vulgarization and decadence of the masses.

A contemporary version of this position can be found in Allan Bloom's best-selling book, *The Closing of the American Mind*. Bloom criticizes popular culture, especially rock and roll, as a "nonstop commercially prepackaged masturbational fantasy,"[15] which has caused a spiritual paralysis among today's youth. In Bloom's terms popular culture occupies a terrain marked by the debilitating escapism of the Walkman radio and the pulsating sexual energy mobilized in rock music. Reading Bloom, one gets the impression that popular culture has ruined the imagination of contemporary youth who, incited by the base and vulgar passion of rock and roll, appear to be electronically wired and and constantly poised to copulate. Today's youth provide for Bloom the evidence of social decay and a new form of barbarism. Of course, Bloom's position is not new and in many ways echoes Bernard James's attack on the counterculture of the 1960s. James writes:

Where the external barbarian pounds at the gates of civilization with battering ram and war club, the internal barbarian insinuates values and habits that degrade civilized life from within. I interpret much of the so-called counter-culture we witness about us today as evidence of such internal barbarism.[16]

In the conservative attack on mass and popular culture, the category of true culture is treated as a warehouse filled with the goods of antiquity, waiting patiently to be distributed anew to each generation. Knowledge in this perspective becomes sacred, revered, and removed from the demands of social critique and ideological interests.[17] The pedagogical principles at work here are similar to those at work in the Left's celebration of high culture. In both cases, the rhetoric of cultural restoration and crisis legitimates a transmission pedagogy consistent with a view of culture as an artifact and students as merely bearers of received knowledge. Though starting from different political positions, both left and right advocates of high culture often argue that the culture of the people has to be replaced with knowledge and values that are at the heart of ruling culture. In these perspectives, the modalities of revolutionary struggle and conservative preservation seem to converge around a view of popular culture as a form of barbarism, a notion of the people as passive dupes, and an appeal to a view of enlightenment that reduces cultural production and meaning to the confines of high culture. Questions regarding the multidimensional nature of the struggles, con-tradictions, and re-formations that inscribe in different ways the historically specific surface of popular cultural forms is completely overlooked in both the dominant radical and conservative positions.

Dominant left views of popular culture have not provided an adequate discourse for developing a theory of cultural analysis that begins with the issue of how power enters into the struggles over the domains of common sense and everyday life.[18] Nor do such accounts provide sufficient theoreti-cal insight into how the issues of consent, resistance, and the production of subjectivity are shaped by pedagogical processes whose structuring prin-ciples are deeply political. Of course, in the exaggerations that characterize popular culture as either imposed from above or generated spontaneously from below there are hints of the political reality of cultural power both as a force for domination and as a condition for collective affirmation and struggle. The point is not to separate these different elements of cultural power from each other as oppositions but to capture the complexity of cultural relations as they manifest themselves in practices that both enable and disable people within sites and social forms that give meaning to the relations of popular culture.

HEGEMONY AS A PEDAGOGICAL PROCESS

The work of Italian Marxist theorist, Antonio Gramsci, represents an impor-tant starting point for both redefining the meaning of popular culture and advancing its pedagogical and political importance. Gramsci did not directly address himself to modern manifestations of popular culture, such as cinema and radio, nor did he write anything of profound worth on the symbolic forms of popular culture that existed in the urban centers of Europe in the early part of the twentieth century, but he did formulate an original theory of culture, power, and hegemony which provides a theoretical basis for moving beyond the impasse of viewing popular culture within the bipolar alternatives of a celebratory populism or a debilitating cultural stupor.[19] Gramsci's theory of hegemony redefines the structuring principles that maintain relations between dominant and subordinate classes in the advanced capitalist societies. For Gramsci, the exercise of control by the ruling classes is characterized less by the excessive use of officially sanctioned force than it is through what he calls "the struggle for hegemonic leadership" — the struggle to win the consent of subordinate groups to the existing social order. In substituting hegemonic struggle for the concept of domination, Gramsci points to the complex ways in which consent is organized as part of an active pedagogical process within everyday life. In Gramsci's view such a pedagogical process must work and rework the cultural and ideological terrain of subordinate groups in order to legitimate the interests and authority of the ruling bloc.

Gramsci's concept of hegemony broadens the question of which social groups will hold and exert power. More importantly, it raises a number of theoretical considerations regarding how power as a cultural, economic, and political set of practices works to define, organize, and legitimate particular conceptions of common sense.[20] Gramsci's hegemony is both a political and pedagogical process. Moral leadership and state power are tied to a process of consent, as a form of practical learning, which is secured through the elaboration of particular discourses, needs, appeals, values, and interests that must address and transform the concerns of subordinate groups. In this perspective hegemony is a continuing, shifting, and problematic historical process. Consent is structured through a series of relations marked by an ongoing political struggle over competing conceptions and views of the world between dominant and subordinate groups. What is worth noting here is that this is not a political struggle framed within the polarities of an imposing dominant culture and a weak but "authentic" subordinate culture(s). On the contrary, by claiming that every relation of hegemony is necessarily an educational relationship, Gramsci makes clear that a ruling bloc can only engage in a political and pedagogical struggle for the consent of subordinate groups if it is willing to take seriously and articulate some of the values and interests of these groups.[21]

Inherent in this attempt to transform rather than displace the ideological and cultural terrain of subordinate groups, dominant ideology itself is compromised and exists in a far from pure, unadulterated state. Needless to say, the culture of subordinate groups never confronts the dominant culture in either a completely supine or totally resistant fashion. In the struggle to open up its own spaces for resistance and affirmation, subordinate cultures have to negotiate and compromise around *both* those elements it gives over to the dominant culture and those it maintains as representative of its own interests and desires.[22]

From this view of struggle within the hegemonic process, it is clear that the relationship between popular culture and the processes of consent requires rejecting any concept of popular culture articulated in essentialist terms. That is, the concept of popular culture cannot be defined around a set of ideological meanings permanently inscribed in particular cultural forms. On the contrary, because of their location within and as part of the dynamics of consent, the meaning of cultural forms can only be ascertained through their articulation into a practice and set of historically specific contextual relations which determine their political meaning and ideological interests. Break dancing, punk dress, or heavy metal music may be sufficiently oppositional and congruent within one social and historical context to be considered a legitimate radical expression of popular culture and yet in another social field may be mediated through the consumer ideology and investments of mass culture. What is important to recognize here is: *the key structuring principle of popular culture does not consist in the contents of particular cultural forms*. Stuart Hall illuminates this issue well:

> The meaning of a cultural form and its place or position in the cultural field is not inscribed inside its form. Nor is its position fixed once and foreever. This year's radical symbol or slogan will be neutralised into next year's fashion; the year after, it will be the object of a profound cultural nostalgia. Today's rebel folksinger ends up, tomorrow, on the cover of *The Observer* colour magazine. The meaning of the cultural symbol is given in part by the social field into which it is incorporated, the practises with which it articulates and is made to resonate. What matters is not the intrinsic or historically fixed objects of culture, but the state of play in cultural relations.[23]

We want to extend this insight further and argue that not only are popular cultural forms read in complex ways, they also mobilize multiple forms of investment. In other words, the popular has a dual form of address: it not only serves as a semantic and ideological referent for marking one's place in history; it also brings about an experience of pleasure, affect, and corporeality. This is not to suggest that these forms of address posit a distinction in which pleasure takes place outside of history or forms of representation. What is being posited is that the popular as both a set of practices and a discursive field has a variety of effects which may be mediated through a combination of corporeal and ideological meanings or through the primacy of one of these determinants.

It must be recognized that while popular cultural forms are productive around historically constructed sets of meanings and practices, their effects may be primarily affective. That is, how these forms are mediated and taken up, how they work to construct a particular form of investment may depend less on the production of meanings than on the affective relations which they construct with their audiences. Pleasure as a terrain of commodification and struggle never exists completely free from the technology of gendered and racist representations but its power as a form of investment cannot be reduced to its signifying effects. This means that the practices associated with a particular cultural form such as punk can never be dismissed as being merely ideologically incorrect or as simply a reflex of commodity logic. The importance of both the semantic and the affective in the structuring the investments in popular cultural forms provides new theoretical categories for linking the terrain of the everyday with the the pedagogical processes at work in the notion of consent.

In summary, we claim that there is no popular culture outside of the interlocking processes of meaning, power, and desire that characterize the force of cultural relations at work at a given time and place in history. This suggests that popular culture is not to be understood as simply the content of various cultural forms. Quite divergently, the concept of popular culture must be grasped in terms of how cultural forms enter into the ideological and institutional structuring relations which sustain differences between what constitutes dominant culture and what does not. In North America today, underlying this struggle to maintain both a difference and an accommodation of dominant and subordinate cultures is a set of institutions, ideologies, and social practices that mark a generic distinction between the realms of popular and dominant culture.

In the context of this distinction, popular culture is an empty cultural form. Its form or representation does not guarantee an unproblematic, transcendent meaning. At the same time, popular culture can be understood as a social practice constituted by a particular site and set of features which point to a distinctive field of political action. The general distinctiveness of popular culture as a sphere of social relations can be made more clear by further elaborating its basic theoretical features.

A theory of popular culture has several cogent features which we wish to re-emphasize. First, the concept of hegemony clarifies how cultural power is able to penetrate into the terrain of daily life, transforming it into both a struggle over and accommodation to the culture of subordinate groups. Second, the cultural terrain of everyday life is not only a site of struggle and accommodation, but also one in which the production of subjectivity can be viewed as a pedagogical process whose structuring principles are deeply political. Third, the notion of consent which lies at the heart of the process of hegemony underscores the importance of specifying the limits and possibilities of the pedagogical principles at work within cultural forms that serve in contradictory ways to empower and disempower various groups. In what follows, we want to extend these insights by pointing to those features and activities that illuminate more specifically what constitutes popular culture as both a site and field of pedagogical work.

CULTURE AS A SITE OF STRUGGLE AND POWER RELATIONS

We enter the process of theorizing the relation between popular culture and critical pedagogy by arguing for educational practice as both a site and form of cultural politics. In this regard, our project is the construction of an educational practice that expands human capacities in order to enable people to intervene in the formation of their own subjectivities and to be able to exercise power in the interest of transforming the ideological and material conditions of domination into social practices that promote social empowerment and demonstrate possibilities. Within this position we are emphasizing popular culture as a site of differentiated politics, a site with multiple ideological and affective weightings. It represents a particular historical place where different groups collide in transactions of dominance, complicity, and resistance over the power to name, legitimate, and experience different versions of history, community, desire, and pleasure through the availability of social forms structured by the politics of difference. Some of the theoretical and political implications at work in this view of popular culture are captured in Larry Grossberg's discussion of a theory of articulation:

> [P]eople are never totally manipulated, never entirely incorporated. People are engaged in struggles with, within, and sometimes against, real tendential forces and determinations, in their efforts to appropriate what they are given. Consequently, their relations to particular practices and texts are complex and contradictory: they may win something in the struggle against sexism and lose something in the struggle against economic exploitation; they may both gain and lose something economically; and while they lose ideological ground, they may win a bit of emotional strength. If peoples' lives are never merely determined by the dominant position, and their subordination is always complex and active, then understanding [popular] culture requires us to look at how they are actively inserted at particular sites of everyday life and at how particular articulations empower and disempower its audience.[24]

The key theoretical concepts for further specifying popular culture as a particular site of struggle and accommodation can be initially organized around a category we label "the productive." In the more general sense, we use the term productive to refer to the construction and organization of practices engaged in by dominant *and* subordinate groups to secure a space for producing and legitimating experiences and social forms. The term productive points to two distinctly different sets of relations within the sphere of the popular.

The first set of relations refers to the ways in which the dominant culture functions as a structuring force within and through popular forms. In this case, the dominant culture attempts to secure — both semantically and affectively, through the production of meaning and the regulation of pleasure — the complicity of subordinate groups. Rather than merely dismiss or ignore the traditions, ideologies, and needs that emerge out of the cultures of subordinate groups, the dominant culture attempts to appropriate and transform the ideological and cultural processess that characterize the terrain of the popular. At issue here are processes of selective production, controlled distribution, and regulated notions of narrative and consumer address.

In the second set of relations, productive refers to the ways in which subordinate groups articulate a distinct set of contents and/or a level of involvement in popular forms that is less distancing and more social in nature than that found in the cultural forms of dominant bourgeois groups. This articulation and set of relations are characterized by a refusal to engage in social practices defined by an abstract rationality, a theoretical mapping, so to speak, that structures cultural forms through a denial of the familiar affective investments and pleasures. For the dominant class, such refusal is often understood as a surrender to the moment, the fun of the event, or the "horror of the vulgar." A more critical reading might suggest that the affective investment and level of active involvement in popular forms such as neighborhood sports, punk dancing, or working-class weddings represent an important theoretical signpost. In this case, it is a particular form of sociality that signals something more than vulgarity, co-option, or what Bloch calls the "swindle of fulfillment." Instead, the sociality that structures popular forms may contain the unrealized potentialities and possibilities necessary for more democratic and humane forms of community and collective formation.[25] This can be made clearer by analyzing the structuring principles that often characterize dominant cultural forms.

Pierre Bourdieu argues that the cultural forms of dominant bourgeois groups can be characterized by the celebration of a formalism, an elective distance from the real world, with all of its passions, emotions, and feelings. The social relations and attendant sensibility at work in bourgeois cultural forms are those which maintain an investment of form—a celebration of stylized detachment. On the other hand, there is often a space in the cultural forms embraced by subordinate groups that is organized around a sensibility in which the needs, emotions, passions of the participants largely resonate with the material and ideological structures of day-to-day life. Underlying these social relations one can find a richly textured collective investment of play and affective engagement in which there is no great disjunction or interruption between the act and its meaning. In other words, there is an active, communal set of experiences and social practices at work in subordinate cultural forms, including a form of public participation in which the dominant practice of distancing the body from reflection is refused. This is the productive moment of corporeality. Mercer illuminates this point in his discussion of Bourdieu's concept of "popular forms":

"Nothing [argues Pierre Bourdieu] more radically distinguishes popular spectacles—the football match, Punch and Judy, the circus, wrestling or even in some cases the cinema—from bourgeois spectacles, than the form of participation of the public. For the former, whistles, shouts, pitch invasions are characteristic, for the latter the gestures are distant, heavily ritualised—applause, obligatory but discontinuous and punctual cries of enthusiasm—'author, author' or 'encore'." Even the clicking of fingers and tapping of feet in a jazz audience are only a "bourgeois spectacle which mimes a popular one" since the participation is reduced to "the silent allure of the gesture." A certain distance, Bourdieu argues, has been central in the bourgeois economy of the body: a distance between "reflexion" and corporeal participation.[26]

Since corporeality may be inscribed in either repressive or emancipatory actions, any uncritical celebration of the body is theoretically and politically misplaced. At the same time, a discourse of the body is needed that recognizes a sensibility and set of social practices that both define and exhibit a possibility for extending unrealized and progressive moments in the production of coporeality. For example, punk culture's lived appropriation of the everyday as a refusal to let the dominant culture encode and restrict the meaning of daily life suggests the first instance of a form of resistance that links play with the reconstruction of meaning. This particular popular form, filled as it is with abortive hopes, signifies within bourgeois culture a "tradition of the scorned." That is, punk culture (for that matter, any lived relation of difference that does not result in dominance or infantilization) ruptures the dominant order symbolically and refuses to narrate *with* permission. It is scorned by the bourgeoisie because it challenges the dominant order's attempt to suppress all differences through a discourse that asserts the homogeneity of the social domain. However, it also presents the possibility of a social imaginary for which a politics of democratic difference offers up forms of resistance in which it becomes possible to rewrite, rework, recreate, and re-establish new discourses and cultural spaces that revitalize rather than degrade public life. Whether conscious or not, punk culture partly expresses social practices which contain the basis for interrogating and struggling to overthrow all those forms of human behavior in which difference becomes the foundation for subjecting human beings to forms of degradation, enslavement, and exploitation. Of course, there is more at work in punk culture than the affirmation of difference; there is also the difference of affirmation, that is, affirmation becomes the precondition for claiming one's experience as a legitimate ground for developing one's own voice, place, and sense of history. It is this dialectic of affirmation, pleasure, and difference that constitutes some of the basic elements of the notion of the productive. Pierre Bourdieu is helpful here, for he defines the productive as that dialectical mixture of pleasure, consent, and unselfconscious involvement that maps out a significant aspect of the popular within everyday life.

The desire to enter into the game, identifying with the characters' joys and sufferings, worrying about their fate, espousing their hopes and ideals, living their life, is based on a form of investment, a sort of deliberate "naivety," ingenuousness, good-natured credulity ("we're here to enjoy ourselves") which tends to accept formal experiments and specifically artistic effects only to the extent that they can be forgotten and do not get in the way of [the affirmation and dignity of everyday life].[27]

As we have stressed, it would be a political mistake to place too much faith in the level of participation and nature of spontanteity that characterize many cultural forms of subordinated groups. Many of these are not innocent. As an area and site of exchange between the dominant and subordinate classes, popular culture embodies a violence inherent in both sides of the processes of hegemony as well as the unrealized potentiality of those needs and desires which reflect a respect for human dignity and a commitment to extend their most ethical and empowering capabilities. We stress here that innocence is not an intrinsic feature of the popular. There is a violence inextricably inscribed in popular forms that must also be addressed as part of the multilayered and contradictory investments and meanings that constitute its changing character.

POPULAR CULTURE AND CONSENT:
THE DIALECTIC OF IDEOLOGY AND PLEASURE

If the popular is to be understood in terms of the unrealized potentialities that inform it, critical educators need to analyze how the production of subjectivity and cultural alliances can emerge within the grammar and codes that make the terrain of the popular significant in peoples' lives. Popular culture as a site of struggle and possibility needs to be understood not only in terms of its productive elements, but also in terms of how its forms articulate processes through which the production, organization, and regulation of consent take place around various social practices and struggles at the level of daily life. These processes can be elaborated through the category we call "the persuasive." In the most general sense, the term refers to the ways in which hegemony functions through a variety of pedagogical processes that work not only to secure dominant interests but to offer as well the possibility of a politics of resistance and social transformation.

The notion of the persuasive illuminates the insight that political power never works without an ideological mediation. By introducing the element of persuasion — how ideological mediation actually functions as a pedagogical process — domination along with resistance can be connected to a broader notion of cultural politics in which the very act of learning can be analyzed as a fundamental aspect of hegemony. More specifically, the category of the persuasive provides a starting point for understanding how the complex relations of dominance and resistance are organized and structured through particular pedagogical forms and practices. Theorizing popular culture in this way lays bare the practical grounds on which transformations are worked and represented through the important and related categories of consent, investment, ideology, and pleasure.

Consent is an important feature of the practice of persuasion. As the term is generally defined in radical theories of hegemony, it refers to two somewhat different perspectives on how people come to be engaged within the ideologies and social relations of the dominant culture. In the more orthodox version, consent refers to the ways in which the dominant logic is imposed on subordinate groups through the mechanizations of the culture industry. In the revisionist radical version, consent is defined through more active complicity, in that subordinate groups are now viewed as partly negotiating their adaptation and place within the dominant culture. In either case, as imposition or as negotiated complicity, consent defines the relationship between power and culture as nothing more than the equivalence of domination. We want to modify these notions of consent so as to illuminate its dialectical importance as a political and pedagogical process.

To us, the notion of consent rightly points to the ways in which people are located within and negotiate elements of place and agency as a result of their investments in particular relations of meaning constructed through popular forms. At work in this notion are the central questions of what it is that people know, how they come to know, and how they come to feel in a particular way that secures for the hegemonic or counter-hegemonic order their loyalties and desires. This perspective is important as a political and social practice and as a framework of inquiry because it raises important questions about how the modern apparatuses of moral and social regulation, as well as resistance and counter-discourse, define what kind of knowledge counts, how it is to be taught, how subjectivities are defined, and how the very dynamic of moral and political regulation is constantly worked and reworked. The political implications of these insights for a politics of popular culture are significant and need further theoretical elaboration.

That consent is learned begs the question of what kinds of pedagogical processes are at work through which people actively rather than passively identify their own needs and desires with particular forms and relations of meaning. Unfortunately, the pedagogical issue of how people come to learn such identites and pleasures through particular forms of identification and cathexis has not been the central focus of study in most radical analyses of culture. Instead, radical analyses usually focus either on deconstructing the ideologies at work in particular cultural forms or on how readers organize texts according to their own meanings and experiences. In both cases, pedagogy is subordinate to and subsumed within a rather limited notion of ideology production. In this approach, the concern over ideology is limited to a particular view of consent in which the study of popular culture is reduced to analysis of texts or to popular culture as a form of consumption.[28] Ideology as a pedagogical process thus is restricted to how meanings are produced by texts and mediated by audiences or to how the market organizes needs in order to commodify popular culture.

What is noticeably missing from these perspectives is the question of how cultural forms can be understood as mobilizing desire in a way that elaborates how such forms are engaged. Through what processes, for example, do cultural forms induce an anger or pleasure that has its own center of gravity as a form of meaning? How can we come to understand learning outside of the limits of rationality, as a form of engagement that mobilizes and sometimes reconstructs desire? We can see that pedagogy is not so neatly ensconced in the production of discourse; rather, it also constitutes a moment in which the body learns, moves, desires, and longs for affirmation. These questions also suggest a rejection of the pedagogy of modernism, one which serves up "ideal" forms of communication theory in which the tyranny of discourse becomes the ultimate pedagogical medium,[29] that is, talk embodied as a logic disembodied from the body itself. In opposition to the latter position, we need to reemphasize that the issue of consent opens up pedagogy to the uncertain, that space which refuses the measureable, that legitimates the concrete in a way that is felt and experienced rather than merely spoken. In this argument, we are not trying to privilege the body or a politics of affective investments over discourse so much as we are trying to emphasize their absence in previous theorizing and their importance for a critical pedagogy. The relationship we are posing between affective and discursive investment is neither ahistorical nor ideologically innocent. Nor do we suggest that ideology and affect as particular forms of investment can best be understood by positing a rigid conceptual opposition between meaning and desire. The cultural forms that mobilize desire and affect along with the struggles that take place over re/producing and investing desire, pleasure, and corporeality are constructed within power relations which are always ideological in nature but which produce an experience or form of investment that cannot be understood merely as an ideological construction—an experience re/presented and enjoyed through the lens of meaning rather than through the primacy of pleasure and affect. Put another way, interpellations in the Althusserian sense are not merely ideological, they also summon particular forms of pleasure, which are always historically situated but not discursively privileged. In what follows, we will argue that by retheorizing the notion of ideology through a reconstructed theory of pleasure, educators can begin to develop a pedagogy that offers a more critical possibility for addressing the purpose and meaning of popular culture as a terrain of struggle and hope.

We are arguing that the relationship between power and complicity is not framed simply around the organization of knowledge and meaning. The power of complicity and the complicity of power are not exhausted by registering how people are positioned and located through the production of particular ideologies structured through particular discourses. The relationships that subordinate groups enter into with respect to cultural forms cannot be understood only through what often amounts to a search and destroy mission based on uncovering the particular meanings and messages that mediate between any given film, popular song, or text and its audience. The limits of ideology and rationality as the interests which structure behavior and move us within particular social forms is neither understood nor made problematic in this position. This position represents a basic misrecognition of the central and important role that pleasure (or its absence) plays in structuring the relationships and investments that one has to a particular cultural form. Colin Mercer emphasizes this point:

> Barthes has it that "ideology passes over the text and its reading like the blush over a face (in love, some take erotic pleasure in this colouring)" and this signals something of the contemporary concern for the contradictory play of ideology. There is a general unease that, within the plethora of ideology analysis which has emerged in recent years, something has quite crucially been missed out: that it may now be important to look over our shoulders and try to explain a certain "guilt" of enjoyment of such and such in spite of its known ideological and political provenance. . . . Any analysis of the pleasure, the modes of persuasion, the consent operative with a given cultural form would have to displace the search for an ideological, political, economic or, indeed subjective, meaning and establish the coordinates of that "formidable underside" (i.e., pleasure, joy). . . . because what we are really concerned with here is a restructuring of the theoretical horizon within which a cultural form is perceived.[30]

Drawing upon the work of Walter Benjamin, Roland Barthes, and others, Mercer calls attention to an issue that is central to a politics of popular culture. He has focused on the ways in which consent is articulated not only through the structuring of semantically organized meanings and messages, but also through the pleasures invoked in the mechanisms and structuring principles of popular forms. The theoretical insight at work in this position is in part revealed through the question of why "we not only consent to forms of domination which we know, rationally and politically, are 'wrong,' but even enjoy them."[31] The importance of this issue is made somewhat clear in the limits of an ideological analysis that might reveal the sexist nature of the lyrics in a popular song or video. Such a critique is important, but it does not tell us or even seem capable of raising the question as to why people enjoy the song or video even though they might recognize the sexist ideologies that the latter embody. At stake here is the recognition that an overreliance on ideology critique limits our ability to understand how people actively participate in the dominant culture through processes of accommodation, negotiation, and even resistance.

The investments that tie students to popular cultural forms cannot be ascertained simply through an analysis of the meanings and representations that we decode in them. On the contrary, affective investments have a real cultural hold, and such investments may be indifferent to the very notion of meaning itself as constructed through the lens of the ideological. This suggests a number of important political and pedagogical principles. First, in hegemonic and counter-hegemonic struggles, the production and regulation of desire are as important as the construction of meaning. This means that the constitution and the expression of such desire compose an important starting point for understanding the relations that students construct to popular and dominant forms. Second, the idea and experience of pleasure must be constituted politically so that we can analyze how the body becomes not only the object of (his patriarchial) pleasure,[32] but also the subject of pleasure. In this case "pleasure becomes the consent of life in the body," and provides an important corporeal condition of life-affirming possibility.[33] This argues for a discriminatory notion of pleasure that is not only desirable in and of itself, but which also suggests "at one and the same time. . . a figure for utopia in general, and for the systemic revolutionary transformation of society as a whole."[34] Third, we must recognize how popular culture can constitute a field of possibilities within which students can be empowered so as to appropriate cultural forms on terms that dignify and extend their human capabilities.

We realize that this raises enormously difficult questions about how, as teachers, we come to analyze a politics of feeling within sites that are at odds with the very notion of the popular. To make the popular the object of study within schools is to run the risk not only of reconstituting the meaning and pleasures of cultural forms but also of forcing students into a discourse and form of analysis that conflicts with their notion of what is considered pedagogically acceptable and properly distant from their lives outside of school. At the same time, the popular cannot be ignored because it points to a category of meanings and affective investments that shape the very identities, politics, and cultures of the students we deal with. Subjectvity and identity are in part constituted on the ground of the popular, and their force and effects do not disappear once students enter school. The political issue at stake here and its pedagogical relevance are suggested by Larry Grossberg:

> It is only if we begin to recognize the complex relations between affect and ideology that we can make sense of people's emotional life, their desiring life, their struggles to find the energy to survive, let alone struggle. It is only in the terms of these relations that we can understand people's need and ability to maintain a "faith" in something beyond their immediate existence.[35]

In the section that follows, we will consider a particular Hollywood film as a demonstrative text in order to illuminate how the formation of multiple identities takes place through attachments and investments which are structured as much by affect and pleasure as they are by ideology and rationality. The importance of this cultural text is in part due to the opportunity it offers for further elaborating the elements of a critical pedagogical practice and our affirmation of the centrality of the body in the processes of knowing and learning.

INVESTMENT AND PLEASURE IN DIRTY DANCING

We have argued throughout this chapter that popular forms both shape and are mediated through the investments of rationality and affect. In attempting to make this observation more concrete as both a way of analyzing popular forms and of using them as part of a critical pedagogical process, we want to take up a specific consideration of the film, *Dirty Dancing*, written by Eleanor Bergstein and released into the North American market during the summer of 1987.

As we stressed earlier, the concept of popular culture cannot be defined around a set of ideological meanings permanently inscribed in particular cultural forms. Rather, the meaning of cultural forms can only be ascertained through their articulation into a practice and set of historically specific contextual relations which determine their pleasures, politics, and meanings. This position straightforwardly implies Roland Barthes's encouragement that "whenever it's the body which writes, and not ideology, there's a chance the text will join us in our modernity."[36] Thus our comments on the text of *Dirty Dancing* are not offered as abstract observations without an observer but as a fully embodied account. The pedagogical significance of this statement should not be minimized. It means that when we engage students through a critical consideration of particular cultural forms (whether they be commodity texts like films or lived social relations like local peace or environmental movements) we must begin with an acknowledgment and exploration of how we—our contradictory and multiple selves (fully historical and social)—are implicated in the meanings and pleasures we ascribe to those forms. The interest here is not so much self-knowledge as it is the understanding and consideration of the possibilities and limitations inherent in lived social differences.

The following interpretation of this particular popular text has been produced, in part, through our own investments in this film. This combination of reason and pleasure is organized not only by our shared work as educators interested in elaborating the complexities of a critical pedagogical practice but as well by biographies within which our earliest sense of social contradiction was formed by the juxtaposition of body movements, textures, timbre, and clothing. We have lived our lives within and against the grain of very different conjunctions of class, gender, and ethnic relations. For Simon, this experience of difference and desire was organized, in part, through being born the son of a marriage constituted across class divisions. Thus, the infrequent visits and family celebrations with working-class relatives and the more frequent moments when adult bodies (father and friends)—in the syntax, semantics, and very volume of speech; in the expansive gestures and use of space—articulated forms of passion and pleasure suppressed by the detachment offered with middle-class rituals of politeness and formalism. For Giroux, the experience of having a different culture inscribe the body in terms that were at odds with his own social positioning occurred when affiliatons organized through high school sport led to hanging out with working-class blacks. Attending weekend parties, dancing to the music of black blues singers such as Etta James, and learning how to dance without moving one's feet made manifest the fact that the body could speak with a rhythm vastly different from that which structured the Catholic Youth Organization dances for white working-class youth. In both situations, our bodies were positioned within different sets of experiences and practices that incorporated contradictions that we neither understood nor were able to articulate. Although our youth was shaped within and against the grain of very different class relations, what we have shared is the shock, awe, and production of desire in confronting bodies that know something we did not.

Unlike many of the teenage films currently sweeping the American and Canadian markets, *Dirty Dancing* locates the formation of youth within a material and social set of contradictory and conflicting practices. This film does not treat youth as an isolated social stratum lacking any wider referent than itself. Questions of class and sexism, culture and privilege come together in a tapestry of social relations that emerges within the unlikely location of an affluent summer resort for the families of the rising class of Jewish businessmen and professionals.

The year is 1963, and Frances "Baby" Houseman, her sister, mother, and father arrive at Kellerman's Resort for their summer vacation. We sense after a few moments into the film that Baby (who is soon to start a university program in the economics of international development and later plans to join the U.S. Peace Corps) is bored and alienated from the pleasures and pastimes of the nouveau Jewish-bourgeoisie who make up the majority of the patrons at Kellerman's. But we also quickly learn that Baby's idealistic political commitments to equality and fairness are just as surely rooted in the rhetorical discourse of liberal democracy historically embraced by her class (embodied particularly by her physician father). Baby is proudly introduced as someone who "is going to change the world" and do it with reason and intelligence.

Except for the college men hired by Kellerman to work the dining room, the hotel staff consists of young people whose experience and corporeality define a location across a solid class and ethnic barrier that marks the landscape of the resort. Such barriers are familiar to us: collectively we have been on both sides.

One evening after escaping the inanities of "entertainment night" at Kellerman's, Baby wanders the grounds and inadvertently discovers an unknown, astonishing and mesmerizing corner of the terrain of the popular, the site of "dirty dancing," a form of music and movement whose coded desires and productive pleasures crumble what to her seems like an empty bourgeois body, only to reconstitute it with new meanings and pleasures. What Baby discovers at this working-class party is the overt sensuality of rock and soul. She learns, in Barthes's words, that "the human body is not an eternal object, written forever in nature...for it is really a body that was constructed by history, by societies, by regimes, by ideologies."[37]

The articulations between Baby's class position and the class location of the employees at Kellerman's are first felt as differences of affective investment in the body. By placing her body within the terrain of working-class pleasures, Baby begins to feel and identify her body as a site of struggle, one which suggests a need to reject her family's view of bodily pleasure and desire for the more pronounced sexuality and bodily abandonment offered by the culture of the working-class staff parties. It is through the sociality of "dirty dancing" that Baby first engages her own class-specific cultural capital and attempts to reclaim her body through a redefined sense of pleasure and identity. For Baby, the body becomes the referent not only for redefining and remaking a sense of her own class and gender identity, but also for investing in a notion of desire and pleasure that reconstitutes her sense of self and social empowerment.

From this position—amazed and attracted to a particular body knowledge—the film's narrative begins to unfold. Baby is drawn to both the male and female personifications of the new cultural terrain, the dance instructor, Johnny Castle, and his partner, Penny. As the story proceeds, Baby is transformed both by a new body knowledge and a new knowledge of her body and its pleasures. Baby seems to embrace the "abandon" of working-class cultural terrain, finding in it perhaps an arena of feeling and emotion that cannot be totally colonized by the expectations of rationality within which her identity has been formed.[38]

Baby learns that Penny is pregnant and that money is needed to abort (illegally, then) the pregnancy. A "doctor" is only available on the night Penny and Johnny are to perform at a nearby hotel. If they miss the performance, Penny would most likely be fired. Deceiving her family (who place perfect faith in her reason and honesty), Baby obtains the abortion money from her father and agrees to take Penny's place as Johnny's partner. As Johnny begins to teach her the dance routine, their relationship develops.

Baby's substitution for Penny as Johnny's partner is a form of lived fantasy that works a reconstitution of explicitly who and what she is. As McRobbie has written:

> Dance evokes fantasy because it sets in motion a dual relationship projecting both internally towards the self and externally towards the "other"; which is to say that dance as a leisure activity connects desires for the self with those for somebody else. It articulates adolescence and girlhood with femininity and female sexuality and it does this by and through the body. This is especially

important because it is the one pleasurable arena where women have some control and know what is going on in relation to physical sensuality and to their own bodies. Continually bombarded with images and with information about how they should be and how they should feel, dance offers an escape, a positive and vibrant sexual expressiveness.[39]

That Baby's investment in the dance of the Other is being anchored through affect seems clear enough from the often-cliched dialogue. As Johnny emphasizes, "It is not enough to know the steps; you have to feel the music." And Baby acknowledges as their relationship deepens, "I'm afraid of never feeling the rest of my whole life as I do when I'm with you."

Even in a setting so well defined to privilege the wealthy, the constraints of class and power move across the terrains of pleasure and work so as to lay bare the relationship between wider social constraints and the formation of differentiated class-specific dreams. In *Dirty Dancing* the desire mobilized by relations of domination runs both ways. Johnny confides to Baby "I dreamt you and I were walking along and we met your father and he put his arm around me just like Robby [one of the Kellerman dining room staff who attends medical school]."

Baby's new investments, however, are not independent from the identity position regulated and organized by liberal discourse. Within the complications of the plot (when Johnny is falsely accused of theft) she acts on the belief that she can and should help those in trouble and less fortunate than herself, fully expecting Johnny and his friends to be treated with the same credibility and fairness as anyone else. When they are not, her naiveté is shattered, and the film seems about to conclude with an honest appraisal of the relations of class power. Even though he is cleared of the theft charge, Johnny is fired when Baby admits to their relationship. They say good-by to each other, and he drives off.

But author Bergstein was evidently unsatisified by such a limited sense of possibility. Consequently, she closes the film with what can either be dismissed as Hollywood schmaltz or celebrated as a glimpse of utopian hope keyed by the recognition of the importance of investments in the pleasures of sensuality. Johnny returns to find the season-closing Talent Night in progress. Confronting Baby's parents, he leads her on to the stage for a final dance performance which evolves into total audience participation. The film thus ends magically, erasing all social divisions (including the patriarchical one between Mr. and Mrs. Houseman) as all the assembled staff and guests rock and roll to the final dissolve into the film's credits.

This concluding scene constitutes dance as a collectivizing process within which individual differences disappear. Rock and roll, like religious singing, seems deftly to bind people together, uniting young and old, performer and audience, white and black, the rulers and the ruled, in a expression of celebration of the American dream in which the relationship between social power and inequality simply fades away.

What then does our understanding of *Dirty Dancing* display regarding the processes of persuasion. Our argument is that Baby's lived relation to the working-class people she engages is mediated by a dual investment mobilized by both the subject position she takes up within the discourse of liberalism *and* the popular cultural forms of working-class life within which she experiences the pleasures of the body. The point of emphasis here is the importance of popular cultural forms in constituting the identities which influence how we engage new challenges and construct new experiences. In this context we are referring to popular culture as a field within which investment is mobilized which is an elaboration of how any given cultural form (text, song, film, event) is engaged. It is worth noting how important it is to be able to hold analytically separate both semantic and affective aspects of investment since they can be mutually contradictory. Thus, it is not uncommon to experience contrary investments in relation to a specific cultural text, e.g., rock music can provide pleasure while being comprehended as very much sexist and racist. Such internal contradictions are integral to experiences of guilt.[40]

IMPLICATIONS FOR CRITICAL PEDAGOGICAL PRACTICE

> Everyday moments of teaching…incorporate the minds and bodies of subjects, as knowers and as learners. When we are at our best as teachers we are capable of speaking to each of these ways of knowing in ourselves and our students. We may override precedents in the educational project that value the knowing of the mind and deny the knowing of the heart and of the body. Students, the partners in these enterprise of knowing, are whole people with ideas, with emotions and with sensations. The project must not be confined to a knowing only of the mind; it must address and interrogate what we think we know from the heart and the body.[41]

Even in agreement with McDade, it is important to clarify that when we consider the relationship between popular cultures and pedagogy, we have a particular form of teaching and learning in mind. This is a critical pedagogical form that affirms the lived reality of difference as the ground on which to pose questions of theory and practice. It is a form that claims the experience of lived difference as an agenda for discussion and a central resource for a pedagogy of possibility.[42] The discussion of lived difference, if pedagogical, will take on a particular tension. It implies a struggle over assigned meaning, over in what direction to desire, over particular modes of expression, and ultimately, over multiple and even contradictory versions of "self." This struggle makes possible and hence can redefine the possibilities we see in both the conditions of our daily lives and those conditions which are "not yet." This is a struggle that can never be won, or pedagogy stops.[43]

What we are stressing is the absolutely crucial dimension of a critical pedagogy in which knowledge is conceived as an integral aspect of teaching/learning. As David Lusted writes:

Knowledge is not produced in the intentions of those who believe they hold it, whether in the pen or in the voice. It is produced in the process of interaction, between writer and reader at the moment of reading, and between teacher and learner at the moment of classroom engagement. Knowledge is not the matter that is offered so much as the matter that is understood. To think of fields or bodies of knowledge as if they are the property of academics and teachers is wrong. It denies an equality in the relations at moments of interaction and falsely privileges one side of the exchange, and what that side "knows" over the other.[44]

This position *does not require teachers to suppress or abandon what and how they know.* Indeed, the pedagogical struggle is lessened without such resources. Within this position, however, teachers and students are challenged to find forms in which a single discourse does not become the locus of certainty and certification. Teachers need to find ways of creating a space for mutual engagement of lived difference that does not require the silencing of a multiplicity of voices by a single dominant discourse. This is precisely the pedagogical motive for our insistence that *Dirty Dancing* be seen as an embodied interpretation that provides an invaluable resource from which to engage lived difference as a possibility for critical dialogue and self- and social formation.

What might teachers need to understand in order to engage in such a struggle? What might they wish to find out? If we take popular culture as that terrain of images, knowledge forms, and affective investments within which meaning and subjectivity function, there are several questions teachers might pursue. What are the historical conditions and material circumstances under which popular culture practices are pursued, organized, asserted, and regulated? Do such practices open up new notions of identities and possibilities? Are they disorganized and excluded? How are such practices articulated with forms of knowledge and pleasure legitimated by dominant groups? What interests and investments are served by a particular set of popular cultural practices and which are critiqued and challenged by the existence of such? What are the moral and political commitments of such practices and how are these related to one's own commitments as a teacher (and if there is a divergence, what does this imply)?

What all this means is that we think the analysis of popular culture is not simply a question of "reading" ideology from either commodity forms or forms of lived everday relations. Rather, we are moving toward a position within which one would inquire into the popular as a field of practices that constitute Foucault's indissoluble triad of knowledge, power, and pleasure.[45] At the same time we want to raise a note of caution. Teachers engaged in a pedagogy which requires some articulation of knowledge and pleasure integral to student life walk a dangerous road. Too easily, perhaps, encouraging student voice can become a form of voyeurism or satisfy an ego-expansionism constituted on the pleasures of understanding those who appear as Other to us. So, we must be clear on the nature of the pedagogy we pursue. Popular cultue and social difference can be taken up by educators either as a pleasurable form of knowledge/power which allows for more effective individualizing and administration of physical and moral regulation or such practices can be understood as the terrain on which we must meet our students in a critical and empowering pedagogical encounter.

As teachers committed to the project of a critical pedagogy we have to read the ground of the popular for investments that distort or constrict human potentialities and those that give voice to unrealized possibilities. This is what the pedagogical struggle is all about — opening up the material and discursive basis of particular ways of producing meaning and representing ourselves, our relations to others, and our relation to our environment so as to consider possibilities not yet realized. This is a utopian practice, to be embraced for its urgent necessity and scrutinized for its inherent limitations. John Berger captured the sentiment in his short story, "The Accordion Player."

> Music demands obedience. It even demands obedience of the imagination when a melody comes to mind. You can think of nothing else. It's a kind of tyrant. In exchange it offers its own freedom. All bodies can boast about themselves with music. The old can dance as well as the young. Time is forgotten. And that night, from behind the silence of the last stars, we thought we heard the affirmation of a Yes.

> "La Belle Jacqueline, once more!" the dressmaker shouted at Felix. "I love music! With music you can say everything!"

> "You can't talk to a lawyer with music," Felix replied.[46]

NOTES

A version of this chapter originally appeared in the journal *Cultural Studies* 2 (Oct. 1988): 294–320.

1. For example, see Ira Shor, *Critical Teaching and Everyday Life* (Boston: South End, 1980); Paul Willis, *Learning to Labor: How Working-Class Kids Get Working-Class Jobs* (New York: Columbia University Press, 1981); R. W. Connell et al., *Making the Difference: Schools, Families, and Social Division* (Sydney: George Allen & Unwin, 1982); Michael Apple, *Education and Power* (New York: Routledge & Kegan Paul, 1982); Henry A. Giroux, *Theory and Resistance in Education* (South Hadley, Mass.: Bergin & Garvey, 1983); Peter McLaren, *Schooling as a Ritual Performance* (New York: Routledge & Kegan Paul, 1986).

2. Examples of this work include Michael W. Apple and Lois Weis, eds., *Ideology and Practice in Schooling* (Philadelphia: Temple University Press, 1983); Margo Culley and Catherine Portuges, eds., *Gendered Subjects: The Dynamics of Feminist*

145,656

Teaching (New York: Routledge & Kegan Paul, 1985); David Livingstone and Contributors, *Critical Pedagogy and Cultural Power* (South Hadley, Mass.: Bergin & Garvey, 1987); Kathleen Weiler, *Women Teaching for Change* (South Hadley, Mass.: Bergin & Garvey, 1988); Jay MacLeod, *Ain't No Makin It* (Boulder: Westview, 1988).

3. Exceptions include the work published in *Screen Education* in England during the late 1970s and early 1980s and the U203 Popular Culture course and writings first offered by the Open University in the 1982 (and only recently terminated). For example, see the entire issue of *Screen Education*, No. 34 (Spring 1980), especially Tony Bennett, "Popular Culture: A Teaching Object," pp. 17–29; Iain Chambers, "Rethinking 'Popular Culture'" *Screen Education* No. 36 (Autumn 1980): 113–17; Iain Chambers, "Pop Music: A Teaching Perspective," *Screen Education* No. 39 (Summer 1981): 35–44; Len Masterman, *Teaching About Television* (London: Macmillan, 1980); Len Masterman, "TV Pedagogy," *Screen Education* No. 40 (Autumn/Winter 1981/2): 88–92; David Davies, *Popular Culture, Class, and Schooling* (London: Open University Press, 1981).

4. Both of these positions can be found in Theodore Mills Norton and Bertell Ollman, eds., *Studies in Socialist Pedagogy* (New York: Monthly Review Press, 1987). A classic example of the privileging of knowledge in the educational encounter can be found in Pierre Bourdieu and Jean-Claude Passeron, *Reproduction in Education, Society, and Culture* (London: Sage, 1977); see also Rachel Sharp, *Knowledge, Ideology, and the Politics of Schooling* (New York: Routledge & Kegan Paul, 1980).

5. Much of the radical work dealing with the hidden curriculum fell into the theoretical trap of privileging social relations and pedagogical processes over the relations between knowledge and power; the best-known example is Samuel Bowles and Herbert Gintis, *Schooling in Capitalist America* (New York: Basic, 1976); see more recent examples in Shor, *Critical Teaching and Everyday Life*, and Robert V. Bullough, Jr., Stanley L. Goldstein, and Ladd Holt, *Human Interests in the Curriculum* (New York: Teachers College Press, 1984).

6. This issue is taken up in detail in Henry A. Giroux, *Schooling and the Struggle for Public Life* (Minneapolis: University of Minnesota Press, 1988); Valerie Walkerdine, "On the Regulation of Speaking and Silence: Subjectivity, Class, and Gender in Contemporary Schooling," in *Language, Gender and Childhood*, Carolyn Steedman, Cathy Urwin, and Valerie Walkerdine, eds. (London: Routledge & Kegan Paul, 1985); Roger I. Simon, "Empowerment as a Pedagogy of Possibility," *Language Arts*, 64 (4): 370–82; Michelle Fine, "Silencing in Public Schools," *Language Arts*, 64 (2): 157–72.

7. The issue of the politics and pedagogy of emotional investment is developed in Lawrence Grossberg, "Teaching the Popular," in *Theory in the Classroom*, Cary Nelson, ed. (Urbana: University of Illinois Press, 1986). For an exceptional analysis of the relationship between pleasure and the popular, see Colin Mercer, "Complicit Pleasure," in *Popular Culture and Social Relations*, Tony Bennett, Colin Mercer, and Janet Woollacoot, eds. (Milton Keynes: Open University Press, 1986). Also see various articles in Fredric Jameson et al., *Formations of Pleasure* (London: Routledge & Kegan Paul, 1983).

8. For a historical treatment of this theme, see Patrick Brantlinger, *Bread and Circuses: Theories of Mass Culture as Social Decay* (Ithaca: Cornell University Press. 1983). This subject has been treated extensively, and we cannot repeat all of the sources here, but excellent analyses of the theoretical and political shortcomings of left and right positions on popular culture can be found in Stuart Hall,

"Deconstructing 'the Popular,'" in *People's History and Socialist Theory*, Raphael Samuel, ed. (London: Routledge & Kegan Paul, 1981); Tony Bennett and Graham Martin, eds. *Popular Culture: Past Present* (London: Croom Helm/Open University, 1982); Bennett, Mercer, and Woollacoot, eds., *Popular Culture and Social Relations*. It is worth noting that Postmodernism's disdain for the "masses" is a more more recent version of left cultural elitism that disdains popular culture; this is particularly true in the writings of Jean Baudrillard, such as *In the Shadow of the Silent Majorities*, Paul Foss, trans. (New York: Semiotext(e), 1983), and *Simulations,* Paul Foss et al., trans. (New York: Semiotext(e), 1983).

9. Max Horkheimer and Theodor W. Adorno, *Dialectic of the Enlightenment* (New York: Herder & Herder, [1944] 1972); see especially, "The Culture Industry: Enlightenment as Mass Deception," pp. 120–67; Theodor W. Adorno, "Television and the Patterns of Mass Culture," in *Mass Culture: The Popular Arts in America*, Bernard Rosenberg and David Manning White, eds. (Glencoe, Ill.: Free Press, 1957), especially pp. 483–84; Theodor Adorno, *Minima Moralia* (London: New Left Books, [1951] 1974).

10. Theodor W. Adorno, "Culture Industry Reconsidered," *New German Critique* No. 6 (Fall 1975) 18–19.

11. Adorno and Horkheimer, *Dialectic of the Enlightenment*.

12. Tony Bennett, "The Politics of the 'Popular' and Popular Culture," in *Popular Culture and Social Relations*, p. 15.

13. Examples of this tradition in the United States can be found in the *Journal of Popular Culture*; see also John G. Cawelti, *The Six-Gun Mystique* (Bowling Green, Ohio: Bowling Green State University Press, 1984). For a discussion of this issue, see Hall, "Deconstructing 'the Popular.'" For a brilliant work that integrates history and theoretical analyses, see John F. Kasson, *Amusing the Million: Coney Island at the Turn of the Century* (New York: Hill & Wang, 1978).

14. Brantlinger, *Bread and Circuses*, p. 23.

15. Allan Bloom, *The Closing of the American Mind* (New York: Simon & Schuster, 1987), p. 75 .

16. Bernard James, *The Death of Progress* (New York: Knopf, 1973), p. 38.

17. For an excellent commentary on this issue, see Robert Scholes, "Aiming a Canon at the Curriculum," *Salmagundi*, No. 72 (Fall 1986): 101–17.

18. Lawrence Grossberg, "Putting the Pop Back into PostModernism," in *Universal Abandon? The Politics of Postmodernism* (Minneapolis: University of Minnesota Press, 1988).

19. Lawrence Grossberg provides a useful theoretical elaboration of hegemony as a struggle for the popular:

> Hegemony is not a universally present struggle; it is a conjunctural politics opened up by the conditions of advanced capitalism, mass communication and culture....Hegemony defines the limits within which we can struggle, the field of "common sense" or "popular consciousness." It is the struggle to articulate the position of "leadership" within the social formation, the attempt by the ruling bloc to win for itself the position of leadership across the entire terrain of cultural and political life. Hegemony involves the mobilization of popular support, by a particular social bloc, for the broad range of its social projects. In this way, the people assent to a particular social order, to a particular system of power, to a particular articulation of chains of equivalence by which the interest of the ruling bloc come to define the leading positions

of the people. It is a struggle over "the popular." Lawrence Grossberg, "History, Politics and Postmodernism: Stuart Hall and Cultural Studies," *Journal of Communication Inquiry* 10 (1986): 69.

20. By focusing on the relationship between power and domination, on the one hand, and consent and struggle, on the other, Gramsci highlights not only the contradiction between the interests of the ruling bloc and the powerlessness of subordinate groups, but also the contradiction between the choices that subordinate groups make and the reality of the conduct they live out. Thought and action, common sense and lived experience, become for Gramsci elements of a contradictory consciousness that should be at the heart of political and pedagogical struggle. Gramsci clarifies what he means by contradictory consciousness in the following passage:

> The active man-in-the-mass has a practical activity, but has no clear theoretical consciousness of his practical activity, which nonetheless involves understanding the world insofar as it transforms it. His theoretical consciousness can indeed be historically in opposition to his activity. One might almost say that he has two theoretical consciousnesses (or one contradictory consciousness); one which is implicit in his activity and which in reality unites him with all his fellow workers in the practical transformation of the real world; and one, superficially explicit or verbal, which he has inherited from the past and uncritically absorbed. But this verbal conception is not without consequences. It holds together a specfic social group, it influences moral conduct and the direction of will, with varying efficacity but often powerfully enough to produce a situation in which the contradictory state of consciousness does not permit of any action, any decision or any choice, and produces a condition of moral and political passivity. Antonio Gramsci, *Selections from Prison Notebooks,* Q. Hoare and G. Smith, eds. (London: Lawrence & Wishart, 1971), p. 333.

For Gramsci, it is the terrain of the everyday and the popular that need to be understood in their contradictory representations of the world; moreover, as the basis for critique, common sense is treated as a discourse which becomes meaningful only if it is linked to those affective investments, practical activities, and elements of daily life that provide the basis both for understanding hegemony and for transforming it.

21. Ibid., p. 350.

22. Tony Bennett, "Introduction: Popular Culture and 'the Turn to Gramsci'" in *Popular Culture and Social Relations*, p. xv.

23. Hall, "Notes on Deconstructing 'the Popular,'" p. 235.

24. Lawrence Grossberg, "Putting the Pop Back into PostModernism," pp. 4-5; see also Lawrence Grossberg interviews Stuart Hall, "On Postmodernism and Articulation," *Journal of Communication Inquiry* 10 (1986): 45–60.

25. Ernst Bloch, *The Principle of Hope*, 3 vol. (Cambridge, Mass.: MIT Press, [1959] 1986).

26. Mercer, "Complicit Pleasure," p. 59.

27. Pierre Bourdieu, "The Aristocracy of Culture," in *Media, Culture, and Society* 2 (1980): 237–38.

28. The emphasis on the study of texts can be seen most clearly in Roland Barthes, *S/Z* (New York: Hill & Wang, 1974); the emphasis on the relationship between

popular culture and consumption is exemplified in Judith Williamson, *Decoding Advertisements: Ideology and Meaning in Advertising* (New York: Marion Boyars, 1978); Judith Williamson, *Consuming Passions: The Dynamics of Popular Culture* (New York: Marion Boyars, 1986).

29. Jürgen Habermas, *The Theory of Communicative Action*, vol. 1., Thomas McCarthy, trans. (Boston: Beacon, 1973).

30. Mercer, "Complicit Pleasure," pp. 54–55.

31. Mercer, "A Poverty of Desire: Pleasure and Popular Politics," in Jameson et al., *Formations of Pleasure*, p. 84.

32. Laura Mulvey, "Visual Pleasure and Narrative Cinema," *Screen* 16 (1986): 6–18.

33. Fredric Jameson, "Pleasure: A Political Issue," in Jameson et al., *Formations of Pleasure*, p. 10.

34. Ibid., p. 13.

35. Lawrence Grossberg, "Putting the Pop Back into PostModernism," pp. 5, 17.

36. Roland Barthes, *The Grain of the Voice: Interviews 1962–80*, Linda Coverdale, trans. (New York: Hill & Wang, 1985), p. 191.

37. Roland Barthes, "Encore le corps," *Critique* 35 (1982): 10.

38. The worst aspect of *Dirty Dancing* is its construction of the polarities of reason and passion as congruent with the class dichotomy portrayed in the film.

39. Angela McRobbie, "Dance and Social Fantasy," in Angela McRobbie and Mica Nava, eds., *Gender and Generation* (London: Macmillan, 1984), pp. 144–45.

40. Lawrence Grossberg, "Teaching the Popular," in Cary Nelson, ed. *Theory in the Classroom* (Urbana: University of Illinois Press, 1986).

41. Laurie McDade, "Sex, Pregnancy, and Schooling: Obstacles to a Critical Teaching of the Body," *Journal of Education* (in press): 1–2.

42. Simon, "Empowerment as a Pedagogy of Possibility."

43. Magda Lewis and Roger Simon, "A Discourse Not Intended for Her: Learning and Teaching With Patriarchy," *Harvard Educational Review* 56 (1986): 457–72.

44. David Lusted, "Why Pedagogy," *Screen* 27 (Sept.-Oct. 1986): 4–5.

45. Michel Foucault, *Power/Knowledge: Selected Interviews and Other Writings, 1972-1980*, Colin Gordon, ed. (New York: Pantheon, 1980).

46. John Berger, *Once in Europa* (New York: Pantheon, 1987), p. 35.

Chapter 2

PEDAGOGY AND THE POPULAR-CULTURAL-COMMODITY-TEXT

Paul Smith

♦ In this chapter I want to sketch out some of the theoretical issues which surround the teaching of popular culture and its texts and to add to these theoretical issues a reading of a couple of Hollywood movies of the genre known as action movies. Part of my aim is to offer some small sense of the theory and practice which constitute my own teaching. I work in a university English department which has, since 1984, run a program entitled "Literary and Cultural Studies." To state its aims as flatly as possible, this program intends to replace traditional English department canons and methodologies with, respectively, a broader and largely different range of texts and a more theoretically oriented and guided pedagogy. Even though the program operates within a very specific context, I hope that some of the issues and procedures I can point to in this chapter will have relevance to the teaching of popular culture in any educational environment.[1]

THE POPULAR-CULTURAL-COMMODITY-TEXT

Popular Culture and Texts

In the era of late capitalism it is no longer possible to think of any cultural object or artifact except in its extreme overdetermination (if, indeed, that ever *was* possible). That is to say, the time has passed when such objects could be viewed, as it were, objectively or as simple elements of a cultural superstructure. Their determinations cannot be explicated only by reference to the economic realm, and their effects cannot be considered as simply the reproduction of "false consciousness." In addition, in the industrial and postindustrial countries of the First World, cultural objects and artifacts are not only the commodity productions of our given historical phase of capitalism, but equally and always they have become the game pieces in a rapidly increasing and increasingly rapid miscegenation of global cultures. While it is probably the case that cultural objects are currently commodified as never before, it is equally true that the living cultures in which these objects circulate are ever more fragmented at the level of consumption, while at the same time they are ever more unified at the level of production. The circuits of capital, in other words, extend ever further and faster in global terms, but even as they do so they create the most fragmented of conditions wherever they reach. Countries and peoples in both the North and the South confront every day in the most extreme terms the cultural gap between their lived conditions and their histories and traditions, on the one hand, and on the other the demands of a global capitalist network of production and circulation which in its hegemonic success renders old-style territorial imperialism largely unnecessary. In the First World we tend, rather blithely, to refer to this cultural condition as "postmodernism," while elsewhere people live like the kids in the The Clash song, "Straight to Hell" – uncertain whether their heritage is Coca-Cola or rice. Any of our cultural artifacts are now deeply inscribed into this, the sharpest of contradictions.

Such a context inevitably demands a pedagogical rethinking of the status of popular culture and its objects – and perhaps the first move here is to distinguish as far as possible between the two. It would seem both necessary and legitimate to recognize that the artifacts, objects, and texts which we all currently consume do not themselves actually constitute popular culture. Rather, they are best seen as interventions into, or specifiable elements of, people's actual lived culture. The cultural object produced by capital always, of course, appeals to lived culture and indubitably has far-reaching effects on it, but, importantly, it cannot be said to *constitute* popular culture which I want to define here as an organic sociality. Popular culture, in this emphasis, can then be seen as the unfinished account of a continually negotiated intersection between relatively discrete, often fragmented social blocs and the productive forces of capital itself.

One of the immediate effects of making this distinction is to help amend those often insistent claims from the Left which would see the cultural products of capital as the bearers of a more or less irresistible ideological force and, consequently, to enable some theorization of the relation between the human "subject"[2] and the cultural artifact in a way which takes in the possibility that ideology can be contradictory for the subject, can fail, and can be resisted. The cultural object can be thence conceived of, not as an omnipotent ideological command, but as a text which the subject can read. Such reading will constitute a negotiation between the subject's experience and the demands, suggestions, or implications of the text.

At the same time, it is important not to try to deny or disregard the text's provenance: cultural objects, cultural texts, are still nonetheless *commodities* which will attempt to situate the subject in some preferred relation to them. Even if we resist a text, we still consume it and thus enter into a given relation to it. The artifacts and objects produced for us by capital must then be seen simultaneously as sites of our interaction and as objects for which we are consumers: they are popular-cultural-commodity-texts (PCCTs).

In the Classroom

In American schools (at all levels, I think) it is still quite rare for PCCTs to be part of the curriculum. Even in cultural studies programs at the college and university level it is by no means a matter of course that film, television, music and music video, mass circulation magazines, "dime-store" fiction, advertisements, and the like should be taken into the classroom. The relatively conspicuous absence of PCCTs from classrooms here might be taken as symptomatic of widely accepted pedagogical practices (and sometimes theories) which assume that culture is a mostly static entity, containable in its most essential and fixed forms in anthologies and in the works of a few privileged writers).[3] Even when such texts are used it is not inevitable that their use should be for progressive purposes. Often PCCTs function in classrooms as lures and come-ons offered by teachers to students reluctant or unwilling to appreciate the virtues of the canonical curriculum. It would seem quite common, for instance, for the lyrics of rock music to be used in the poetry section of an English course or for film versions of particular fictions to be used to animate discussion of the literary. In such cases, the PCCT is evidently only a teaching aid; its own specificity is rarely addressed, and its interest resides in the light that it can shed on more routine concerns.

The PCCT can, however, act in classrooms as the most apt place from which to develop precisely an opposition to canonical texts and to the interests which subvent them. This is a slightly different function from the one which many radical educators would give to such texts. Deriving from the liberal-progressivist educational tradition which reached its acme (or nadir) with the call to relevance in the late 1960s, whatever increased interest there is in PCCTs often leads teachers to use them to facilitate students in expressing or assessing their own experience. The logic is that the nearest access that most students have to culture is through and in mass culture and that their interest and participation in that realm can be turned toward self-expression and self-consciousness. In this process, so the argument goes, students will see their own experiences reflected and thus be more satisfied with the classroom experience than if they were taught canonical texts.

This little logic has many pitfalls when put into practice, so it seems to me. Not least, it tends to encourage the unwarranted validation of individual experience and thence often leads, via relativism, toward a kind of cultural quietism: the students' supposed propinquity to what might be called the cultural ethos of such texts allows them to assume that their understanding or interpretation of the texts is as sufficient as the next person's. If that were the case, then nothing need be done: the subjective reception of the text is adequate, can be celebrated as somehow an authentic response, and — more disturbing — leaves the individual student's response stunted and isolated in relation to even the most pressing social issues.

Of course, in making those observations I do not wish to deny the importance of subjective responses, or to suggest that they cannot be built upon and finally turned to more radical ends. Rather, I am concerned that the mere fact of facilitating the production of students' voices often remains an end in itself — a celebration after which we return to the everyday. There is, of course, much theory written about the place of student voice and experience in pedagogical method, but my sense is that it is this celebratory mode that usually marks practice.[4]

In such contexts, where pedagogical theory and practice have demonstrated a willingness to enhance students' participation and to encourage their voices but prove unable or unwilling to pass beyond this level of celebration, the crucially missing pedagogical element is often the recognition of contradiction. Faced with any PCCT, students and teachers alike have the task of investigating that text's role in both the proffering of meaning and, more generally, social relations.

Meaning is often already understood by students to reside within texts of a traditional kind (novels, poems, stories) but is not always recognized by them as a component of the PCCT. Students already tend to think of PCCTS as texts which do not need to be analyzed; rather, they often seem self-evident or obvious, texts which, to adopt a distinction of Roland Barthes's, *signal* rather than *signify*.[5] The first pedagogical task, then, can be conceived as the production of contradiction in and among students' views of the PCCT, simply by treating it as meaningful and significant. The text, any text, delimits a particular field of meaning, displays internal contradictions, offers particular interpretative choices, alludes to given histories and circumstances.[6] These need to be put into play in all their contradictions, not necessarily as contradictions which need to be resolved, but as contradictions which the students should be encouraged to puzzle. Similarly, the conflict among different students' receptions of the PCCT can be encouraged, further undermining the text's previously silent, unanalyzed passage through their lives and marking it as the site of disagreement, not to say struggle.

The second pedagogical task would concern the PCCT's production of social relations. This need not be undertaken (as I think it often is) at the level of ideology. Rather than encourage students to think primarily in terms of what has come to be known as the positioning or the interpolation of themselves as subjects, more effective, I think, is to ask them to address precisely the commodity status of the text. How do they obtain, say, a movie ticket or a rock album; what is the price of the commodity in monetary terms; where do they get that money; whose work – theirs, their parents', someone else's – pays for it; do they find the text cheap or expensive in relation to that work? Questions such as these are necessarily to be supplemented by others: among whom is the price of the commodity distributed; do the students admire, resent, or feel indifferent towards the beneficiaries of the sale; and so on? The contradictions usually brought to light by the students' answers to such questions locate the PCCT firmly in their own daily lives.

At bottom the intention of this double investigation is to foster a particular recognition of the distinction with which I started, between the PCCT itself and popular culture. The stress on the text's variable, contradictory, and not necessarily shared meaning, on the one hand, and the discussion of students' place in a pragmatic social relation to the text, on the other hand, can produce something very important – a sense of the central position and role of a PCCT in constructing, upholding, or perhaps even resisting a context of interests which students will no longer automatically accept as identical to the interests of their own lived culture. This seems to me important not only because it will counter teachers' frequent classroom use of PCCTs under the assumption that they are the students' own culture, but much more because it breaks through students' own embedded silence about both their own experience and their relation to PCCTs.

The PCCT in Action

The preceding remarks have been largely theoretical in nature, even though I hope that they adumbrate a feasible pedagogical practice. Certainly they reflect my sense that some generalized notions of both pedagogy itself and the public aims of that pedagogy need to precede and prefigure any actual classroom dealings with texts. But I want now to turn to an actual analysis of a couple of PCCTs. This analysis is not exactly a composite or mimetic version of readings that have come up in classroom situations, but is nonetheless a reading which was made possible by those experiences, and it points toward a few, further observations in the shorter, final section of this chapter.

This particular analysis – involving two recent Hollywood action movies, Clint Eastwood's *Heartbreak Ridge* and Richard Donner's *Lethal Weapon* – arose most directly from discussions of popular women's magazines. Class members were asked to give their reactions to journals such as *Vogue*, *Cosmopolitan*, *Mademoiselle*, *Playgirl*, *Ms.*, and others of the sort.[7] Among the issues that the students found to be foregrounded by articles in these magazines was (predictably) relations between men and women. In particular, the magazines often dealt with an entity known variously as "the new man," "the sensitive male," or "the man of the Eighties." The readiness with which students picked up this theme was undoubtedly the product of our having previously read some parts of Rosalind Coward's *Female Desires*, a book which attempts to demonstrate how images of women are constructed in the various media and internalized by female subjects.[8] This book and the students' projects on women's magazines were followed by several assignments designed to help them locate similar constructions of masculinity. The most frequently mentioned locus for such constructions was the movies; many had recently seen the Eastwood movie, and they were asked to see the then newly released *Lethal Weapon*.

Hollywood's long and persistent tradition of action movies has been centered on the most traditional of masculine heroes and rarely paused to take stock of alternative social trends and moralities. Throughout the last fifty or more years the action movie has continued on with a business-as-usual attitude and has functioned as a kind of universal Hollywood standard, positing its male hero as the unquestionable and timeless essence of masculinity. Action movies in the late Eighties, however, seem to break this mold in a certain way. The discourse on masculinity which action movies generally constitute has begun to find space for explicit consideration of a quality that at first blush would seem alien to it: sensitivity in the male, a motif in both *Lethal Weapon*, with Mel Gibson and Danny Glover, and *Heartbreak Ridge*.

Lethal Weapon is about a partnership between Gibson and Glover, and both characters contribute in different ways to one of the movie's central problematics: the contradictory impulse — between utter macho and relative sensitivity — which a male in the Eighties is considered to have to cope with. In both these movies the new sensitivity motive might be interpreted as a belated response to the kind of pop feminism of the women's magazines, or at least as a response to an area of popular culture which is trying to recuperate and popularize the concept of strong womanhood. In both *Lethal Weapon* and *Heartbreak Ridge*, sensitivity as a response (and later as a riposte) to a particular kind of woman is a central motif.

In *Lethal Weapon*, playing the older, black, half of the central male partnership, Danny Glover is shown trying to be the sensitive male when, for instance, he deals with his wife at breakfast. He is a traditional Hollywood male in many ways, that is, he'll do things such as peremptorily ask his wife what's the spot on his tie or make a snide comment when she accidentally breaks an egg on the floor. But greeted by her patient though sarcastic responses, he accepts her implicit rebuke of his manner and seems to express any further annoyances with very deliberate and clumsy good humor. His sense of his family's integrity and importance is there acted out in such a way as to express his need not to alienate a basically strong and supportive wife. And with his family generally his tactic is good humor and tolerance, to the point that he will act childishly and join in with his children's antics without any apparent self-consciousness.

Although he acts young with his family, at work he is often harassed and confused, continually complaining that he is "too old for this shit." The family is thus offered as the fulcrum of his sanity, as the calm center around which the dangers of his job and the apparently psychopathic behavior of his partner, Mel Gibson, circulate. Indeed, it is through this sense of family that the villains of the movie attack him — they kidnap his teenaged daughter.[9]

After his concessions to, and his implied need of, his wife and family have been established, however, Glover is shown worrying about precisely his "sensitivity." In a sequence at the police station, Glover is shown anxiously considering the term "an Eighties man." In the context of his work he is clearly not sure that he should be an Eighties man since such a man can be easily confused with a nonmacho man, bending to women's will, showing his sensitivity, and generally being what Glover calls "a pussy." His anxiety is played upon by a colleague who, taking Glover's anxiety rather lightly, tells him, "You know, I cried in bed last night." Glover asks with some alarm, "Were you alone?" and the colleague replies, "That's why I was crying, 'cos I was on my own." In that short set-piece exchange, the movie undermines the style of Glover's dealing with family life, interrogates the whole notion of the new male's sensitivity, turns it into a joke, and suggests that it's all some kind of sham.

The movie's plot itself also undercuts Glover's clinging to the uxorial and childish ethos of the home. The Mel Gibson character, all the things that Glover is not (young, single, unsettled, living in a trailer, immoderate in his tastes, violent), not only ends up being the effective protector of the black man's home, he also brings his own lifestyle into that home.

The climactic scene of Lethal Weapon involves Gibson's combat (in a vaguely kung-fu style) with the arch-CIA-villain right on Glover's front lawn. In a sense Gibson brings a demonstration of empowered masculinity precisely home in order to correct Glover's wavering masculinity. At least, the implication is that the security of home cannot be guaranteed without the intervention of such a man — an implication which has further, political implications and which is familiar enough in Hollywood, especially of late. This message is underlined by the film's closing scene in which Glover invites Gibson to share the family's Christmas turkey and Gibson arrives with a dog which immediately duels with the family's cat. The last dialogue in the movie has Gibson say that he would "put five on the mutt." Thus the Gibson brand of masculinity is imported into the home as its heroic emblem, but also as a disturbance.

In those two ways Lethal Weapon undermines or negates its initial dealings with the idea of the sensitive male, the Eighties man, as adumbrated in the Glover character. The strategy is paralleled in the Gibson character's development throughout the movie. What the audience knows about Gibson at the beginning is that he is a wildly violent but obviously successful cop who gets transferred to become Glover's partner in part because the movie's police psychologist—a woman, of course—keeps warning that he is becoming dangerously suicidal. In one of this movie's best sequences, shot mostly in very tight close-up, we see Gibson at the point of committing suicide. Like Eastwood's Dirty Harry, he apparently has lost the woman he loved: with his wedding pictures on his lap and his gun at his head, he agonizes and comes within a millisecond of shooting himself. Later he tells Glover that what keeps him from suicide is his job—basically killing bad guys. His sensitivity, arising from a definite but unelaborated suffering over a woman, is converted, predictably enough, to the good, to the defense of the nuclear family, and to the removal of corruption from the civic body.

What is also predictable is the way the movie climaxes, as it were, with the two main characters consummating a homoerotic relationship that has been running throughout the movie. Standing very close, one behind the other, they draw their guns (Gibson's has earlier been shown to be bigger than Glover's) and finish off the villain. This medium shot is reminiscent of one of the final scenes in *Beverly Hills Cop*, in which Eddie Murphy and the older policeman similarly line up one behind the other to shoot that movie's villain, a crooked art dealer who is specifically portrayed as gay.

Such allegories of the true male spirit, manifested in cooperative relationships and consummated in an act of joint violence, are not unusual in Hollywood, nor is it unusual that one element of such relationships is the simultaneous exercise of homophobia and exorcising of homosexuality. But what is perhaps most interesting about these two characters is the extent to which, especially with Gibson in the suicide scene, their emotional vulnerability is allowed to be portrayed. Certainly for the Gibson character, this is no mere resentment or frustration with bureaucracy in the Dirty Harry mold, but something closer to a genuine existential angst. For Hollywood to be portraying explicitly this degree of male vulnerability—in a movie which, moreover, has already committed itself to some kind of discourse about the Eighties man and male sensitivity—provokes some interesting questions for the classroom. Why this, now, in an era when the dominant political ethos would seem to be antagonistic to such a version of masculinity? What are the aspects of such a move which might empower the Eighties man? What changes occur in the more traditional or familiar of popular culture's paradigms of gender relations? Is there any sense in which such a portrayal of the Eighties man can be functional in a progressive way?

My own implicit answer to at least the last question is that such a movie, although to some extent internally conflictual, finally succeeds in negating any radical potential it might have included within itself. That conclusion will be unsurprising in many ways. The discourse of left criticism on popular culture—with a few exceptions, such as in moments of Benjamin's work—has chronically consisted in either a straightforward condemnation of the false ideologies foisted by the culture industry upon subjected audiences or what has always appeared to me as a rather whistling-in-the-dark kind of celebration of the radical energy of both popular cultural artifacts and their mass audiences. This dichotomy certainly doesn't point to the whole story (I'll return to this toward the end), but it does seem to me to pose a central and perpetually unresolved dilemma for the Left in general and for the teaching of PCCTs in particular: the issue of how to deal with the ubiquitous symptoms of a popular culture which we suspect of both *subjecting* (in relatively clear ways) and of *empowering* (in more mysterious ways) the mass audiences of contemporary cultures. To put this contradiction differently, it is relatively simple and common to read from the cultural text its ideological messages and to critique them; yet at the same time it is currently politically *de rigueur* not to regard mass audiences as merely the passive dupes of the overpowering ideological products of their culture.

I don't pretend to offer—here or elsewhere—the solution to that dilemma; I want merely to try to negotiate a way toward a space from which to view and thus to teach the issues, while maintaining a certain oppositional tendency and while concentrating on the production of meanings around a crucial part of popular culture's repertoire of ideologies—its images of sexual identity.

Late in 1986, in her syndicated newspaper column, Ellen Goodman wrote about another movie in which the hero's sense of masculinity is specifically addressed: Clint Eastwood's *Heartbreak Ridge*.[10] In this movie Eastwood directs himself in the role of a career marine sergeant put in charge of a bunch of misfit recruits who have no respect for marine discipline, tradition, officers, or work. Eastwood whips them into shape, just in time for them to become the cutting edge in the U.S. invasion of Grenada (no less!). Eastwood's marine sergeant persona (that is, Eastwood at work) is anything but the figure of the Eighties man who subvents the discourse of *Lethal Weapon*. Indeed, his character here is perhaps even more unreconstructed and dinosauric[11] than in most of his movies as he ruthlessly resocializes his recruits and cold-bloodedly executes a surgical strike on the mostly Cuban enemy in Grenada.

It is not this action-man persona that is of interest to Ellen Goodman. She picks up on the movie's romance plot. In the town where he is sent to train these recruits Eastwood discovers his ex-wife who had left him precisely because of his macho behavior and his commitment to the lifestyle and ethos of the marines. Eastwood, determined to win her back, begins to look for clues about what went wrong with their marriage. In his spare time he reads women's magazines, does *Cosmopolitan*-type quizzes, pores over the pop-psych articles about relationships, and so on. He then attempts to use these in dealing with his ex-wife, asking her, "Did we mutually nurture each other? Did we communicate in a meaningful way in our relationship?" Goodman wants to see these unfamiliar words in Eastwood's mouth as a positive and hopeful sign that men in the Eighties perhaps are willing to "wrestle with new words and emotions" in order to deal with a new generation of women and their demands. The movie itself seems to support her point of view in that the ex-wife, purely on the grounds that Eastwood "really [is] trying to understand," takes him back on his return from Grenada. Goodman then generalizes what she sees as this movie's positive point by applying it to other male figures in popular culture who seem to be struggling with the conflict between macho strength and the newly acquired sensitivity of the Eighties men. Among such men, she says — somewhat to my amazement — are Frank Furillo of "Hill Street Blues" and the public image of Bruce Springsteen.

By leaving aside some of the more offensive aspects of *Heartbreak Ridge* (specifically those involving the invasion of Grenada) and concentrating only on this romance plot, Goodman distorts a movie in which male sensitivity is in fact presented only to be discarded or undermined by the movie's overall strategies. For instance, the sensitivity toward the woman and her demands is undercut by her final acceptance of the more traditional side of the man into the home, as it were, just as in *Lethal Weapon*. At the end of *Heartbreak Ridge*, Eastwood is still refusing to abandon his marine career — a refusal that had indeed been one of the primary reasons his wife left him in the first place. In other words, nothing has changed except that the male's courting ritual has promised sensitivity.

Furthermore this much-vaunted quality is in contradiction to other movements in the film's rhetoric. The opening sequence shows Eastwood, jailed for being drunk and disorderly, delivering himself of a little discourse to his cellmates about the merits of various women he has penetrated while on duty abroad. This scene and many that follow are marked by their extravagant use — even for Hollywood R-rated movies — of obscenities and sexist descriptions of women and their bodies. Equally, the training of the recruits themselves involves turning them away from being effeminate, fashion-conscious, ornamented, sexually liberal young men, and toward being the good men that the marines demand. One of the sergeant's main strategies in this enterprise is to impugn the recruits' sexuality, telling them in various obscene ways that they are gay, and if not gay then mere "pussies" or "ladies."

Here again, just as with *Lethal Weapon*, the spectacle of what Goodman wants to see as a "window of vulnerability" being opened is in fact just a lure, a strategy by which the traditional Hollywood male can, without essentially changing, have it all. Both these narratives seem to be not about merely the heroes' triumph over social or political evil, but also and once more over women. A touch of sensitivity or vulnerability brings another arm, a further resiliency to masculinity's dominatory arsenal.

In other words, none of this discourse of male sexuality in contemporary action movies is anything but a lure. Even the problematic of sensitivity itself has hardly been absent from over fifty years of Hollywood action movies. The traditional male hero of these films has always been a divided being, in that the direct expression of his heterosexuality has always been somewhat disjunct from the demonstration of his action-man qualities. This disjunction has chronically been used to promote the same kind of division of the sexes as we find in these contemporary action movies in which women, in order to be wooed, won, and kept, have to have their natural appreciation of sensitivity, interpersonal communication, and beauty flattered by the men to whom that discourse is naturally alien. And Hollywood's male heroes have always been presented as masters of the seductive discourses necessary for the satisfying of women and, equally and simultaneously, as the homophobic masters of the external world (the world of work) and its villains.

Women too, have always been at the receiving end, as it were, of that mastery. So what is interesting about the current crop of action movies is that precisely the discourse of sensitivity has become a specific target. As women are perceived to have become more demanding, more independent, more ready to make decisive ruptures in the masculine view of things and as some men have necessarily become aware of the rights of women to do these things, so the image of masculinity in the movies has more of which to purge itself, has another obstacle to its final triumph.

I asked early why this discourse of the Eighties man is being put into place right now, and I think the answer is so that it can be discredited. There are, in my view, no aspects of these movies which might empower the actually existing Eighties man. Male audiences, to judge from students' reactions, know this. The discrediting of the sensitive man on screen, and a con-comitant increase in the intensity of macho violence, acts as yet another imaginary, almost cathartic, in an old fashioned sense, allaying of social contradictions. Audiences know to laugh when Gibson brings his mutt into the settled bourgeois household; they know to laugh when Eastwood, his face twitching as if to keep from laughing, asks whether his relationship has been a mutually supportive one. And so it goes. Little has changed, except *mode*, in the more traditional or familiar of popular culture's paradigms of gender relations. The hopeful signs that someone like Goodman grasps at are subsumed under an even more resilient and even cynical mastery.

POPULAR CULTURES AND GENDER DIFFERENCE

The kind of performative analysis of texts that I have just given probably seems at first blush to sit quite uneasily with my general worries and claims in the first section of this chapter. It might be suggested that this kind of analysis (which, even with its brevity and specific focus, shows a kind of professorial, knowledge-based reading skill at work) does nothing to help advance radical pedagogical practice and might indeed even serve merely to intimidate students. However, what I want to claim is that such an analysis can be produced (indeed, in this instance largely was produced) by students themselves under certain conditions. Those conditions, it seems to me, demand a series of recognitions if they are to come into existence: first, that the PCCT can best be taught only within the framework, or scaffolding, of a clearly articulated pedagogical theory; second, that the role of the teacher in the classroom cannot be reduced to that of empty sounding-board for students' reactions but must be seen as something more akin to that of an orchestrator; and third, that both the pedagogical theory and the practice of text analysis should together be geared toward some specific substantive goal or telos.

The structure of this argument is intended to reflect a certain ordering of those conditions and also to point up some of the necessary problems that arise from contradictions between them. My initial concern with generalized pedagogical questions is intended to stress my conviction that pedagogical theory cannot be seen as a mere afterthought to content. Equally, content analysis, even when coded into discourses which might be alien to students, should not be abandoned because of some vaguely defined professorial guilt. Then (and this is the gist of this section), I want to emphasize the importance of having both theory and practice turn toward a specifiable and substantive social issue which would be the point where the teaching of the PCCT will most fully implicate students.

It would seem an absolute truism that one of the most difficult pedagogical problems remains the contradiction between what might be called the lecturing, professorial stance and the desire to have students articulate their own experience. It is clearly not satisfactory to resort here to a notion of dialogue, or something of that sort, in order to resolve such a contradiction. Still less is it appropriate to fall completely on one side or the other of this dichotomy. Rather I suggest that the contradiction itself needs to be worked in any specific context and that the presentation of what literary theorists sometimes call a "strong reading" from a teacher is not *per se* a retrograde pedagogical act. What I am getting at here is the idea that in order to learn to resist a text or texts students need to come up against resistance from it and, by extension, from teachers. Teachers, in my view, not only cannot abrogate their responsibility to their own voices and their own cultural experience and knowledge; they are obliged to present those elements as needing to be taken into account by students. But (and this seems to me crucial) such resistance thrown up by teachers can only operate effectively (and by that I mean in part in a nonintimidatory manner) when it is articulated to and towards a particular question or set of questions which open out beyond both pedagogical theory and classroom analysis. In this instance, with the two texts that I have briefly analyzed here, that more general context is the question of gender and gender relations.

Now it may seem that, far from opening up a space from which to see the issues of popular culture, my analyses adopt something like a Frankfurt School tone and mode by pointing to an overwhelming and utterly resilient ideological effect in such movies. This may be a tone adopted to counter my understanding that, perhaps in overreaction to what has been seen as the harsh determinism of structuralist and functionalist accounts of mass-media culture, left criticism and theory have of late been tending too far in the direction of celebrating a perceived multiplicity of voices in that culture (with the authority of Derrida and/or Bakhtin often being called upon to bolster the claim). This celebratory tendency, marking out a dialectical implication of resistance in both the products and consumers of our culture, often lends itself to a certain kind of inconclusive dance of difference or differences. At any rate, it is certainly true that I myself would not wish to celebrate anything in these movies as the authentic voice of any resistant subculture or oppressed group. It is important to stress, in opposition to that tendency, that such voices are not to be found in texts, but obviously rather in the lived social relations of the students, of which the classroom situation is but one.

What are often lost in the current championing of multiplicity and difference are the necessarily *moral* and *teleological* dimensions of culture critique. These elements in oppositional thinking have fallen into some disrepute, or at least disuse, and along with them falls the idea that oppositional analysis could possibly have some sense of itself as liberatory rather than merely critical. The Frankfurt School, perhaps our nearest major proponent of a genuine ideology critique, at least never lost sight of those dimensions not only of the Left's tradition, but also of its ongoing tasks. True, Adorno and Horkheimer, in their massively dark condemnations of the culture industry, for instance, carried the moral dimension precisely into a largely sterile moralism and suffered from a couple of the predictable debilities of such a moralism: pessimism and elitism. Nonetheless, it seems obvious still that oppositional criticism must refuse to give up precisely its dimension of moral and political insistence.

In relation to the movies briefly looked at here, the simple but rather condemnatory reading I have given of them offers an example of something which is important to remember. The PCCT, however internally conflictual it might be or however it might accommodate itself to changing social conditions, always contains the specific interests that underpin it and produce it. My claim is that those specific interests cannot be brought out in the classroom by any straightforward kind of encounter with the texts nor, in other words, by the unmediated pedagogical plan of offering students the opportunity to react to them. This would be to adopt a pedagogical approach which is ultimately too text-centered and leaves to much unbroached. The task is, instead, to direct attention and learned skills to something outside texts.

In general, contemporary PCCTs more and more refuse to offer them-selves as unequivocally right wing or liberal in terms of ideological provenance.[12] But as politics in that sense is made ambivalent and some-what murky, popular culture shows itself more and more fascinated by, more and more interested in, the vagaries of sexual difference and, at the same time, tends to adopt increasingly flexible strategies for the protection of male dominance. This figure of the Eighties man might have arisen from a fairly solid and stolid filmic tradition, but is does seem to be a specifically Eighties obsession. In that sense, it points towards one of the possible areas which pedagogy must broach beyond text and immediate textual experience.

There is a clear contradiction within these particular PCCTs which can be exploited. Even as the PCCT installs the sensitive man as its newest or favorite target, it nonetheless puts it up, that is, the question of sexual difference and gender relations is at least no longer taken as chronically and automatically settled in that sphere, and in particular the whole idea of masculine identity has been put into play once more.

There is a certain irony in this. While it has become almost a cliché for feminism to point out that men still have everything to say about their own sexuality, it seems to be the texts of popular culture that are responding to the challenge—defensively, to be sure, but responding just the same. In other words, feminism has over the last ten or twenty years provoked a battle ground of sexuality, and this is a battle that men on the Left still have not wholeheartedly joined. One of the ways to start, perhaps, might be to contest from the grounds of our own sexuality, from our own experience of gendered identity, the versions of masculinity that the culture offers. More specifically, we could begin by naming our sexuality and contesting a number of the notions currently being put forward about the Eighties man. That figure is marked by a homophobia which is then disavowed by the resolution of rivalry between allies, is nonetheless unproblematically heterosexual, is covertly and cynically both the enemy and the seducer of women's ex-pressed desires, is fervid supporter of home and country by whatever means, is constructed in a division between hysterically dutiful violence and merely ingratiating sensitivity, and is surely nothing more than a fiction.

For pedagogical practice this fiction is ripe to be exploited. Most class-rooms in most contexts today are coed, even if (especially at North American universities and colleges) they are in other respects pretty homogeneous. Now that class and even race distinctions are mostly silent (that is, silenced or passed over in silence) in many educational institutions, gender distinc-tions are perhaps the most powerful ones that actually exist among students. They can and need to be exploited as a way of marking and remarking the experience of contradiction between PCCTs and the actual lived lives and cultures of their audiences/consumers.

NOTES

1. For information purposes, the particular context, Carnegie Mellon University, is a small, expensive American four-year college, mostly dedicated to technological and vocational education and into which the introduction of this kind of program is already an anomaly. The incoming student classes are not universally literate to the level of most major universities, and the institutional incentive for them to become so is negligible. The students' class backgrounds are quite varied; ethnically the school seems to have more Asians than it does blacks.

2. I put this word in quotations here only, following my practice in *Discerning the Subject* (Minneapolis: University of Minnesota Press, 1987); the book's argument—in its most basic reduction—is that contemporary discourses in the human and social sciences employ theories of the "subject" which foreclose upon any notion of human agency. The book attempts, in other words, to weaken the hegemonic use of the term subject.

3. The arguments and rationales for using such texts at all levels of education have often been proffered, of course, and I don't wish to restate them here. Many of these rationales are offered in the course of making a general distinction between process-oriented and product-oriented pedagogy. For a reworking of that distinction, see Robert Scholes, *Textual Power: Literary Theory and the Teaching of English* (New Haven: Yale University Press, 1985). For particular theoretical arguments of the teaching of popular culture, see Henry Giroux, David Shumway, Paul Smith, and James Sosnoski, "The Need for Cultural Studies: Resisting Intellectuals and Oppositional Public Spheres," *The Dalhousie Review* 64 (2): 472–86.

4. For a lucid theoretical discussion of the issue of student voice and experience, see Henry Giroux, *Schooling for Democracy: Critical Pedagogy in the Public Sphere* (Minneapolis: University of Minnesota Press, 1988).

5. Roland Barthes, *Le Degré zéro de l'écriture* (Paris: Seuil, 1972), p. 7.

6. See Henry Giroux, "Citizenship, Public Philosophy, and the Struggle for Democracy," *Educational Theory* 37 (2): 103–20, particularly the section "Celluloid Patriotism in Hollywood Films and TV Programming," where these characteristics are discussed more fully.

7. This class was an introductory writing and reading one, English 101, "Reading Texts." It is a university-required course which is tailored to fit with the Literary and Cultural Studies Program mentioned in the text.

Most of the women's magazine discourse on the "new man," as found by students, seemed to assume the existence of such a creature and to want to question his usefulness. Among the texts the class discussed were the following: "Does the New Woman Really Want the New Man?" *Working Woman*, May 1985, pp. 54–56; "The Book on Men's Studies," *Newsweek*, April 28, 1986, p. 79; "The New New Man," *Mademoiselle*, August 1986; "Has the '80s man become the superwimp to superwoman?" *USA Today*, November 26, 1986.

8. Rosalind Coward, *Female Desires* (New York: Grove Press, 1985). This book is, I take it, intended to bring the feminist case to the postfeminist generation, and in doing so it tries to hide or disguise the Freudian, Marxist, and feminist arguments upon which it rests. In the classroom this proved to be a strategic error, in that Coward does not supply the warrants for many of her arguments about popular culture. Students found the book to be poorly argued. They also objected, rightly I think, to Coward's generalizing about "all women" and to her apparent refusal to recognize that male desires, too, are constructed in the way that she claims women's

are. These latter objections catalyzed our class subsequently to address the question of masculinity.

9. This is actually a strange proposition in *Lethal Weapon*'s rhetoric. The villains are ex-Special Forces operators, and it is heavily implied that they still work for the CIA in a peacetime drug-running capacity. Given the Reagan administration's committed sustenance of large-scale illegal activity on the part of its secret operators and its more than occasional attacks on the decadence of black family values, this aspect of the movie can perhaps be seen as a corrective of some kind. However, it is an aspect that is not sustained and even itself my be corrected or negated in some of the ways I mention.

10. Ellen Goodman, "A Nurturing Eastwood?" *Boston Globe*, December 23, 1986.

11. I use this term, dinosauric, to advertise a book I am currently writing on Clint Eastwood, provisionally titled "Dinosaurs: Eastwood/Hollywood."

12. It is true that movies like the two I am referring to could be understood as containing politically liberal, certainly populist, political ideologies, but my sense is that the word containing is absolutely apt there. Such movies do seem to include oppositional moments, contradictory impulses within their narratives, but these are ultimately held in check or discredited by the movement of the narrative and specifically its closure. At the same time, it would not be quite appropriate to dub such movies "right wing." They are certainly conservative in a certain sense, but I would argue that Hollywood has constructed its own unique and specific ideology which very rarely coincides exactly with the path of traditional ideologies of the Right or the Left. For instance, I think it would be tempting to label as reactionary movies like the two recent Vietnam retrospectives, Oliver Stone's *Platoon* and Francis Coppola's *Gardens of Stone*, but a close reading of those two movies would show them struggling *not* to recognize any particular political provenance and returning, rather, to the history of Hollywood itself and not the history of Vietnam.

Chapter 3

EDUCATIONAL MEDIA, IDEOLOGY, AND THE PRESENTATION OF KNOWLEDGE THROUGH POPULAR CULTURAL FORMS

Elizabeth Ellsworth

♦ Throughout the history of education in the United States, educators and educational media producers have disguised school lessons in the attractive costumes of popular cultural forms. In some cases, educators have used this pedagogical strategy to make the unfamiliar familiar. In the 1800s, the McGuffey *Reader* presented unfamiliar reading vocabulary through recognizable parables and sayings of contemporary oral culture. In the 1940s and 1950s, educational films employed popular cultural forms such as romance and melodrama to humanize otherwise impersonal, scientific information. In a 1947 educational film provocatively entitled *Miracle in Paradise Valley*, even farm safety techniques were presented through a Hollywood-like romance to demonstrate their human consequences. Today, educational media producers turn to popular cultural forms with the hope that they will create a glittering diversion from curricular material that students resist as boring or tedious. A recent article about the Children's Television Workshop's (CTW) new program, called "Square One TV," applauds the producers for hiding the "often dreary topic" of mathematics under a "fast-paced series of sketches that mimic what children know best: other TV shows." The article quotes Assistant Secretary of Education Chester Finn, Jr.'s favorable reaction to the show: "Math is spinach and television is candy" (Tynan 1987: 86). *Sex, Drugs, and AIDS*, a 1986 film for use in health education classes, conforms its curricular content to the sound

47

and rhythm of rock music videos and wears that popular youth culture form as a signifier of legitimacy.

The incorporation of popular cultural forms into educational films and videos has a long history and enjoys wide acceptance as a welcome and legitimate teaching strategy. Yet popular cultural forms like dramatization, television commercials, and rock videos are not neutral carriers of educational content. They inflect curricular content with changes in meaning and significance. Nevertheless, research into the ideological work of educational media that incorporate popular cultural forms is virtually nonexistent. This pedagogic practice remains one of the most hidden of the hidden curricula.

Sociologists of education have produced sophisticated and persuasive analyses of how and why textbooks, prepackaged curricula, and the structure of everyday life in classrooms select some ways of making sense of the world out of the many available and present them as objective, factual, school knowledge. They have argued convincingly that educational theory is not merely the application of objective scientific principles to the concrete study of learning. Rather, it is a "political discourse that emerges from and characterizes an expression of struggle over what forms of authority, orders of representation, forms of moral regulation, and versions of the past and future should be legitimated, passed on, and debated within specific pedagogical sites" (Giroux 1986: 36).

However, as a field of research, the sociology of education has paid little attention to intersections between popular media and the curriculum. These intersections are complex and constant. They occur when educational media incorporate popular cultural forms for the teaching of concepts, processes, and the modeling of behavior. They occur when educational media attempt to legitimate school knowledge by associating it with the positive connotations that popular cultural forms carry about leisure, entertainment, and socially sanctioned or socially dangerous pleasures. Students construct their own intersections when they legitimately or illegitimately use popular cultural forms in everyday classroom life to elaborate upon, resist, subvert, or escape the subjectivities schools attempt to construct for them. The relation between popular cultural forms and the curriculum becomes even more complex when we recognize that all popular cultural forms are knowledge forms in and of themselves.

This chapter demonstrates the importance of placing the investigation of these intersections high on the agenda of educational research. I will briefly examine three recent analyses by media critics that address the incorporation of popular cultural forms by educational film and television. My purpose is to locate patterns and develop categories of analysis related to the issue of how such incorporations inflect curricular content with particular meanings and significance. These patterns and analytical categories can then inform further work in this direction. To grasp fully the ideological work of such films, we must address their specific modes of distribution, exhibition, and reception, as well as their texts. I will indicate the need for research in education that contextualizes the use and reception of educational media texts in specific pedagogical sites and point to the implications that such research raises for pedagogy and media use in education.

One would think that researchers within the fields of educational technology or contemporary media studies would have already taken up such work. Instead, research in educational technology remains preoccupied with questions of how viewers learn through media and what isolated effects specific media techniques have on the learning process (color *vs.* black-and-white images, moving images *vs.* still images). The goal of such research is to increase efficiency in meeting educational objectives by increasing predictability and control of the effects of media viewing on the learner. Such research privileges questions of how individuals process information from educational media over and above questions about the ideological work of meaning construction, content selection, setting of objectives, and media use. The concept of information processing as developed within cognitive psychology and applied in educational technology research cannot explain meaning, intent, and significance.

Historically, theorists and critics in television and film studies have shunned educational media texts as inadequate or insignificant objects of analysis. As long as debates about auteurs, aesthetics, popularity, and filmic enunciation dominated media studies, the highly formulaic and seemingly banal styles and structures of educational media and the institutional nature of their use and exhibition, insured their marginalization.

However, new directions in media studies seem to hold potential for shifting what could amount to significant critical attention toward educational media texts. Since the late 1960s, economic and political crises in France and Britain, along with the development of feminist film criticism, have prompted media critics to add to their aesthetic concerns questions about the relation of media to social change, social subjectivities, and power. This shift in focus required researchers to broaden their concerns beyond close textual analysis of classic Hollywood or avant-garde films. They found questions regarding heterogeneous audiences, oppositional interpretations, diverse reception contexts, and uses of media texts within social institutions well suited to studies of documentaries, political film and television, popular television, and educational film and television practices. For a few media critics (Gardner and Young 1981; Kuhn 1985; Mattelart 1985), analyses of educational film and television have proven helpful in refining and challenging conceptualizations of the role of media in the ideological work of social institutions and consciousness industries. However, these studies have employed methods and critical categories of analysis developed to address the place of film and television not in classrooms or schools, but in popular culture, leisure, and the social construction of pleasure. As a result, they only faintly suggest a framework for addressing the implications of presenting school knowledge through popular cultural forms.

The bridge between sociology of education and media studies is not yet built. But the conceptual tools required for such a task are becoming available on both sides. A full analysis of the similarities and points of divergence between sociology of education and media studies is beyond the scope of this chapter. However, the analytical categories of "knowledge forms," "modes of address," "hidden curriculum," and "modes of reception" have begun to emerge in the recent studies as useful to the task of developing an understanding of how incorporation of popular cultural forms is related to the legitimation of school knowledge. I will look at how these categories have informed three recent analyses of educational feature films, educational dramatizations for school use, and educational television.

While there has been no systematic investigation of the incorporation of popular cultural forms in educational films and television, media educators and educational technologists have long recognized and discussed its application as a pedagogical strategy. A review of the terms in which educators have understood this strategy is helpful for setting the stage for the examination of more critical approaches.

In the 1940s, Charles Hoban (1942, 1946) offered a detailed rationale for incorporating Hollywood-like dramatization into educational films. The principles at work in this rationale continue to inform current literature written to guide teachers in media evaluation, selection, and production. In Hoban's view, dramatization is one among several forms of information carriers, including exposition, documentary, and propaganda. Each has attributes that make it better suited for carrying some kinds of information compared to others.

According to Hoban, cold war educational imperatives required that schools "insure peace," not only through academic instruction, but also through "habit formation in good conduct or general moral and social orientation" (1946: 23). He saw dramatization in the tradition of Hollywood films to be an effective vehicle for social orientation because it examined processes "not in isolation but in their human settings and in their social significance" (1942: 37). Furthermore, because dramatization relies upon creating suspense, it is well suited to creating interest, holding attention, and generating enthusiasm for continued activity in the curriculum. In addition to these characteristics of the form itself, dramatization supported the educational project of social orientation because of the kind of viewer involvement it solicited from students. Based on research involving questionnaires and tests administered to students, Hoban concluded that students tended to identify themselves with characters who were shown "doing desirable kinds of things that other people of the same age and sex do" (1942: 49). By using "emotionally possessive" dramatization, an educational film could end "in a way that leaves the audience with a feeling of personal responsibility for continued learning activity, for performance similar to that shown in the film, for direct application of the principles involved in the lesson, or for further inquiry or investigation, as appropriate" (1946: 99). As one character in a 1947 educational dramatization declared, "Now that they've got their hearts into it, they'll be putting their heads into it" (*Miracle in Paradise Valley*). Hence, an educational mission that called for the teaching of correct action as well as correct knowledge could rely on dramatization to motivate students to act properly.

Finally, Hoban argued that the extracurricular media environment of students necessitated the incorporation of popular cultural forms into educational media. Students who watched educational films in school also went to the movies in neighborhood theaters. They brought standards and tastes that originated in the entertainment world into the school and viewed educational films in terms of theatrical movie standards. Thus, while the content of a school film should be derived from the subject matter, its form, style, and execution must be able to compete with the professional quality of theatrical films (1946: 80–81).

Hoban addressed the proper use of educational dramatizations in the curriculum as well. They belonged in introductory or refresher curricula intended for general audiences, and their primary function should be to make the subject interesting and important, to arouse curiosity to know more. Because they were appropriate for "dealing with the ethical and social obligations of technical subjects," they could also be shown as refresher films for specialists already familiar with a body of knowledge (1946: 97). Non-dramatic, expository films were best suited for teaching technical material to audiences who were already interested and motivated in a subject area.

Unlike the films Hoban describes, the CTW's new product, "Square One TV," is intended for after-school viewing at home and incorporates many popular visual forms besides Hollywood-like dramatization. Yet promotion for the program and comments by reviewers show that educational media producers' and educators' rationales for the incorporation of popular media forms have changed little since Hoban presented his arguments.

"Square One TV" consists of fast-paced imitations and parodies of television commercials, sit-coms, rock videos, game shows, and movies. The characters are either "now," "with it" role models whose mastery of popular youth styles, music, entertainment, rhythm, encourages viewer identification, or they are comic "others" whom viewers can reject as outside the boundaries of acceptable youth cultural style. Like the films Hoban describes, "Square One TV" is not intended to teach technical skills. Rather, its purpose is to provoke specific emotional responses that will motivate novices to change their attitudes and behaviors toward mathematics. According to its promotional flyer, the program sets out to generate enthusiasm for and interest in mathematics by developing positive attitudes toward mathematics and to encourage the use of problem-solving processes in everyday life. A positive attitude is apparently the result of positive emotional responses to watching popular cultural forms that children know best, enjoy immensely, and value.

Underlying this rationale, which has informed educational media for at least forty-five years, are unexamined assumptions that must be interrogated if educational media production and use are not simply to replicate the dominant ideologies of commercially interested popular cultural forms. These assumptions hinge on what amounts to taken-for-granted, common-sense notions about the process of mediated communication, including: why students watch and enjoy some media and not others; how media motivate people to change their attitudes and take action; how form and style work to construct meanings in texts; and what meanings viewers actually construct out of their viewing experiences. In addition, this rationale leaves dramatization untheorized as a form of organization and presentation that affects the knowledge itself, embodies specific conceptualizations of learners, and implies what constitutes proper use of the meanings learners are encouraged to construct.

In the examination of media critics' analyses of educational media texts that follows, I will attempt to make dramatization in educational film and television problematic by focusing on three questions: If popular cultural forms are not neutral carriers of explicit educational "content," what is the nature of the ideological work they attempt? How is this ideological work attempted through mechanisms of form and style[1] peculiar to the popular cultural forms in question? What kind of knowledge is privileged by the textual effects of this deployment?

KNOWLEDGE FORMS

The concept of knowledge form is a familiar one in sociology of education literature. It refers to a category of ideological work that is specific to the construction of meaning in educational settings. However, neither media studies nor sociology of education has applied this concept systematically to the study of educational media and their use within classrooms.

Knowledge form refers to the level of organization of the knowledge itself. It embodies the position that knowledge is socially constructed and the methods and forms of conveying knowledge affect the knowledge itself. Apple argues that the key to uncovering the role of ideology in education "is to see its work at the level of form" (1982: 139). This refers to a number of characteristics of the curriculum, including organization of time and space, movement of encoded meanings at different rates of speed, definition of what counts as knowledge, assumption about what goes on in the learning process, how it requires certain kinds of attention to what is happening, its norms of ambience and style, and its structuring of interpersonal implications (Postman 1979: 63; Apple 1982: 139).

Apple demonstrates that, as an analytical category, knowledge form allows the researcher to identify ways in which the level of organization of material functions ideologically as knowledge control. He argues that the logic of capital may enter most effectively into schools not at the level of overt or bureaucratic control of teacher activities (since, unlike other kinds of workplaces, schools are still relatively free from those kinds of control), but at the level of the "encoding of technical control into the very basis of the curricular form itself. The level of curricular, pedagogic, and evaluative practice within the classroom can be controlled by the forms into which the culture is commodified in schools" (1982: 149). For example, school curricula organize our experiences "in ways similar to the passive individual consumption of prespecified goods and services that have been subject to the logic of commodification so necessary for continued capital accumulation in our society" (1982: 32).

This concept, then, prompts us to locate within our textual analyses the ways in which the very structure of educational film or video operates as an intentional or unintentional attempt to inflect curricular content with particular meanings or significance.

In a recent ideological analysis of educational films that incorporate Hollywood-like dramatization (Ellsworth 1987b), I argue that dramatization privileges some kinds of knowledge over others. I would like to restate that argument here with a new focus on the way in which dramatization constitutes a knowledge form.[2]

Classic Hollywood cinema is characterized by a clearly defined set of norms that prescribe particular types of forms and structures of storytelling (Bordwell, Staiger, and Thompson 1985). In order to be intelligible and to evoke a pleasurable viewing experience similar to watching a Hollywood film in a theater, educational dramatizations must make their curricular material conform significantly to these norms.

The norms of Hollywood storytelling include: cause-and-effect chains of events; psychologically individualized "good" and "bad" characters, who function as causal agents, thereby hiding the fact that a commercially motivated industry outside the fictional world of the story is actually constructing and manipulating the story; and a happy ending that provides closure in which all questions appear to be answered. Educational dramatizations reformulate these norms to serve the specialized interests of their educational projects. However, while their interests are quite different from the interests of feature film producers, the overall Hollywood-like narrative structure remains intact. This has a profound effect on the level of organization of the knowledge being presented in an educational dramatization, and therefore on the nature of the knowledge itself. For example, while characters in Hollywood films are motivated by individualized psychological traits and desires, characters in educational dramatizations are vaguely drawn and consistently appear as if they are unmotivated to learn what they do not know — even if this is causing danger or difficulty. If left to themselves, it often seems that they would simply persist in their habits, traditions, or illusions that things are fine the way they are.

This lack of motivation leaves a particular type of gap in the story's cause-and-effect chain of events. Without clearly defined character motivations for change and action, educational dramatizations need some other engine for propelling their stories forward. In the films studied, this engine consistently turns out to be an expert. Characters move from a state of ignorance to a state of enlightenment only as a result of the expert's intervention.

Reformulation of the norms of characterization so that experts become primary causal agents is linked to the ideological projects of educational dramatization. Obviously, educational films would be unnecessary if nonexperts learned all they needed to know from their practical experiences of everyday life. Educational films must convince viewers that the kind of knowledge possessed by the experts is different from that of the other characters, and better. This ideological work is supported structurally by the norms of Hollywood-like storytelling. For example, expert knowledge is portrayed as being analytical, capable of breaking processes and objects down into stages and elements, to reveal for the characters, and for the viewer, the underlying causal and structural relationships. As a result, it can be abstracted into general principles applicable to many situations, rather than linked to the personal, practical knowledge gained by people solving problems in the unique circumstances of everyday life. Thus, the expert's knowledge is rational, linear, and generalizable, as opposed to experiential, local, and intuitive. The structures of educational dramatizations imply that if we understand the causal relations between actions and effects, we will be better able to control events and prevent negative outcomes.

The cause-effect structure underlying Hollywood narrative of course demands, and accommodates, the presentation of knowledge organized according to stages, elements, discrete parts, sequential relationships, and linear, chronological order. Thus, even the most experiential, traditional, and intuitive learning situations, such as the day-to-day parenting by a mother whose daughter is going through adolescence, as told in *Social Sex Attitudes in Adolescence* (1952), is made to take on a story form that divides the daughter's experiences into stages, crises to be managed, and clear-cut cause-effect relationships that demand precise and timely parental interventions.

Despite vaguely drawn, unmotivated characters who rely on experts to define their desires, educational dramatizations persist in presenting knowledge through stories about individuals. Stories do not have to be told this way. Alternatives to character-originated causes and effects include supernatural causes, natural causes, historical causes, and unmotivated coincidences. Film critics have argued that character-centered causality reinforces a dominant ideological position within American culture – individualism and an ethic that places the responsibility for success or failure in society on the individual's willingness and ability to work hard within the system as it is (Cook 1985). Educational dramatizations reproduce this position by linking the knowledge they offer to the fortunes of individual characters, rather than to those of social groups. The stories link characters' happiness to their knowledge about a subject. By contrast, individuals who resist learning a lesson or have no access to it are portrayed as miserable – even risking death.

Further, the reformulated process of characterization in educational dramatizations is the primary mechanism by which the film proves the correctness of the expert's knowledge. Educational dramatizations seldom refer to evidence from experiments, research, or testimony about real people's actual experiences to demonstrate that the knowledge of the story's expert is correct. Rather, characterization becomes its own proof. For example, when characters act using the expert's knowledge, the story shows their efforts to solve a problem to be a guaranteed and unqualified success. When characters act out of ignorance or resistance to the expert's knowledge, they might fail to solve a problem, suffer injury on the job, or grow worried and confused. Of the sixty educational dramatizations analyzed for this study, not one has an unhappy ending. The norm of the happy ending demands, and accommodates, the guaranteed success of characters who learn the expert's lesson. Viewers are thus encouraged to interpret knowledgeable characters in educational dramatizations as they would the good characters in Hollywood films.

In addition, characterization proves the experts right by making the fictional world appear to be the real world, existing separately from the experts' discourses and able to be used as independent, empirical evidence in support of the experts' knowledge. One mechanism for accomplishing this is voice-over narration which consistently explains events in the story as if they were really happening, and not constructed as illustrations of the already-determined narration. In *A Day at the Fair* (1947), the narrator says, "Here in the cattle barn on the fairground, the folks are at work early, tending and grooming their cattle." A second mechanism for offering the fictional world as proof is to imply that the characters are acting independently of the narrator's voice-over, that the narrator has no control over their actions. In the case of *Social Sex Attitudes in Adolescence*, we watch as Bob's and Mary's parents act from their own knowledge and experience, without access to the narrator's more complete understanding of the situation. As a result, they sometimes make mistakes and forget important information. That the narrator does not intervene reinforces the illusion that he cannot intervene, that the parents are real people in the real world. Classical realism's construction of its fictional world systematically denies the mechanisms of its own constructedness and thus demands, and accommodates, a similar presentation of curricular material as natural, unconstructed, and waiting to be discovered.

The films I have studied consistently imply that the characters in their stories suffer from a double lack: lack of information about a particular subject, issue, or process plus lack of knowledge about how to use or interpret that information properly. It is this second layer of knowledge — how to use and interpret the expert's discourse — that is unique to educational dramatizations when compared to classroom teaching films or educational documentaries. The same mechanisms of characterization that present the curricular material itself organize that knowledge in such a way that its correct use is implied. In the films analyzed, proper use is that which leads to positive social implications. The films personalize the social by showing the effects of proper use on individual characters' lives. However, what constitutes positive social implications is never made explicit in these films or acknowledged as a contested issue requiring public debate. Instead, once again, characterization is called upon to prove that the expert's version of the social good is the correct version. This happens when characters who use their knowledge properly are rewarded by the story not only with success in problem solving or individual happiness, but with security, social acceptance, and leadership. While their rewards are social, their motives to act properly are presented in terms of individualized desires. This removes the issue of proper use of knowledge from the social domain and places it in the personal domain, outside of public debate. In *Social Sex Attitudes in Adolescence*, for example, Bob and Mary are not shown to be motivated to use their information about sex properly out of a concern for social order and the reproduction of middle-class values and a patriarchal family structure; rather, proper use is shown to cause satisfaction of their individual desires for happiness and meaningful love.

However, educational dramatizations, like all social constructions of knowledge, ultimately fail in their attempts to deny their own interests and assumptions and conflate the social and political with the natural. Inevitably, contradictions appear in the experts' discourse. At those moments, characterization is often used in what are ultimately unsuccessful textual attempts to cover over the contradictions and magically resolve them. In *Social Sex Attitudes in Adolescence*, some crises and transitions in Bob's and Mary's development cannot be addressed by the expert's discourse without exposing the socially constructed values and assumptions embedded in what it is trying to present as a neutral, scientific discourse about adolescent development. These crises include Mary's emotional attraction to other women, Bob's interest in pornography, Mary's involvement with the wrong boy, and Bob's and Mary's attraction to the inappropriate knowledge and attitudes that come from books, jokes, friends, teenage culture, and jazz music. Instead of modeling resolutions for these crises through parental action influenced by the expert's discourse, *Social Sex Attitudes in Adoles-*

cence resolves them "naturally," as when Bob and Mary simply "pass through a stage" or "magically," as when the wrong boy suddenly moves out of town or Bob solves his problem with pornography off screen. The expert cannot address these contradictions because that would force him to move his explanation of social sex adjustment out of the domain of biology (or the natural) and into the domain of ideology (or the social and the political). As socially and politically interested knowledge, social-sex adjustment is the (unacknowledged) site of struggle requiring public debate over which meanings about sexuality, normality, and typicality will prevail as legitimate school knowledge. As MacCabe (1974) argues, classical realism cannot admit contradiction, because it would threaten the inner stability of the text. Insofar as they conform to the norms of classical realist texts, educational dramatizations both demand and accommodate knowledge organized as seamless, uncontested, and already achieved. But the inner stability of the text is constantly threatened and ultimately displays contradictions and gaps in its logic as a result of the strain of making the socially constructed appear to be natural, given, inevitable.

The underlying structure of dramatization thus organizes knowledge in such a way as to accommodate and reproduce — but not without tension — the privileging of expert, scientific knowledge over practical, intuitive, everyday knowledge; the personal benefits of knowledge over the social; and the discovery of knowledge over its social and political construction.

MODES OF ADDRESS AND HIDDEN CURRICULUM

Dramatization functions not only as a knowledge form that recasts curricular material in the service of interests embedded within the form, but also as a mode of address that attempts a specific type of manipulation of the audience and solicits a particular type of learning experience. The effect of this is to privilege some knowledges over others, thereby constructing a hidden curriculum.

We have seen how Hoban and the producers of Children's Television Workshop specified the ways in which their incorporations of popular cultural forms attempted to capture and organize the learner's attention for particular purposes. Hoban's purpose was social and moral orientation, and the purpose of "Square One TV" was to change attitudes toward mathematics. Neither interrogated the ideological nature of these goals. Nor did they see the use of dramatization as a strategic one involving relations of power, manipulation, or control. Here, "strategic" refers to a relationship in which ideology is used in an attempt to calculate or manipulate the power relationships of students to other students, to teachers, and to ways of knowing and relating to the world outside the school (de Certeau 1984: 35–38).

Only in the past few years have some media critics (Ellsworth 1987a,1987b; Kuhn 1985; Mattelart 1985) begun to look at the question of mode of address in educational media using popular cultural forms. Mode of address has become an important critical concept in film studies concerned with the relation between the film viewer and the text (Cook 1985). To identify a film's mode of address is to show how the formal operations of a film solicit from the viewer a particular kind of involvement in the unfolding of the film's story or discourse. The concept of mode of address points to the fact that the film needs viewers to give it its meaning. Viewers are not passive recipients of an already meaningful message. Depending on the their social, political, economic, racial, and gender positions within a culture, viewers are likely to attach a wide variety of interpretations to any one film. In their attempt to impose some limits on the kinds of meanings that viewers attach to a film, filmmakers consciously and unconsciously manipulate form and style in ways that appeal to filmmaking conventions.

In order to make sense of the film in its own terms, the viewer must be able to adopt — if only imaginatively and temporarily — the social, political, and economic interests that are the condition for the knowledge it constructs. In this way, the film seeks to engage the viewer not only in the activity of knowledge construction, but in the construction of knowledge from a particular social, political, and economic point of view as well. A textual analysis that seeks to understand the strategic use of dramatization in educational films will attempt to specify how it functions as a mode of address that solicits and demands from the viewer a closely circumscribed involvement in constructing a particular kind of knowledge.

Media researchers have made some initial attempts to question how mode of address in educational media attempts to manipulate viewers and to solicit a particular type of learning experience both textually and contextually. In separate efforts, both Kuhn (1985) and Mattelart (1985) ask how the incorporation of popular cultural forms into educational media constitutes a strategic attempt to capitalize on the spectatorial apparatus — "a mental machinery through which spectators could engage with, be drawn into, a film" (Kuhn 1985: 101) — that was already in place for viewing popular cinema and television and how this benefits particular interests. I will look at each in turn.

In her analysis of educational feature films on venereal disease produced in Great Britain after World War I, Annette Kuhn argues that "if fictional narrative was the chosen medium for VD propaganda films, the choice was a strategic one — even if not always consciously so, and not always with the results allegedly intended" (1985: 101). The choice of fictional narrative form "constitutes an attempt to capitalise" (Ibid.) on certain aspects of a situation which included the facts that an audience, an apparatus for reception, and a spectatorial apparatus already existed. These could be employed to gain access to an audience in a way that carried with it a certain amount of cultural authority and legitimacy. Using Hollywood-like dramatization, then, would allow these films to be seen in commercial cinemas and thereby be accessible both physically and conceptually to large audiences.

By comparing the spectator involvement solicited by feature films to that solicited by educational films, Kuhn suggests what type of learning experience the VD films attempted to construct, and with what interests. Dramatization in the VD films solicited a kind of viewer involvement in the process of acquiring knowledge and information different from that of feature films. In classic realist narrative, the spectator is encouraged to identify with characters and their fates. In the VD films, however, characters are not well-rounded individuals with clear psychological traits. Instead, they are representatives, "if not of social types, certainly of moral positions" (Ibid., p. 102). The films took on the stylistic and formal characteristics of simple, folktale-like melodramas.

The moral position of the characters was constructed in terms of their sexual practices and their placement in relation to discourses around the body and its health. Within the fiction, certain of these practices and discourses become privileged. For example, some characters and the practices associated with them were signified as good or bad through the iconography of costume, *mise-en-scene*, and gesture. However, the project of the film was not to label people as good or bad. Rather, it was to define a narrative through which characters' eyes are opened to knowledge, and therefore to the truth. "Characters are not positioned as bad but merely as ignorant or misinformed" (Ibid., p. 109). The films then offer themselves as means of filling the gap in knowledge that is shown as being the cause for characters' suffering or evil.

Kuhn demonstrates how the films insure that this gap will be filled not by just any knowledge. A correct knowledge is presented as being of a particular kind, spoken from a particular source. In *Damaged Goods*, the character of the doctor represents and enunciates knowledge that is provided by science, specifically by science harnessed to discourses of medicine and social purity and institutionalized within practices of public health. We are encouraged to identify with the doctor's discourse because of the special position it occupies within the structure of the film. His voice is a central motivator of both image and intertitles; he is shown in settings connoting status and specialized knowledge; he is presented in individual close-up or in medium two-shot alongside whichever character is at the moment receiving the benefit of his wisdom. His appearance and expression convey rectitude, sternness, strictness, and rigorously unbending correctness. He has a great deal more to say than any of the other characters. "Taken together, these conditions produce a specific mode of address for the films, a mode of constructing spectators as 'moral subjects' of a particular kind" (Ibid., p. 101). Thus, viewers are offered a moral and social position from which to construct the kinds of knowledge that are integral to the processes that constitute those positions.

In a critical analysis of "Sesame Street," Mattelart (1985) foregrounds the ways in which the text's mode of address interacts with the context of reception to solicit a particular kind of involvement from the viewer. Mattelart specifies the type of learning experience that "Sesame Street" attempts to construct when it links educational content with the modes of address and reception contexts of commercial television. Because the producers saw any lack of attention as rendering the message inoperative and threatening to stop the learning process, their central preoccupation was to get the child interested, to capture attention and teach via entertainment (Ibid., p. 178). The linchpin of the didactic method for learning letters and numbers would be the technical event which lies at the heart of the discourse of television commercials. This is a matter of holding attention by creating around a minimal piece of information the maximum number of visual and sound changes. This is strictly codified by television advertising as twenty to thirty events per minute (Ibid., pp. 179–80). Mattelart argues that because "Sesame Street uses television as a tool inscribed not within the schooling system, but within the private space of leisure, it took up a strategy of "organizing attention through desire," instead of through constraint (Ibid., p. 178). While Mattelart's assertion is based on television intended for home learning, it could be argued that the incorporation of dramatization into educational media intended for classroom use is a similar attempt to create within a public space sites that are momentarily private (darkened rooms in which students interact individually with a film) and inflected with connotations of leisure and entertainment (which can be offered or withheld by teachers for the purposes of winning control and consent). As such, educational films and television intended for classroom use also attempt to organize student attention through desire rather than coercion.

Whereas Kuhn locates mechanisms of mode of address that construct spectators as particular kinds of moral subjects, Mattelart concludes that "Sesame Street" seems to have unwittingly adopted a mode of address that constructs students as consumers. "Sesame Street" reinjects into the pedagogic field "all the stimuli of the consumer universe, all the injunctions so normative for the imaginary and sensorial dimensions of the child" (Ibid., p. 181). Textually, it operates by "the seduction of rhythm, and of diversity," but above all, it operates contextually by "stimulating the immense arsenal of signs from the universe of mercantile culture, stimulating the integration of the child with this world" (Ibid.). In Mattelart's view "the producers of 'Sesame Street' do not seem to have measured the contradiction that exists between the 'educational' style and advertising techniques which bring to a climax of alienation the unequal relation of exchange which is the basis for a material and symbolic mode of production and distribution....One may legitimately ask whether the true educational message of 'Sesame Street' doesn't reside in this initiation into the consumer universe with its modalities of mass space and time" (Ibid., pp. 181–82).

By locating textual strategies that privilege particular kinds of knowledge and showing their links to particular social institutions and interests, Kuhn and

Mattelart provide evidence of Foucault's claim that knowledges are an integral part of the processes that constitute the social domain and contribute to the exigencies and constraints that form the administrative and regulative processes of the population (Henriques et al. 1984: 92). Further evidence can be found in the analysis of educational dramatization as a knowledge form presented above, where I attempted to demonstrate that norms of Hollywood narrative structure not only reproduce the logic and subjectivities that constitute the social domain; they also become productive in the sense that they have definite effects on the objects one seeks to know. This is a key moment in the ideological work such films attempt because "these effects are not separable from the practices of administration to which they are tied" (Ibid., p. 92).

RECEPTION CONTEXTS AND IMPLICATIONS FOR EDUCATIONAL RESEARCH AND PEDAGOGY

While the analyses of the relations between popular culture and educational media examined above are preliminary and partial, they have serious implications for educational research and for pedagogy. Based on semiotic analyses of the educational films and television, all three offer speculations about what meanings would get made and what positions assumed when students and teachers actually use the texts. However, in the past ten years, significant developments have taken place in audience research within the fields of critical cultural studies and film and television studies (Morley 1987). And it has become clear that textual analysis alone is unable to grasp how meaning arises through the *interface* of audiences and texts. Dahlgren summarizes this criticism:

> [T]he structuralist procedure behind many semiotic studies incorporates a view of meaning and consciousness (and even the unconscious) where the Subject is essentially dominated by the Object—the formal sign or code. This position is at base empiricist: the cultural text is reduced to an abstract grammar, with meaning residing wholly in its confines. The negotiation of meaning and the historicity of consciousness is denied. (1985: 240)

"Negotiation of meaning," is a concept that has emerged out of empirical studies of audience interpretation (Hall 1980); it refers to evidence that audiences are not passive recipients of the communications of others. Rather, they actively, and unpredictably, construct diverse and sometimes contradictory meanings for the same text. The meanings given any particular text will be constructed differently depending on the discourses, knowledges, prejudices, or resistances brought to bear on it by the audience (Morley 1987: 7).

Elsewhere, I have argued that this process of negotiation is not merely an unproblematic picking and choosing between the multiplicity of meanings that a text seems to suggest (Ellsworth and Selvin 1986). Rather, each process of media interpretation takes place within a context of socially constructed, unequal, and competing versions of reality embedded within the text, the institutions of its production and reception, and the social history of the participants. Not all versions of reality enjoy equal legitimacy within a given historical moment. Not all negotiators of meaning get a fair hearing. Not all negotiators have access to powerful negotiation skills or repertoires of discourse. When a media text becomes the site of struggle over which meanings are to prevail, it signals a situation in which "we are not in agreement." If we were, the text's meaning would appear to be obvious—in no need of interpretation or negotiation. To construct or impose a correct classroom interpretation of a film or videotape is to end the negotiation process temporarily, to privilege one set of meanings over alternatives, and to displace the alternatives as illegitimate, irrelevant, expendable, or marginal.

Understanding interpretation in this way places the analytic category of reception at the center of concern for researchers interested in the legitimation of knowledge in classrooms. This is not to say that textual analysis like those reviewed above becomes unnecessary or ideologically complicit. As Masterman argues, it is important to uncover the dominant meanings and values encoded within texts and the techniques their producers employ in order to win assent to and complicity with their ways of seeing (1985: 219).

In addition to being able to uncover the privileged meaning of a text, textual analysis can help in understanding the historically unique cultural and technical qualities that constitute a medium's particular way of organizing and structuring perception. "Each medium fosters a somewhat different dispositional relationship between itself and its audiences; the audiences must 'work' in different ways to attend to the output and make sense of it. I call this feature of a medium its 'epistemic bias'" (Dahlgren 1985: 242). Dahlgren advocates an analytical process that shuttles back and forth between studies of the reception process and textual analyses of the epistemic bias that will help to clarify both, in a reciprocal fashion.

In their study of how children make sense of popular television, Hodge and Tripp (1986) demonstrate the power of shuttling back and forth between textual analyses of television programs and "ethno-semiotic" analyses of how children construct interpretations of those texts in their discussions with each other and with interviewers. Drawing on recent developments in audience studies, Hodge and Tripp argue that educational research on media and pedagogy must realize that semiotics, or the study of meanings; psychology, or the study of mental processes; and social and political theory, or the study of social agency, are inseparable aspects of the methodology that must be employed in understanding the relation among media, education, and power (1986: 3).

Hodge and Tripp attempt to construct such a methodology by combining semiotics, psychology, and ethnography. First, they selected a television cartoon and performed a semiotic analysis on its text. Their analysis showed that the program was not a single stimulus, but a vast meaning-potential complex that is realized onto meaning only through the intensely active process of interpretation. They then established the interpretive codes available to children by giving a developmental account of the complex structures and processes of the minds that can create such meanings offered by developmental and cognitive psychology. To account for how children watch television as part of their social existence, they used ethnographic methods informed by a critical cultural studies approach. The result was an analysis of how the power relations between children in discussion groups affected the transformations of meanings that children produced in interpreting the cartoon. They concluded that children interpret the context of viewing and discussion of viewing through general social relationships and the meanings they carry about power, solidarity, authority, peers, and sex roles.

Hodge and Tripp's conclusions about how children watch popular television led them to recommend a particular kind of media education. They found that television watching was not necessarily a passive, mindless activity for children, but viewing television was an important aspect of general cognitive and social development (Ibid., p. 159). Implicit in popular television programs were issues which children regard as important to their lives and which already circulate through their interpersonal relations and social contexts. Yet such issues were largely ignored and condemned by teachers and excluded from the curriculum (Ibid., p. 188). In addition, the ability to make subtle and adequate reality judgments about television was a major developmental outcome that could only be acquired from children's experience of television (Ibid., p. 216).

On the basis of these conclusions, Hodge and Tripp argue that television should be brought into the school curriculum to teach students how to make modality judgments about television and other message systems and to teach media literacy, appreciation, and discrimination. The goal of such education is to equip "students to be adequate citizens in the society in which they live" (Ibid., p. 218).

As evidenced by the recent work of Masterman and the special issue of *Screen* (Vol. 25, No. 5, 1986) on media and pedagogy, other media educators are beginning to recognize the relevance of certain concepts within media studies to a more critical classroom practice. The highly successful challenge by media studies to notions of passive spectatorship and simple stimulus-response models of communication holds particular significance for critical educators. As Masterman (1985) argues, the social relationships of interpretation and discussion hold true not simply in front of the television screen, but within every classroom. As a result, "for teachers of all subjects, knowledge of and sensitivity to what students themselves bring to a subject becomes at least as important as knowledge of and sensitivity to the subject itself" (Ibid., p. 218).

It is worth quoting Masterman at length on the type of pedagogy a recognition of the process of meaning negotiation entails:

[D]ifferential decodings, traditionally either repressed in many classrooms or treated as a "problem" to be overcome through the combined authorities of teacher, author, and text, should be given the fullest articulation as reflections or refractions of important subcultural differences within the group. Finally, the transformation of students, from being passive recipients of the communications of others to active meaning-makers—from objects to whom education happens to subjects who create knowledge and make it their own—should be liberating for students and teachers alike and should help to promote the development of genuine dialogue within the classroom....(p. 218)

This is not to say that appeals to individual experience as the basis for meaning construction are unproblematic. Masterman calls for a type of classroom dialogue that "denaturalizes" particular judgments (including the teacher's) and "tracing out some of the ways in which they are systematically related to wider sub-cultural codes and formations" (Ibid., p. 218). In a similar gesture, Richards describes a teaching strategy which he calls "depersonalization." He takes classroom discussion of a media product and asks students to uncover the "structured social basis" of their apparently "personal responses" by addressing and redefining what is constitutive of their interpretations. This is accomplished by inviting "examination and questioning of those boundaries between what is thought of as the individual, and the social matrix out there, an external body of institutions, society" (1986: 77).

Hodge and Tripp argue that schools should bring television into the curriculum for the purpose of teaching media literacy and appreciation so students can become adequate citizens, and Masterman advocates a type of viewer liberation that recognizes and fosters the power of students to be ultimately responsible for the differential interpretations that get made in their society. However, an understanding of media as sites of social and political struggle over which meanings are to be legitimated demands an even more radical reformulation of the relation between media and pedagogy. Elsewhere (Ellsworth and Larson 1986; Ellsworth and Selvin 1986), I have argued for the possibilities of a transformative media education aimed at developing skills for initiating and participating in social change. The concepts of knowledge form and mode of address examined here can become part of curricula for critical thinking and transformative media education. They can help students understand the mechanisms educational media and other curricular materials use in attempts to structure their relations to themselves, their teachers, their classmates, and alternative ways of making sense of the world held by social groups struggling for legitimacy. Such curricula would be transformative to the extent that they enable students to understand their "places" in the networks of social differences they inhabit, how they relate to others across these differences, and how educational media attempt to organize learning experiences in ways that constrain or facilitate their abilities and desires to change. The primary goal of such a future-oriented pedagogy for change is to aid students in establishing action guides where none exist. The strength of transformative media education lies in its ability to demonstrate that the meanings we construct and the ways we negotiate their construction cannot be separated from the skills necessary to review and restructure the systems in which we participate.

NOTES

1. "Form" refers to ways of structuring the filmed material (such as narrative, topical, or argumentative structures); "style" refers to the ways the film includes some stylistic elements available to filmmakers (such as voice-over narration, animated graphics, types of camera movements).

2. My work with educational dramatizations is part of a larger research project on the form, style, and ideology of educational films. I have analyzed sixty educational dramatizations as part of that research. The films sampled were produced between 1930 and 1970 and are located at the American Archives of the Factual Film at Iowa State University. I chose that period because it represents the time during which the aesthetic and ideological characteristics of educational dramatizations became similar and stable across films, before significant changes in industrial practices and norms began to take place. I selected seven study films representative of the range of forms and styles apparent in the larger sample and performed close shot-by-shot analyses of each. Those were: *Film Tactics* (1945); *School Bus Patrol* (1963); *Atom Smashers* (1952); *Social Sex Attitudes in Adolescence* (1952); *Using Visual Aids in Training* (1947); *A Day at the Fair* (1947); and *Miracle in Paradise Valley* (1947).

REFERENCES

Apple, M.
(1982)   *Education and Power*. London: ARK Paperbacks.
Bordwell, D., J. Staiger, and K. Thompson
(1985)   *The Classical Hollywood Cinema: Film Style and Mode of Production to 1960*. New York: Columbia University Press.
Cook, P., ed.
(1985)   *The Cinema Book*. New York: Pantheon.
Dahlgren, P.
(1985)   "The Modes of Reception: For a Hermeneutics of TV News." In P. Drummond and R. Paterson. *Television in Transition*. London: British Film Institute.
de Certeau, M.
(1984)   *The Practice of Everyday Life*. Berkeley: University of California Press.
Ellsworth, E.
(1987a)   "Fiction as Proof: Critical Analysis of the Form, Style, and Ideology of Educational Dramatization Films." Paper presented at the Convention of the Association for Educational Communications and Technology and Sponsored by the Research and Theory Division. Atlanta.
(1987b)   "Educational Films Against Critical Pedagogy." *Journal of Education* (Boston University) 169(3): 32–47.
(1986)   "Interpretation Is a Social and Political Act." *Journal of Visual and Verbal Languaging* 6(2): 23–29.

Ellsworth, E., and M. Larson
(1986)   "Critical Media Analysis, Radical Pedagogy, and MTV." *Feminist Teacher* 2 (1): 8–13.

Ellsworth, E., and A. Selvin
(1986)   "Using Transformative Media Events for Social Education." *New Education* 8(2): 70–77.

Gardner, C., and R. Young
(1981)   "Science on TV: A Critique." In T. Bennett et al., eds. *Popular Television and Film*. London: British Film Institute.

Giroux, H. A.
(1986)   "Curriculum, Teaching, and the Resisting Intellectual." *Curriculum and Teaching* 1 (1&2): 33–42.

Hall, S.
(1980)   "Encoding/Decoding." In S. Hall et al., eds. *Culture, Media, Language*. London: Hutchinson.

Henriques, J., et al.
(1984)   *Changing the Subject: Psychology, Social Regulation, and Subjectivity*. London: Methuen.

Hoban, C. F., Jr.
(1946)   *Movies that Teach*. New York: Dryden Press
(1942)   *Focus on Learning: Motion Pictures in the School*. Washington D.C.: American Council on Education.

Hodge, R., and D. Tripp
(1986)   *Children and Television: A Semiotic Approach*. Cambridge: Polity Press.

Kuhn, A.
(1985)   *The Power of the Image: Essays on Representation and Sexuality*. London: Routledge & Kegan Paul.

MacCabe, C.
(1974)   "Realism and the Cinema: Notes on some Brechtian Theses." *Screen* 15 (2): 9–15.

Masterman, L.
(1986)   "Reply to David Buckingham." *Screen* 27 (5): 96–100
(1985)   *Teaching the Media*. London: Comedia.

Mattelart, M.
(1985)   "Education, Television, and Mass Culture: Reflections on Research into Innovation." In P. Drummond and R. Paterson, eds. *Television in Transition*. London: British Film Institute.

Morley, D.
(1987)   "Changing Paradigms in Audience Studies." Paper presented at symposium "Rethinking the Audience: New Tendencies in Television Research," Tübingen, West Germany, February.

Postman, N.
(1979)   *Teaching as a Conserving Activity*. New York: Dell.

Richards, C.
(1986)   "Anti-Racist Initiatives." *Screen* 27 (5): 74–79.

Tynan, W.
(1987)   "Multiple Fun on 'Square One'." *Time*, February 23, p. 86.

Chapter 4

PLAYING…CONTRA/DICTIONS, EMPOWERMENT AND EMBODIMENT: PUNK, PEDAGOGY, AND POPULAR CULTURAL FORMS (ON ETHNOGRAPHY AND EDUCATION)*

Philip Corrigan

We are engaged in the production of a discourse which is cut against the grain of science, a discourse which is informed by a peculiar sense of urgency, a sense of the emergent, one tilted to deliver a particular knowledge, a knowledge of the particular, a knowledge which threatens within the academic sphere to present a simulacrum of those other kinds of knowledge generated underneath, outside, within (for instance) the subcultural milieu, a knowledge which cannot be systematized, generalized, a knowledge that doesn't travel at all well.

Engaged in deconstruction, reflexive deconstructions, discursively promiscuous, we aim to fabricate a logic which is diverse and discontinuous, a science, if you like, a science of the concrete, which is to say an unscience, a science of things happening, a discourse which breaks a silence in order to produce dis. . . quiet, this quiet. (Hebdige 1983: 87–88)

♦ Happily identifying myself with the "we" here—and in that spirit—I want to begin by making this stranger (sociologist as Other), *stranger*.[1]

A confession. I have always found my theory in practices. Yes, of course, I have used Theory, but it was never mine (until I made it by montage, collage, flourishingly "Look at this! . . . and this! . . . "). For obvious "professional" reasons I first kept quiet about this, the degree to which all that I write (as justified belief and not tired replication, obligation, and obedience) are fragments of autobiography.[2] I've read a few books, articles on Theory, but they only made sense (for me) when I could misread them, see them like films, hear them like rock and roll; when I did not just polish them up for further exchange, but could decorate them, inscribing annotations made in the light of sources and resources normally denied any theoretical validity, except, perhaps, as instances, as pre-texts for proper Theory. Graffiti. Adornment. Transgression. Kaleidoscope. Hiding in the Light.

Then, suddenly, in a rush, a happy confluence took place. First (and this disciplinary imperialism is a mixed blessing), what could be studied (claimed, conquered, charted, frozen in those noisy cartograms of conceptual clarity) increased apace (the 1960s, say). Then — a more significant moment (for me) — *how* study could take place shifted: Form appeared as a question, or a series of the same. What was (as I now know and shall shortly show) sayable affected the features of the saying. A happier isomorphism was made necessary: if some real sense is to be made of sensed (meaningful) realities, then the realization must partake of the same forms of making sense. Poets and musicians as *realizateurs* were vindicated. The fragmentary and the particular were (re)centered. The third moment, that of the spiral embodied here, is still marginal, still, strange, Otherly. Since there can be no observation without an observer, the I/Eye has to be the acknowledged and embodied paradigm in any account which, moreover, can no longer be explanatory, but exploratory; no longer telling ("it" like *it* is), but offering (a gift, a picture, a song, a poem) to share, to converse, to discuss. Let us talk together.

By chance, I very recently discovered a basis (in terms of the discontinuous lineages that connect my obsessions) for the above: James Clifford's "On Ethnographic Surrealism" (1981). A remarkable writing — a sense of which I already had before I read it, in the modes of modern writing/visuality that I had found and made mine, that I *use* — especially that of Roland Barthes, Walter Benjamin, and unmentioned by Clifford, Gertrude Stein. Clifford tells a story. His story could be replicated in another theatre of the absurd which he also does not connect, only to distinguish: that dawn when joy it was to be alive of Proletkult, *Novy Lef*, the Commissariat of Enlightenment, in the USSR from 1917 onward, for a little while, of which the last traces — brutally annihilated for so long — are those "late Bolsheviks" Pashukanis, Rubin, Bakhtin/Volosinov. Their, in turn, "co-existence" with Simmel, Kracauer, Benjamin, Bloch should not, in turn, be dissociated from both the signifying "Americans in Paris" *and* the distinctive revolution of Charlie Parker, Thelonius Monk, Charlie Christian, Bud Powell, Art Blakey in Mintons, New York City. This *is* the modern world, my modern world of "amorous fits," trying different styles of (ad)dress. These were all, in their fashion, "youth cultures": words, sounds, signs, in time.

Clifford's story is of Paris, of a moment (1917–1939) when surrealism *was* ethnography and ethnography *was* surrealism: simulacra terminated with the institutionalization of two Museums — Musée de l'Homme and Musée d'Art Moderne.[3] This "violent abstraction" left a little group who refused those disciplinary divisions — Le Collège de Sociologie. This College met for two years from 1937–1939 in the dining room of a Latin Quarter café to continue the open, collage-montage project of the previous twenty years. Central to the longer-term, as to the short-term, projects was to see culture as contested. In the ideogram of the key figure — Georges Bataille — cultural order includes both the rule and the transgression. Le Collège de Sociologie[4] involved Bataille, Michel Leiris, Roger Caillois, and was frequented by Jean Wahl, Pierre Klossowski, Alexandre Kojève,[5] Jean Paulhan, Jules Monnerot, and Walter Benjamin. To exemplify the project of this College, Clifford quotes his own translation from an article by Jean Jamin, whose translated title is "A sacred college or the sorcerer's apprentices of sociology" (1980: 16):

> The notions of distanciation, exoticism, representation of the other, and difference are inflected, reworked, readjusted as a function of criteria no longer geographical or cultural but methodological and even epistemological in nature: to make foreign what appears familiar; to study the rituals and sacred sites of contemporary institutions with the minute attention of an "exotic" ethnographer, and using his methods: *to become observers observing those others who are ourselves*—and at the limit, this other who is oneself.... The irruption of the sociologist in the field of his research, the interest devoted to his experience, probably constitutes the most original aspect of the Collège. (Clifford 1981: 561, my emphasis)

As Clifford concludes his article so shall I this necessary prologue:

> The surrealist elements of modern ethnography tend to go unacknowledged by a science that sees itself engaged in the reduction of incongruities rather than, simultaneously, in their production. But is not every ethnographer something of a surrealist, a re-inventor and shuffler of realities? Ethnography, *the science of cultural jeopardy*, presupposes a constant willingness to be surprised, to unmake interpretive syntheses, and to value—when it comes— the unclassified, unsought Other. (my emphasis)

UNSOUGHT OTHERS — AT THE LIMITS, ON EDGE. SHUFFLING/FAST-FORWARD

From all that I have said, there must be one recognition in this writing, this reading, one which is *retro*-spective and *pro*-spective. Studies of popular cultures generally, and youth cultures particularly, have been resolutely masculinist. That is, not only have the ethnographed persons been of a male gender (and usually heterosexual) but the discursive regime and image repertoire, plus the general illumination, of all such studies has been masculinized.[6] It is timely both to recognize this and then to move on, recognizing thus a twofold implication: (1) that such studies can be used within these newly recognized limits of validity, and (2) in keeping with all that has been said — here is the pre-scription — any inscription that claims the status of a re-presentation has to entail the gendered embodiment of the "Initial Eye" (Corrigan 1987a).

Rendered thus, the paradigm setting studies (Willis 1977; Hebdige 1978) can contribute to the project that I would wish to place alongside the opening quotation from Dick Hebdige, thereby specifying the content of the "we" I was happy to endorse. Among the ways of sensing and seeing, which the ethnography I endorse here entails, is one recently argued by Elaine Showalter.

> Male intervention in feminist criticism has to be about masculinity. It doesn't have to end there, but it does have to start there.... You have to exercise power and criticize it at the same time. Male critics see feminist criticism as an opportunity to exercise power. There's no criticism, no interrogation of what masculinity means in terms of practice, in terms of discourse.... It would be interesting to problematize masculinity. Then we could have a dialogue. It's a necessary gesture that very few men ever have made.... (1986:17; cf. Lewis and Simon 1986)

In quoting this at the start of my exploration of "Masculinity as Right" (1986c; cf. 1983a).[7] I am also trying to recover, and thus trace the lineaments of the specific empowering involved, the revolutionary kernel of "1968" for me: we do not only have to make different Xs (name your own favorite cultural production/form) but we have to make different Xs, *differently*. This may well entail a lot of hesitation, uncertainty, a welcoming of a "loss of the old verities" and of the multivarious "crises of Marxism" because it involves being careful: taking care that we do not replicate (with our bodies, in our voices, behind our backs) the old forms that constrain and maim in our embracing of the political romance and the leadership drives and performance instincts associated with both avant-gardes and vanguards. The suffering male Artist; the agonizing, dismal male Intellectual: being smart, being clever.

But there are two other related points, by way of a prolegomena which is more methodologically and epistemologically extensive than the focus of what follows. First, some contradictory unities within "Masculinity as Right" have to be recognized. At the end of Paul Willis's *Profane Culture* (1978: 183f.) is an Epilogue which lists the violent deaths of several hippies. In 1984–85 Dick Hebdige "broke down" (went over the edge, beyond the limits, into a different quiet; Hebdige, 1985, 1986a). Male-Power (which is conferred generically by masculinity, however much we have then to qualify, but never erase, such power in relation to the embodied combinatory of sexual preference, race, ethnicity, class, religion, age and language) is also compatible, as social analysis, with violent desensitization and imploded responsibility/rage of men, with wounding. This neither says that the latter justifies the former (or that recognition and understanding of the latter explains the former), nor that there is some kind of gender-free human essence to be recognized and worked for (usually as individual efforts of mind-changing will). What it says is what it shows: until men recognize the full range of male power (whether that form of the social which is displayed in the architectonics of the public realm or that other social, which we men too often inscribe as private and havenlike, where masculinity lives as common sense) a revolutionary trans-*form*-ation is impossible. As well as what Kafka aptly entitled "the slime of a new bureaucracy," we shall have patriarchy paraded as correct ideas — (and we all know where they come from!). Initial Eye. Who is writing, who is reading, who is written?

Second, popular cultural forms, as embodied enactments, have their place, their play in — or, better, as — *always already regulated relations*. Whether in those productions we identify as performances or on the real terrain of making meaningful (making public), persons are aged, sexed, raced, ethnicized, classed, and otherwise socially identified. Modes and means of performance, as modes and means of making meaningful, are likewise *already always organized as difference(s)*. This is, as I now see, an axiological conundrum. Any accounting and reading which claims a general human validity is flawed against the profound historical experiences, dressed/embodied as these most Obvious (and most ignored, even — usually implicitly — denied) *social facts*. Old Answers have to be re-cognized as New Questions.

These two statements should not be ignored in what follows. They connect, directly, with my Prologue above, but they take the deconstruction further as they also announce that there are other authority claims and selecting-dividing practices more important than those which abstracted and assundered surrealism into the tamed arenas of ethnology and art, and classed them. I am trying to connect, without merging, ethnology and education in raising questions about any *general* claims concerning embodiment and empowerment. Cultural forms are not constitutive positions, but regulated plays, works.

PUNK SOCIOLOGY: THOSE FAMILIAR OTHERS

Punks, as the Other familiarized within the gaze of a national socialscape, have always been there. In contrast to the sanctified and diabolized exoticism of the foreign, blurred like a film out of sync, a poorly developed photograph — all sepia and smears — there is the Other within. Alien. Omen. *Nemo*. Youth, like the Child (childhood), has been long in the making. What makes an ethnography of "now" so much more difficult is that we are always dealing with kaleidoscopes, in which patterns become focused in terms of one predominant term as embodiment within a signifying chains. These denied chains, as loud claims, are part of the forms that constrain, dilute, deny, deride, derange, and de-form the voices of the Other. What is being said, all ways, is that conversation with these people is (almost) impossible. Annihilation.

Punk, in the 1970s, gathers the crystals in the kaleidoscope around Youth, but the coding of Otherness is multiple, and any punk sociology must go beyond the immediate (blinding, dispersing, pictorial) identification to see the graphic in the hieroglyphic *mugging* sociology which (snatches and runs with the immediate sign). In contrast to annihilation is a fake plenitude, where stolen adornments crystallize in *curricula vitae*, refereed journals, big tomes, and reputations; as they also do in *Sid & Nancy* Hollywood specular dis-satisfactions. As Dick Hebdige has argued (1982, 1983) by such immediacy of signing punks get *noticed*, but the notifications partake of dichotomization, the murderous quality of the conceptual. Imagine, to make this clearer, the theft done by photography and ethnography as a material action, the journalists and sociologists run down the streets carrying the signs they have stolen, shiftily, into taxis, subways, buses, cars, to worship them in the sacred museums of the academy, the Press. As violently abstracted categories — deconstruction as disembodiment and denial — they can then circulate safely. The Others are familiar, like us but weird, and not like us: inside the outside *or* outside the inside. Alien Omens.

Two voices. Randomly found, in dispersed texts. First, one from my place — a trace of a history in a small piece of open land, a Common, a very political English place, and a moment that brings together that for me fascinating Oxford University/Town and the area of South East working-class London where I, my parents, and their parents "grew up": this common was owned by Queen's College, Oxford (a sign of some long-ago royal reward to the rich). An Irish Republican, John de'Morgan, formed a Commons Protection League, to stop further encroachments on Plumstead Common, Woolwich, S.E. London, England, in 1876. On 1 July 1876, several hundred people took down the fences that a private individual (actually the Vestry Clerk and later the local Member of Parliament, Edwin Hughes) had affixed as a claim to make the Common part of his garden (yard). On 2 July 1876, the crowd returned and removed the already-rebuilt fences. Hearken to how the local newspaper described these events:

> A shocking scene of brutality and revelry…the infection has spread and every section of the rougher population participated in a lawless and sensual holocaust of animal enjoyment.[8]

"Brutality and revelry," "lawless and sensual" ("animal enjoyment")…and Holocaust!

Secondly, in Jack Fuller's 1985 novel *Mass*, Majewski (a newspaper editor, who changed his name to John Majors and works for *The Herald* in New Haven) reflects generally on the relationship with his son:

> Somewhere *along the lines* something had gone terribly wrong with the young. It was as if a deep ravine separated you from them, and all you could do was *shout* across it, *pleading* with them to watch their step as they staggered *along the edge*. He did not know what it was that kept them apart. But they were different, so completely different, and when you *begged* them

to be careful, they *looked* at you as if you were the one who was about to fall. (p. 14, my emphases)

"Along the line," "along the edge": shouting, pleading, begging, looking. The familiar becomes the Other, the son as a stranger. Loss and Lack: "something had gone terribly wrong with the young."

Although contemporary, such depictions and designs have very deep historical roots. Dick Hebdige in his work has come to see these roots as a series of dichotomies that coalesce and intersect (intertext) as a category or focus, a way of seeing and naming. Once these relational and perspectival categories are in place then they become ingredients for those thus *placed*, thus *sighted*.[9] One setting (set-up) is "youth as fun" and "youth as trouble," but contextualized in the specific urban settings of the crowd, where the free juveniles, in gangs, occupying their own idle time in these new delightful spaces, are taken as a symptom of the general problem: the legibility of a novel Otherness. One response to this "deep ravine" was a lot of shouting across it, shouting *at* the Other whilst keeping a necessary distance. Another, and these are not, of course, distinct and their blending is part of the genealogy of "Youth"/"Style," hence "Punk"; another, is to shift this distance (without at all diminishing either the ravine or the Otherness), to go beyond the police surveillance gaze to that of ethnographic exploration, to go into darkest England. A third set-up is that of salvation road, to see the barely legible as writable and thus savable; if conversation was not possible, conversion was! Combinations of these are found in documentary investigations, whether journalism or sociology. Child saving became an extensive production; if we could disaggregate national and subnational expenditure budgets (during the social democratic or liberal welfare era that has just ended *and* into the monetarist present) we would find them dominated by monies and programes oriented to child and youth saving and regulation: *reform as reconstruction*.

Central to this genealogy is the more and more detailed specification of the proper embodied signs of development. These media of modernity relate both what modernity is (civilization as modernization) and what are the stages of human maturation, within a simultaneously constructed pattern of governance and state formation. This cultural revolution — normalizations, identifications, standardizations, institutionalizations — continues coherently and flexibly through to today. Both senses of development are folded into the wider frames of governance, all rest upon patriarchal paternalism: Father knows best; Daddy is always right. The pervasiveness of this paternalism is well established in Alan Fox's recent survey of industrial relations, that very site of masculinity:

The key principle...the junior, subordinate or inferior participant is defined as having certain "true" or "real" interests which he or she is incapable of perceiving or pursuing. Responsibility for those interests is therefore vested in the senior or superior, who demands to receive in return the willing obedience of the person under his or her protection. *Reciprocity is of the essence. To assert protection is very often to assert control.* (my emphasis)[10]

This displays coherently the pedagogy of governance, patriarchal paternalism located as much within domesticity, schooling, and religious belief and observance, as within those other private institutions of work *and* that public realm constructed around rational, responsible respectability.

What is important in Hebdige's argument[11] is that the projected alternations of youth as fun and youth as trouble form and founder around the construction of categories drawn from the various surveillance techniques I outlined (from his work) earlier: the cartographs (documentation as texts, statistics and images) result from ways of looking *and* offer representations for ways of seeing. It is but another example of how descriptions as prescriptions become inscriptions. Since the bodies were not legible (a feature of their not being governable) they have to be assigned, written over, embodied in and as signs. Thus named they are claimed as simultaneously Other and Familiar; they are given their place in an order, albeit at the edge, over the ravine: border-lined boundary markers. Infectious. In-vested Reciprocity.

It is here, at this point, that I argue a move beyond any phenomenology of subordination and subculture, to enter the form of life, the language game with a pragmatics of use. There *are* bodies being subjected to the above objectification. There are persons who look back, who gaze and stare, who have to live, that is to handle, the categories applied to their being and becoming.

As McRobbie says of adolescent and adult women:

> [A]ll the signs and meanings in the way we handle our public visibility play a part in the culture which, like the various youth cultures, bears the imprint of our collective, historical creativity. They are living evidence that although *inscribed* within structures, no one are not wholly *prescribed* by them. For many of us too, escaping from family and its pressures to act like a *real girl remains the first political experience.* For us the objective is to make this flight possible for all girls, and on a long term basis. (1980: 49, my emphases)

McRobbie goes on to stress that this *cannot* be accomplished by being "like" the boys/men, but requires *separate* culture and political "pre-figurative forms and sets of social relations" to *disrupt* "normal" development "with a sense of oppositional sociality, and unambiguous pleasure in style, a disruptive public identity and a set of collective fantasies."

PUNK SOCIOLOGY (TAKE 2): REGARDING THE REAL "OTHER"

Some years ago I polemicized against dichotomies and dualisms as part of what I now see as the either/or pseudo choices of hegemonic moral regulation, whereby descriptives operate as both prescriptions – (the totalizing "ought" of normalizations) – and inscriptions – (the individualizing "is" of identifications (Foucault 1982)). I subsequently embraced Roland Barthes's twin notions of "spiralling" and finding a third way, a third term to refuse the either/or-ism of rule and regulation. Recently I have come to see a new trap in this triadic perspective which has relevance for the punk/surreal ethnography I am elaborating.

Carl Pletsch, in his important discussion of three worlds theory (in its dominant U.S. modernization frame), recalls the quote from Paul Valery I used earlier:

> Only if we can remember that "the Other" is never defined in intrinsic terms, but always in terms of the difference from the assessor, will we have the epistemological basis for a differential understanding.... (1981: 590)

What seems to happen is the use, and simultaneous denial and erasure, of one point-of-view, highly specific and yet claimed as both natural and normal. The other is constructed in relation to this perspectival, grammatical *figure in dominance*. But is is also empirically the case that there remain beyond the purity/impurity, good/bad, either/or-ism of the founding classification, *residual categories*. If we see the normal as Masculinity (as Right) then we can see the other as Femininity (as Wrong?) and then see children and — subsequently — both youth and deviant sexualities, constituted as a "third group," the residual ambiguous other. This could then be illuminated by Pletsch's comments above, insofar as we can trace empirical attention to the correction or conversion of the "wrongs" of the third group (they *can* be "righted" to be fitted into the norm/other dichotomy). *But* none of this need alter the basic "social algebra" — the other side remains "wrong" ideologically and "wronged" morally.

This means, again, that we have to call to mind the always- already differenced organization of all cultural forms, including those of "youth cultures" like Punk. Insofar as we can see Punk as a more general *refusal* than many other youth cultural forms, it is organized within gendered sexualized subjectivity relations. Thus, insofar as we can see this culture — in all its disquiet — as empowering via embodiment, we have to see its shadow also; the accents of its collective language, the grammar of its fashioning, do not break from the dominant code. This is why I referred to the kaleidoscopic (viewed as flashing signs) construction of Punk earlier.

It is necessary to qualify this direction, this stretch of language, in case I am misunderstood. There is no doubt that Punk recalls and reveres a longer tradition that refuses rather than resists, that opposes rather than alternates (Corrigan 1981a, 1986c). As such it does refuse a design from without, the de-signs of fashion are constantly gone beyond or refused, ultimately, by *an exotic that permanently marks the body*. As such there is a recall of the moment of surreal ethnography described by Clifford (1981). Val Hennessy registers this in her book of Punk photographs, *In the Gutter* (1978), where images of a Fulani woman, Upper Volta (p.14); Samburu warrior, Kenya (p.

18); Dinka boy, Sudan (p. 22); Hindu ceremony, Kuala Lumpur, Malaysia (p. 26); Chinese opera, Singapore (p. 29); Masai elder, Kenya (p. 34); Kelaket man, Sarawak (p. 39); warrior, New Guinea (p. 42); Kamayura Indian warrior, Brazil (p. 60); Tuareg girl, Algeria (p. 64); Cuna Indian, Panama (p. 71); Kew Yah girl, Sarawak (p. 76); Kayon male, Malaysia (p. 80) Suya Indian, Brazil (p. 84); and others (notably the nine color photograph spread, pp. 56–57), intertex the ninety-four-page book.

If that catalogue offers one intersection, another would have to be seen in Malcolm MacLaren's sense of *this* otherness and the promotion of the Sex Pistols, whose "God Save the Queen/Fascist Regime" (in the year of Her Imperial Majesty's 25th Jubilee, 1977) made it *all* worthwhile, for me. The way, however briefly, this opened spaces for other cultural productions is traceable to Val Hennessy's story of Danny Baker, like MacLaren from Deptford, S.E. London, England (Hennessy 1979).

But there is a darker shadow here in this fleeting working-class, largely male, access to fame (for 15 minutes or 15 years). On page 91 of *In the Gutter*, in an English (London?) pub (public house = bar) sits a male in full SS (Nazi) regalia, under a sign for the National Abortion campaign! On page 74 of the same collection, a bare-breasted woman stage performer wears a Nazi armband, and other NSDAP insignia feature in the book. These features of Punk are no more innocent than, and are, in fact, intimately connected to, those of masculinity.

In all, I reluctantly think, Punk involves as its dominant code of refusal what Saul Friedlander calls an "archaic utopia" (1984: 4, 13, 17, 21). Fried-lander concludes his book by arguing (as others have before) that Nazism involves the "fusion of opposites," a particular *reactionariness*, a refusal of modernity.

> Now, this fusion is only the expression of a kind of malaise in civilization, linked to the acceptance of civilization, but also to its fundamental rejection. Modern society and the bourgeois order are perceived both as an accomplishment and as an unbearable yoke. Hence this constant coming and going between the need for submission and the reveries of total destruction, between love of harmony and the phantasms of apocalypse, between the enchantment of Good Friday and the twilight of the gods. Submission nourishes fury, fury clears its conscience in the submission. To these opposing needs, Nazism—in the constant duality of its representations—offers an outlet; in fact, Nazism found itself to be the expression of these opposing needs. Today these aspirations are still there, and their reflections in the imaginary as well.

> But this duality is grafted onto a much more profound contradiction made up of a dream of all-powerfulness and the accepted risk of annihilation. This is certainly part of the romantic tradition, but above all it is a vision that, better perhaps than the liberal or Marxist vision, explains the profound conflict of man facing modernity. The liberal creed and the Marxist creed imply as-surance of salvation by the cumulative acquisition of knowledge and power.

Neither liberalism nor Marxism responds to man's archaic fear of the trans-gression of some limits of knowledge and power (you shall not eat the fruit...), thus hiding what remains the fundamental temptation: the aspiration for total power, which, by definition, is the supreme transgression, the ultimate chal-lenge, the superhuman combat that can be settled only by death.

Linked as it is to a great extent to the rise of modernity, does this vision still run through our imagination, does it remain a temptation for today and for tomorrow? We know that the dream of total power is always present, though dammed up, repressed by the Law. Also constant is the temptation to break the Law, even at the risk of destruction. With this difference—which perhaps tempers, or on the contrary exacerbates, the apocalyptic dreams: This time, to reach for total power is to assure oneself, and all of mankind as well, of being engulfed in total and irremediable destruction. (1984: 84–85)

As such, this pedagogy returns us to the ethnography illuminated by Hebdige and Clifford — an *Unscience of the Other* — and at the limit, this other who is oneself. Insofar as Punks have allowed me to see myself and my limits they have great importance, as also their practical critiques of romance and gendered music or dancing. Never likely — because of *how* they timed their words — to be recognized like the intellectual/avant-gardes I describe above, I want here to register them sentimentally, recalling nights in the electric Ballroom, Camden Town, London, England. *They are disquieting*. Disquiet and unease remain fundamental resources for a critical ethnography and political pedagogy that goes beyond simply affirming the Other or the Residual as not-like-us, not-ourselves; *or*, where "I" would like to be/How "I" would like to live. While we welcome the Other, we have to know these limits of dis...quiet, this quiet. "The mirror *lies* in — — — pieces" (Hebdige 1985: 39, my emphasis).

PEDAGOGY, PUNKS/FLUENCY, FLUIDITY: TOWARD A POETIC PRAGMATICS (TAKE 3)

There is a film which Roger Simon and I have used in our Winter Forum Workshops with teachers at OISE in Toronto — *The Class of Miss McMichael* (1978).[12] It is, in many ways, fanciful — in a different, approving, language, it displays the marks of its constructivity. For me, the film's rendering offers provisions, glimpses on behalf of a social world I half knew but never lived and which I know I do not now inhabit. My reason for mentioning it now is because it also illustrates a major moral/political dilemma: Do we *reach* those who reject "our" learning, in order to *teach* them? Are alternative pedagogies — progressive, liberatory, emancipatory — caught up in the more solid problematic of exchange (Walkerdine 1986a, b, c). Not here as "obedience for knowledge" but, the weak variant of the former and similarly prescribed by teachers' work, as "attention for" what? Being "taken" serious-ly, being "found out" hiding in the light, "known" as performance, sign makers of the otherwise ignoring ignorant world, being kept quiet within this alternative "permissive" pedagogy? Teachers as warders and wardens, zookeepers for this deviancy,[13] this quiet. Disquieting again.

I fear this, as I also fear that this writing is an ethnography of exploration and discovery, a late twentieth century version of a voyage into Darkest England, a mapping which (pretends) hands-on access to that which was so carefully displayed and yet held back; de-signated. Is not this exploration simply another masculine petty pedagogy typical of the petty bourgeoisie as Dick, Paul, the other Paul (Corrigan 1979), and many others, including me, make available our very male, highly particular, glimpses and imaginations of a world we do not, after all, really *inhabit*, but overview, visit, remember and report from, or fantasize, project, dis-member?[14]

What *The Class of Miss McMichael* displays is the impossibility of pedagogy, no less and no more than that! Miss McMichael is defined, as we are all of us, by social relations of a far wider reach and intensity then those actually imaged in the film, both those beyond the school (as a woman, as a professional, as, importantly, an outside observer of those students/pupils she is trying to teach) and those within that special institution, the school for maladjusted students (for those called, in another rhetoric, "Educationally Subnormal"), with the hierarchy of students, teachers, headmaster (principal), governors (trustees), visitors, directors of education, and chairman and members of the education committee of the local education authority/local municipality. But she is also defined by the Idea of Education. But that "Idea" is far from innocent, as it is also far more than what the etymology of Idea suggests.[15]

First, these students are within months of being sixteen years old and thus then free to leave school; or, rather, henceforth their parents are not subject to potential prosecution for failing to send their adolescent sons and daughters to such a school. Second, although the film is free of Punk personal style,[16] it is sociographically accurate in depicting the persons who are students in such a school as lower-working-class white and black, i.e., West Indian by descent. There was not then (1978), and there is much more *not* so now (1987), *any* coherent career for these students, although there remains the charisma of a fantasy. The school signals "This Is A Dead End" and in that way, quite rationally, *corresponds* to the Dead End of the world, in what nineteenth century educationists called "The After Life," i.e., after school. There is then no point in learning, no reason to do well, *at school*; there is every reason to learn the ways, values and ecology of the other world outside—that of white and black lower-working-class survival in the monetized but not regulated economy (a social economy) of marginal, small-scale activities, crimes, and profitable (for some) pleasures (Belinda announces that she is going on "the Game," i.e., into prostitution, with the approval of her father).

On the other hand, pulling away from the miasma of *ennui*, depression (displaced anger), and deep despair concerning *how* we know and what we know,[17] I move, move on. For this place, this sight/site is where I (and, I know, some of you, readers) have often been: it is the oscillation (frenzied immobility) between optimism and pessimism. I wobble between "It's all wonderful, everything is fine" *and* "It's all terrible, everything is awful." "anything can be done" *and* "nothing can be done."

What I think we need is a realism done differently, even a pragmatism of a certain kind. We need to shift our images of education and pedagogy in at least three ways: to widen our understanding of how we are taught, *and* how we learn, *and* how we know, noting that none of these is the same. What I think is happening in education now is a pragmatism which describes its politics as "administration" (a return of "What is best administered, is best") and its morality as necessity (what our society needs and/or what the people want). This pragmatism can shrug off the critique of the last ten, twenty, or 150 years by an innocent directness: "Yes, schooling stratifies and organizes persons for position, *and that is good.*"[18] The old economy of *exchange*[19] (of obedience for knowing; attention for relevance) has gone. It never worked anyway, for the majority; it did not deliver either the goods or The Good Life insofar as mature capitalism allows such distinctions anyway. But now it is simply not intended, it is no longer necessary to have *that* to mandate a course of action. Moreover, this new pragmatism is absolutely international, for the Fiscal Policing here is methodological, descriptive, and tactical; the moral prescriptions are envisaged strategically. Here that old repressed — the Hidden Curriculum — returns as declarative utterance. As Margaret Thatcher said sometime during her first reign: "Economics is the method but the target is the soul."[20]

There is, of course, an opposing paradigm which resides in the irrepressible lived critique of capitalism (and "actually existing socialism") that will never, can never, disappear, for it is about use values: needs, wants, longing, desire, and pleasure, or better — bliss. "Pleasure is always bliss seen from a distant shore" (Roland Barthes). So, pedagogically (which is not a term in the Punk lexicon) what is to be done What *is* the current situation? What are our tasks? How do we know what we know? Well, one place to start, of course, is language: who are these "we" and "our" of whom we speak and write? The collecting, depicting, interpellating, hailing, addressing/dressing *force* of this we (our) is extremely powerful. If you cannot hear (find) yourself and that of your primary identity group in such an address then you are not there, but it is not you who are partial and peculiar, but the modes of discourse and depiction themselves. It is the speaking and writing that is crazed, not you. This, and so much more, is where we have to take care, recognizing our own power/desire/knowledge, not least the confluence of desiring and fearing, and thus terror or fear being coped with by control, and, above all, in academic cartography, by *ruling out* that which is dangerous![21]

Here then, for no other reason than that my hand has five digits, are five strategic considerations on and for a Punk Pedagogy.

First, we have to be careful. We have to take care. First of all, we have to take care of ourselves (the suicide of Nicos Poulantzas pervades this part of my text, for him, terrifyingly, the lonely hour of the last instance actually arrived!). Being careful here is to critique and shift the enormous pressures to dualize and dichotomize, to enter that dark cloud of preoccupation where it is a matter of us not getting it right, where it is a matter of *will*; or to objectify the problem (and hence the registration of our own powerlessness) as beyond us, as matters of *force*. All my writing life I have struggled in this space, unable to teach myself (often, curiously, more able to teach others) that the dialectic of constraint and construction is a third place from which to understand and oversee the flip-flop dualisms of Internality and Externality, to begin to *feel* and *live* determination as the "setting of limits of variation," as Raymond Williams phrases it.[22]

Second, we have to be "caring-and-yet critical" of the views and lives of others, their ways of knowing. Simple affirmation of common-sense forms leads nowhere (except it leads somewhere, e.g., (a) Death Camps and Genocide and (b) Defeat and Depression). If Academic knowledge is partial, so too is that other, multiple Others, enfolded in "Common senses." Affirmation/Denial dualisms also erase the degree to which all dichotomies are contradictory unities, embodied as persons and socialized as differences.

Third, we must stop being afraid: everything we've been afraid of happens to us[23] and adolescence is the third general moment of such fearfulness. The first is that of birth/infancy; the second is that of childhood; and the fourth is terrifying – being "grown up," an *adult* – responsibility for men[24] and constant caring/forgiveness for women.[25]

Fourth, everything and everybody is connected, but we cannot write it like this. We can recall and work to make visible the dialexis of context-form-content, that triad that always loses its middle term. Punks *declare* themselves, their elocutionary force resides in their willing, forceful acknowledgment (desire for acknowledgment) of how they want to walk forward preceded by their masks. To teach courses in Punk is to deny this embodied "hiding in the light", to entice and ensnare, to capture them within the very force field they seek to avoid in *making their differences*. Not *making* a difference because that does not matter. It is all denial, so the moment of marking is to refuse all that, to say goodbye to all that. It is to try to evade being "collected" (pinioned in a case of exotica; formaldehyded and deadened: "those poor fish," as W. B. Yeats once wrote, "who lie gasping on the strand").

Fifth, my title means something. "Playing" is a problem of the movement What is necessary? What is possible?, as with the play in the door, the play with signs. "Contra/diction" is to remind us to attend to our remembering; there is no grammar without disturbance, improperness; there is no rule without transgression. We (differently) invented Punks as marked bodies in remarkable places. Émile Durkheim, Marcel Mauss, and — recently — Mary Douglas have identified our central ruling categories; how, for example, that dirt is "matter out of place." This centers a contaminating fear, but that fear is also a desire — to be in the place of the Other (to be, in that special sense of the metaphor, the Other). And this desiring fear, this fearful desire, produces a Terror. Terror becomes then "Terror" the terrorizing of the Other to achieve the eradication and the restoration of the Norm. As Theweleit has argued regarding Male Fantasies,[26] it is contamination at the periphery which is the most fearsome. Or as a friend of mine, proposing feminist courses in graduate education was told: this was an "invasion of the corpus" (so saith the Dean!).

There is another way of seeing, showing, saying, and *sharing*. That of the earlier moments of a modernism which finds/founds our multiple contradictory unities and in that finding, founds also in the Other *that other* who is ourselves. Punks here could function in the way I experienced in the early days of watching television, interruptions encoded on the screen (textually) as "NORMAL SERVICE WILL BE RESUMED AS SOON AS POSSIBLE." During those interludes I became aware of what Patrick Meredith calls "Orthogonality" — that I was watching, and *how* I was watching, these *magic rays of light*.[27]

Punks, I am arguing, punctuate not so we can learn to talk their language (it is the grammar that is being refused), but so we can come to a sense, akin to wondering, of how normal service works and whom it serves. It is neither an issue of communication, conversation, or conversion, nor an issue that they are across the divide, alien omens, contaminating pollutants. It is to begin to find ways in which we can translate, to find in the security of a framing, hopeful, easy pedagogy, the awful intent that we live — that we know and have something to say, and this knowing and saying regulates and regularizes, provides a refuge, a place to be, that is replicative, not of — for we all know we are against that — The System, but of our own desire for rules, boundaries, frames, methods. There embodied (but of course usually lost in talk and text) are our projects, but as well the being and becoming gratefulness of those we teach. We teach to be loved.

This is, then, an uncomfortable realism, a place where it is not easy to be, to live, to work. But, first, what *then* is new? And, second, what would being at ease mean in a world of endemic, chronic, and acute suffering, oppression, exploitation, domination, and subordination? By translation I do not intend a learning grammar, the lexicon, and the style, but a a recognition of the differences that frame and in/form desire and fear. Of what and whom are we afraid? Who dies when methodological protocols are not obeyed but clouded, lost from sight, transgressed? Who gets hurt when what is found (accidentally) becomes treasured? Becomes gold, even if later the dust pours through the fingers and is dispersed in a sudden rush of air? It is our fear(ing) that is the issue, and from that place, knowing and naming the desire to be (become) the Other. Perhaps, through listening and caring we can hear what is so special and so unique, a social difference that is being made contradictorally with the signifying grammar of hesitation, in the hard, hard play of constraint and construction....fabrication of "a logic which is diverse and discontinuous, a science, if you like, a science of the concrete, which is to say an unscience, a science of things happening..." (Hebdige 1983: 88).

It means also, and communicatively, that certain words and phrases are hard to say, or say to so easily, they do not "trip off the tongue," but stick, are sticky phrases, leading to stuttering and stammering, to hesitations and heartburn, even heart attack, because in arriving here, this, now, this disquiet, we have arrived at someone new, a person who is embodied, who feels, has a memory, is scarred and starred by their educative context, and we are now mindful of all of this. Ideas are no longer – in any possible way – ideational; we cannot trade in violent abstractions[28] for to do so, hurts.

And the learning? Who knows, and why do we need to know? What is the fearplace here that we have to have some, as cyberneticists say, feedback – are we that hungry? Well, it is not for them, in them, of them; but for, in, and of ourselves. Let me finish with that quiet *Punkista*, in his fashion, Michel Foucault, whom I do not think we should forget:

> I have a dream of an intellectual who destroys evidences and universalities, who locates and points out the inertias and constraints of the present, the weak points, the openings, the lines of stress; who constantly displaces himself [*sic*], not knowing exactly where he'll be nor what he'll be nor what he'll think tomorrow, because he is too attentive to the present; who, in the places he passes through, contributes to the posing of the question of whether the revolution is worth the trouble, and which (I mean which revolution and which trouble), it being understood that only those who are prepared to risk their lives to reply can do so.[29]

And then, the year before he died, Michel Foucault, whom I insist, we should never forget:

> Maybe the target for nowadays is not to discover what we are but to refuse what we are. We have to imagine and build up what we could be....We have to promote new forms of subjectivity through the refusal of this kind of individuality which has been imposed on us for several centuries.[30]

Or, as Gertrude Stein said it, in her usual perfection of bliss:

> Here I am and Look at me Now!....Now!!....Now!!!

For she also said, brutally, yes, "History Teaches that History Teaches." Instead: *Faites rire dans l'âme*, laughing (like singing) against the State, against Schooling. We breathe differently when we laugh, we struggle to catch our breath, we shake, we cease to be ruled (exactly as normally), and we can, peripherally, catch sight of our selves, floppy, in the mirror, in the kaleidoscope. Punks are cubists after all; they also embody be-bop, montage, "quotation." Glance at an angle, listen on the ledge, edgily engage. This quiet. Dis...quiet.

NOTES

*For Dick Hebdige, Surrealist, Ethnographer, My Friend

1. e.g., Corrigan 1975; 1981a, b; 1983a, b, c; 1984a, b, c; 1985a, b, c, d; 1986a, b, c; 1987a, b, c, d.

2. Paul Valery:

> [I]t is more useful to speak of what one has experienced than to pretend to a knowledge that is entirely impersonal, an observation with no observer. In fact, there is no theory that is not a fragment, carefully prepared, of some autobiography. I do not pretend to be teaching you anything at all. I will say nothing you do not already know....(quoted S. Burnshaw, *The Seamless Web*, Oxford 1970: xi,, n2)

See also Bernstein 1973: 2; Williams 1979: 15; Althusser 1969: 81; Willis and Corrigan 1980; and Corrigan 1985e.

3. What follows relies extensively upon Clifford's 1981 article, whose importance for me I cannot overemphasize. It needs to be montaged with, for example, David Frisby's *Fragments of Modernity* (1985) and other work I annotate in "Re/Membering Modernity" (1986b) which centers Ernst Bloch's *Principle of Hope* (1986).

4. The major texts used by Clifford are Jamin 1980; Duvignaud 1979; Hollier 1979; and Lourau 1974.

5. Kojève's involvement is of significance because of his place (or, better, the place of his seminars on Hegel) in a different filiation to structuralism. See Descombes (1981). What returns in post-structuralism and, or, better, *as* post- modernism is the Other, the repressed, forgotten from the 1917–1939 epoch—a refusal of general schemata, of systems, and of disciplinary boundaries, *and* of those doubling dichotomies that are the contagion of the rational masculinized mind: Self *vs.* Society, Content *vs.* Form, and with that, a necessary and not contingent refusal of the Good/Bad ethics which are the bad conscience of capitalism. Of the same nexus of relational necessity, the differenced body is shown and embodied. The "crises of Marxism" flourish this necessity, *from* demythologizing/demystification *to* deconstructing objectivity (changing the object itself) *to* find our subjectivities, differenced, multiple, dispersed, diffuse. The very question is thus "whose Body, whose Signs?" (Corrigan 1981a; 1985e; 1987b)

6. A. McRobbie (1980). Also: A. McRobbie and J. Garber (1976); McRobbie (1978, 1982); McCabe and McRobbie (1983); McRobbie and Nava (1984); A. Campbell (1984) and P. Mahony (1985). For a different working, within the same nexus of relations, see Steedman (1982; 1985a, b; 1986); Walkerdine (1981; 1983; 1984a, b; 1986a, b, c; 1987); D. Smith (1978, 1983, 1986a); and the whole collections by Heron (1985) and Owen (1983).

7. Key features of the presentation (realization) of "Masculinity as Right" come from significant conversations with, and draw from the work of K. Rockhill (1986, 1987a, b, c). See also Lewis and Simon (1986).

8. I am most grateful to my mother, N. R. F. Corrigan, for supplying me with the summary text by John Wilks (1986). The quoted source would be the *Kentish Independent*, 3 July 1876. The whole history of "common" rights, places, activities is a *crucial* ingredient for any theory of popular cultures: see P. R. D. Corrigan and

D. Sayer (1981; 1985:94–113); Marx (1842); Linebaugh (1976); Ditton (1977); Corrigan & Gillespie, 1974; Corrigan & Corrigan, 1979; Yeo and Yeo, 1981; Yeo, 1974, 1979, 1980, 1984; Spitzer, 1975.

9. In what follows I am relying both on Hebdige's texts (1982, 1983, 1985) and on many long and important conversations with him.

10. Quoted from Fox 1985, in John Lloyd "Chronicles of Bitter Confrontation," *Financial Times* (London) 24 August 1985. See Willis 1977, 1979 and Beynon, 1975.

11. It is not, of course, *only* Hebdige's insight I draw on here. For a review of how constraints are resources for construction, see Corrigan 1975, 1981a, 1983a, c, 1984a, 1985c, 1986c, 1987a. Of particular importance are Hudson 1984, Prendergast and Prout 1980, and Smith 1986a, b—the latter being book length— studies of the documentary/textual organization (and disorganization) of lived relations. The importance of Foucault (in one dimension—that of power/knowledge/subjectivity) and Barthes (in another—that of refusal by dispersal, by shifting, by excursion) cannot be overemphasized. They provide two related means of *refusing* power, "baffling" control, centering transgression as the rule.

12. (England, 1978. 90 minutes); production: Brut/Kettledrum, distributed by Rank-EMI; Director: Silvio Narizzano, based on a novel by Sally Houston; starring: Glenda Jackson, Oliver Reed. (Note: Brut also funded *A Touch of Class* (starring George Segal and Glenda Jackson, 1973); the director of *The Class of Miss McMichael* was born in Montreal in 1927 and directed *Georgie Girl* [1966] and *Loot* [1972]. Other films of relevance include *Educating Rita* [England, 1983]; *Teachers* [USA, 1984]; *Breaking Out* [USA, 1986]; and David Leland's four plays "Made in Britain" [Channel Four, 1983–4, especially the second play, which can be compared with both *The Class of Miss McMichael* and *Teachers*].

13. I am recalling here Jock Young's depictions of policing agents as "zoo-keepers of deviancy."

14. This "Desire for the Other" in much academic writing is often repressed to the point of invisibility (invisibility of the socially-material is a feature of all intellectualizations of the obvious and normal and natural and universal, cf. Corrigan, 1984a; Walkerdine, 1985; 1986a, b, c). For one example see the opening lines of Adam Ulam (in the symposium "What's happening in Moscow?" *National Interest* 8 (1987): 11) which quotes (but does not, typically, reference) a poem by Verlaine which compares his Desire for the Other (here the USSR) to the "woman of his dreams." In all of this (see Walkerdine 1986c) it is predictable that Desire slides into a dichotomy that equates *glasnost* (Openness!) and Terror! Recall here both Clifford (1981) and Pletsch (1981).

15. Materializations of this "Idea of Education" are now, thankfully, plentiful; for Scotland, see Fiona Patterson, Ph.D. diss., University of Edinburgh, Scotland, 1986; M. Hawksworth, M.Sc. (Econ) thesis, Institute of Education, London, 1982; Cheryl Hudson, M.A. thesis, OISE, Toronto, 1987. For strategic planning in Ontario education, see Cheryl Gorman, M.A. thesis, OISE, Toronto, 1987; for the earlier formative moments see B. Curtis, 1987 and the OISE Ph.D. theses of Satu Repo (1986), Ananda Kodikara (1986), and Shmuel Shamai (1986) and the forthcoming work from others of the 1850s–1950s Historical Sociology Group, Kari Dehli, Bob Morgan, David Welch, Ken Banks, Gary Kinsman, Debi Broch, together with the M.A. theses of Donna Varga Heise (1986) and Bob Lanning (1986).

16. Although the graffiti on the wall of the school playground states "BORING OLD FARTS RULE OK." There is an important sociology that relates this moment of BOFFING (in that context) to that of HAMMING in elite educational/intellectual/literary/political contexts, where "HAM" equals Heavy Academic Male. For

glimpses of that moment in England see the editors' first introductory chapter in Barrett et al. (1979) and Corrigan and Sayer (1978); a fuller critical survey is traceable in Sheila Rowbotham's chapter in the collective work *Beyond the Fragments* (Newcastle Upon Tyne: Socialist Centre, 1979), or such moments as the gendered split in the editorial board of *Politics of Power* around the feminist issue (See *P&P*, 3, 1981 "Women's editorial," "Men's editorial," and Chris Stretch "Women must lead," *Leveller* 57 (1981): 14—16, prefigured in *Women Take Issue* (Centre for Contemporary Cultural Studies, Women's Group, 1978). In part what is being narrated here are versions of a conflation between the Political and Academic Romances.

17. I am grateful to Marion McMahon for this insight. Her M.A. thesis (OISE, Toronto, 1987) presents a rare tracing of the educated body and its scars. See also McRobbie 1980; Rockhill 1986; Steedman 1986; Walkerdine 1986a, b, c.

18. See Walkerdine 1983, and the section "Terms of Debate" in that collection.

19. Willis 1977: 64; Walkerdine 1986b.

20. See, here, (1) United States Department of Education (a) *What Works* (Washington D.C., the Department, 1986); (b) *First Lessons* (The same); (2) American Federation of Teachers (a) *Education for Democracy* (Washington D.C., A.F.T., 1987); (b)*Democracy's Untold Story: What World History Textbooks Neglect* (The same); (3) Ontario Ministry of Education (a) *Towards the Year 2000* (Ontario, the Ministry, 1984); (b) *Behaviour: A Resource Guide* (The same, 1986); (c) *Discipline* (The same, 1986).

21. Cf. A. Dybijowski and others (eds.) *In the feminine: women and words/les femmes et les mots* (Edmonton, Alberta: Longspoon Press, 1983); E. A. Meese *Crossing the Double-Cross: The Practice of Feminist Criticism* (Chapel Hill: University of North Carolina Press, 1986).

22. R. Williams, *Problems in Materialism and Culture* (London: Verso, 1980).

23. "We've been *so* frightened and everything we've been frightened of, has happened...we need light, we've in the dark too long, we need some light to be seen and if we can't have natural light, we'll have some financial light..." (coal miner, BBC Durham Region, radio broadcast "It's Saturday," 19 February 1972).

24. Cf. Corrigan 1983a, 1986c.

25. Cf. Rockhill, 1986, 1987c, and the work of Marion McMahon.

26. Klaus Theweleit, *Male Fantasies*, vol. 1; *Women, Floods, Bodies, History* (Minneapolis: University of Minnesota Press, 1987); but see also C. W. Ferguson *The Male Attitude* (Boston: Little Brown, 1966) and G. Hofstede, *Culture's Consequences* (Beverly Hills: Sage, 1980, Ch. 6, "Masculinity")

27. P. Meredith, *Instruments of Communication* (Oxford, Pergamon, 1963).

28. D. Sayer *Violence of Abstraction* (Oxford, New York, Blackwell, 1987).

29. From a 1977 interview "The history of sexuality" translated in *Oxford Literary Review* (4): 1980, 14. For a complementary and contemporaneous emphasis see Roland Barthes's "Lecture" of 1977, translated in *Oxford Literary Review* (4): 1979, especially p. 42, cited in context in Corrigan 1985e and in Lewis and Simon 1986. The issue of intellectuals and intellectuality is as worthy of study as that of Punks (cf. note 16 above). For a varied (and largely not wondrous) range of references see: G. R. Kress "Toward an analysis of the language of European intellectuals' *Journal of European Studies*, 7, 1978; R. Williams *Culture* (London: Fontana, 1981, Ch. 8); *Telos* (50) 1981–82 Special Symposium on the role of Intellectuals in the 1980s; P. Schlesinger "In search of the intellectuals: some comments on recent theory" *Media, Culture and Society*, 4, 1982, and so on.

30. M. Foucault "The Subject and Power" *Critical Inquiry*, 8, 1982, p. 785. See also C. MacKinnon, "Feminism, Marxism, Method and the State," *Signs* 7 (1982); "Towards Feminist Jurisprudence" *Signs* 8 (1983); *Feminism Unmodified* (Boston: Harvard University Press, 1987); A. Dworkin, *Intercourse*.

REFERENCES

Althusser, Louis
(1969)   *For Max*. London: Allen Lane.
Anderson, Penny
(1984)   *In the Tracks of Historical Materialism*. Chicago: University of Chicago Press.
Barthes, Roland
(1984)   *A Barthes Reader*. ed. S. Sontag. New York: Hill & Wang.
Bernstein, Basil
(1977)   *Class Codes and Control*. vol. 3. rev. ed. London and Boston: Routledge.
Beynon, H.
(1975)   *Working for Fords*. London: Penguin.
Bloch, Ernst
(1986)   *The Principle of Hope*. Oxford: Blackwell. 3 vols.
Campbell, A.
(1986)   *The Girls in the Gang*. Oxford: Blackwell.
Centre for Contemporary Cultural Studies, Women's Group
(1978)   *Women Take Issue*. London: Hutchinson.
Clifford, James
(1981)   "On Ethnographic Surrealism." *Comparatve Studies in Society and History* 18.
Clifford, James, and George E. Marcus, eds.
(1986)   *Writing Culture*. Berkeley: University of California Press.
Colls, R., and P. Dodd, eds.
(1986)   *Englishness*. London: Croom Helm.
Corrigan, Paul
(1979)   *Schooling the Smash Street Kids*. London: Macmillan.
Corrigan, P. R. D.
(1987a)   "Initial Eye." *Photocommunique*. forthcoming.
(1987b)   "Innocent Stupidities." In G. Fyfe and J. Law, eds. *Sociological Review Monograph*. London and Boston: Routledge.
(1987c)   "'Commatization' and 'Add-ons': How Central Social Issues Become Optional Extras." forthcoming.
(1987d)   ed.*Education Now: Essays in Exploration*. forthcoming.
(1987e)   *X/S: for Roland*. forthcoming.
(1986a)   "Spadina Avenue." *Border/lines* 6.
(1986b)   "Re/Membering Modernity." forthcoming.
(1986c)   "Masculinity as Right." forthcoming.
(1985a)   "Embodying Ethnicity Educationally." In J. Young, ed. *Breaking the Mosaic*. Toronto: Garamond.
(1985b)   "Informing Schooling." In D. Livingstone, ed. *Critical Pedagogy and Cultural Power*. South Hadley, Mass.: Bergin & Garvey.
(1985c)   "In/formation." *Photocommunique* Fall.

(1985d)   "Did I hear bark...." *C. Magazine* 8.
(1985e)   "The Body of Intellectuals...." *Sociological Review*.
(1984a)   "Doing Mythologies." *Border/lines* 1.
(1984b)   "Spadina Avenue: Re/View." *Parachute* 37.
(1984c)   "The Politics of Feeling Good: Reflexions." In R. Gruneau, ed. *Popular Cultural Forms*. Toronto: Garamond.
(1983a)   "'My Body'/'My Self?' Trying to See (with) My Masculine Eyes." *Resources for Feminist Research* 12.
(1983b)   "Hard Machines/Soft Messages." *Nineteeneightyfour in 1984*. London: Comedia.
(1982)   "What is the Subject of (a) Cultural Production?" *Undercut* (3–4).
(1981a)   "Towards a Celebration of Difference(s)." In D. Robins, ed. *Rethinking Social Inequity*. London: Gower Press.
(1981b)   "On Moral Regulation." *Sociological Review* 29.
(1980)   ed. *Capitalism, State Formation, Marxist Theory* . London: Quartet; N.Y.:Orizen.

Corrigan, P. R. D., with V. Corrigan.
(1979)   "State Formation and Social Policy Before 1871." In N. Parry. *Social Work, Welfare and the State*. Leeds: Arnold.

Corrigan, P. R. D., with V. Gillespie
(1974)   *Class Struggle, Idle Time and Social Literacy* Brighton, Moyes: Labour History Monographs.

Corrigan, P. R. D., and D. Sayer.
(1985)   *The Great Arch: English State Formation as Cultural Revolution*. London and New York: Blackwell.
(1979)   "How the Law Rules." In B. Fryer et al. eds. *Law, State, Society*. London: Croom Helm.
(1978)   "Hinders and Hirst." *Socialist Register*.

Corrigan, P. R. D., and P. Willis.
(1979)   "Cultural Forms and Class Mediations." *Media, Culture and Society* 2.

Curtis, Bruce
(1987)   *Building the Educational State*. London and Philadelphia: Falmer Press.

Descombes, Vincent
(1981)   *Modern French Philosophy*. London and New York: Cambridge University Press.

Ditton, J.
(1977)   "Perks, Pilferage and the Fiddle." *Theory and Society* 4.

Duvignaud, J.
(1979)   "Roger Cailloix et l'imaginaire." *Cahiers internationaux de sociologie* 66.

Foucault, Michel
(1982)   "The Subject and Power." *Critical Inquiry* 8.
(1981)   "Questions of Method." *Ideology and Consciousness* 8.

Fox, A.
(1985)   *Heritage and History: The Social Origins of the British Industrial Relations System*. London: Allen & Unwin.

Friedlander, Saul
(1984)   *Reflections on Nazism*. New York: Harper & Row.

Fuller, Jonathan
(1986)   *Mass*. Toronto and New York: Paper Jacks.

Hebdige, Dick
(1987)   *Hiding in the Light*. London: Comedia.
(1986)   "Notes on the Sublime." *New Formations* 1.
(1985)   "Some Sons and Their Fathers." *Ten-8* (17).
(1983)   "Posing...Threats, Striking...Poses: Youth, Surveillance, Display." *Sub-Stance* (37–38).
(1982)   "Hiding in the Light." *Ten-8 Magazine* (9).
(1978)   *Subcultures*. London, Toronto, and New York: Methuen.

Hennessy, V.
(1979)   "Every Which Way But Boring." *Evening Standard* (London).
(1978)   *In the Gutter*. London, Melbourne, and New York: Quartet.

Heron, L., ed.
(1985)   *Truth, Dare or Promise: Girls Growing Up in the Fifties*. London: Virago.

Hollier, D., ed.
(1979)   *Le collège de sociologie*. Paris: Gallimard.

Hudson, B.
(1984)   "Femininity and Adolescence." In A. McRobbie and M. Nava. *Gender and Generation*. London: Macmillan.

Jamin, J.
(1980)   "Un sacre college ou les apprentis sorciers de la sociologie." *Cahiers internationaux de sociologie* (68).

Lewis, Magda, and Roger Simon
(1986)   "A Discourse Not Intended for Her." *Harvard Educational Review* 56 (4).

Linebaugh, P.
(1976)   "Karl Marx, the Thefts of Wood and Working-Class Composition." *Crime and Social Justice*.

Lourau, R.
(1976)   *Le gai savior des sociologues*. Paris: Union Generale des Editions.

McCabe, T., and A. McRobbie eds.
(1983)   *Feminism: An Adventure Story*. London and Boston: Routledge.

McRobbie, A.
(1982)   "The Politics of Feminist Research: Between Talk, Text and Action." *Feminist Review* (12).
(1980)   "Settling Accounts with Subcultures: A Feminist Critique." *Screen Education* (34).
(1978)   "Working-class girls...." In Centre for Contemporary Cultural Studies. *Women Take Issue*. London: Hutchinson.

McRobbie, A., and J. Gerber
(1984)   "Girls and Subcultures." In S. Hall et al., eds. *Resistance Through Rituals*. London: Hutchinson.

McRobbie, A., and M. Nava, eds.
(1984)   *Gender and Generation*. London: Macmillan.

Mahony, P.
(1985)   *Schools for the Boys? Co-Education Reassessed*. London: Hutchinson.

Marx, Karl
(1842)   "Proceedings...Thefts of Wood." *Collected Works of Marx and Engels*. vol. 1. London: Lawrence & Wisehart; N.Y.: International, 1975.

Owen, V., ed.
(1983)   *Fathers—Reflections by their Daughters*. London: Virago.

Parry, N., ed.
(1979)   *Social Work, Welfare and the State*. Leeds: Arnold.
Pletsch, C. E.
(1981)   "The Three Worlds, or the Division of Social Scientific Labor, Circa
           1950–1975." *Comparative Studies in Society and History*.
Rockhill, Kathleen
(1987a)   "Gender, Language and the Politics of Literacy." *British Journal of
           Sociology of Education* B (2).
(1987b)   "Literacy as Threat/Desire: Longing to be SOMEBBODY." In J. T. Gaskel
           and A. T. McLaren, eds. *Women and Education: A Canadian Perspec-
           tive*. Calgary: Detselig.
(1987c)   "Violence Against Wives." Presentation, Graduate School of Social
           Work, University of Toronto.
Rowbotham, Sheila, et al.
(1980)   *Beyond the Fragments*. London: Merlin Press.
Shamai, Samuel
(1987)   "Critical Theory of Education and Ethnicity." Boston University *Journal
           of Education*.
Shamai, Samuel, and Philip Corrigan
(1987)   "Social Facts, Moral Regulation and Statistical Jurisdiction." *Canadian
           Journal of Higher Education* 17 (2).
Showalter, Elaine
(1986)   "No Star Turns." *Women's Review* (8).
Smith, Dorothy
(1986a)   "Femininity as Discourse." Unpublished paper, OISE, Department of
           Sociology.
(1986b)   *Social Organization of Knowledge*. forhtcoming.
(1983)   "Women and Class." *Socialist Register*.
Spitzer, S.
(1975)   "Towards a Marxian Theory of Deviance." *Social Problems* 2 (2).
Steedman, Carolyn
(1986)   *Landscape for a Good Woman: A Story of Two Lives*. London: Virago.
(1985a)   "Prisonhouses." *Feminist Review* (20).
(1985b)   "The Mother Made Conscious." *History Workshop Journal* (20).
(1982)   *The Tidy House: Little Girls Writing*. London: Virago.
Steedman, Carolyn, C. Urwin, and V. Walkerdine, eds.
(1985)   *Language, Gender, Childhood*. London and Boston: Routledge.
Walkerdine, Valerie
(1987)   *The Mastery of Reason*. 2 vols. London, New York, and Toronto:
           Methuen.
(1986a)   "Video Replay." In *Formations of Desire*. London: Routledge.
(1986b)   "Progressive Pedagogy and Political Struggle." *Screen* 27 (5).
(1986c)   "Surveillance, Subjectivity and Struggle." Minneapolis, University of
           Minnesota Center for Humanistic Studies, Occasional Papers 11.
(1985)   "On the Regulation of Speaking and Silence." In Steedman, Urwin, Walker-
           dine. *Language, Gender, Childhood*. London and Boston: Routledge.
(1984a)   "Developmental Psychology." In Henriques and others.
(1984b)   "Someday My Prince Will Come." In McRobbie and Nava.
(1983)   "It's Only Natural." In A. M. Wolpe and J. Donald, eds. *Is There Anyone
           Here from Education?* London: Pluto.

(1981) "Sex, Power and Pedagogy." *Screen Education* (38).

Wilks, J.
(1986) "A Look Back...Plumstead Common." *Connections* (4 Dec.)

Williams, Raymond
(1983) *Towards 2000*. London: Chatto & Windus.
(1979a) *Modern Tragedy*. rev. ed. London: Verso.
(1979b) *Policies and Letters*. London: New Left Books.

Willis, Paul
(1979) "Shop Floor Culture, Masculinity and the Wage Form." In J. Clarke et al., eds. *Working-Class Culture*. London and Boston: Routledge.
(1978) *Profane Culture*. London and Boston: Routledge.
(1977) *Learning to Labour*. London: Saxon House; New York: Lexington Books.
(1976) *Working Papers in Cultural Studies* 9.

Willis, Paul, and P. R. D. Corrigan
(1980) "The Orders of Experience." *Social Text*.

Yeo, Elaine, and Stephen Yeo, eds.
(1981) *Popular Culture and Conflict, 1530–1914*. Brighton: Harvester.

Yeo, Stephen
(1987) *Whose Story?* forthcoming.
(1986) "Socialism, the State and Some Oppositional Englishness." In Colls and Dodd.
(1980) "State and Anti-State...Social Forms and Struggles from 1850." In Corrigan.
(1979) "Working-Class Association, Private Capital, Welfare and the State." In N. Parry.
(1974) "On the Uses of Apathy." *European Journal of Sociology*.

Chapter 5

PEDAGOGY IN THE PRESENT: POLITICS, POSTMODERNITY, AND THE POPULAR

Lawrence Grossberg

◆ One cannot question the politics of pedagogy without simultaneously questioning the pedagogy of politics.[1] There is an obvious struggle over the links between education and politics. From the Right, there is an effort to win back control — defined largely by content — of the various educational apparatuses, but education is not limited to schooling and cannot be isolated from the the broad terrain of popular cultural forms. The Left remains largely on the defensive, neither feeling in control of the dominant ideological apparatuses nor able to articulate the masses, and most especially youth, to their explicit ideological positions. But then, the role of popular culture is rather small in left pedagogies, serving usually as evidence of the sorry state of our cultural industries and mass audiences (except for that small minority who like the "right" texts or who read ambiguous texts in the "right" way). The Left's limited comprehension of the role of popular culture in the organization of power points to its own complicity in failing to find a convincing pedagogical practice for the current political conjuncture.

That complicity is defined by the pedagogy of politics, by what our political practices communicate to those we are attempting to teach. Whatever one might say about the dominant culture, youth is not silenced, ignored, or marginalized. It is noisier, more visible, and more central than ever. It is the Left that silences youth, not merely by its continued political and cultural elitism, but by systematically erasing the dominant sites of youth's experiences. By denying the validity and complexity of their cultural tastes, political values, and social experiences, left politics doesn't seem to be situated in the same world. Unless one begins where people live their lives, one will be unable to engage with the struggles over larger and more explicit ideological positions. That world is not only the real world of labor, capital, school, family, and law; it is also the equally real world of leisure, love, loyalty, pleasure and pain, and very real threats of unemployment, death, and boredom. Unless we approach the complex and specific relations among culture, power, and pedagogy, we risk surrendering the victory before the battle has been fought.

The elistism of the Left, the major stumbling block to a radical pedagogy, takes three forms: hierarchical, dialogic, and praxical. A hierarchical practice assumes that the teacher already understands the truth to be imparted to the student. The teacher understands the real meanings of specific texts and practices, the real relations of power, and the real interests of different social groups. The teacher draws the lines separating the good, the bad, and the ugly. A dialogical practice allows the silenced to speak; only when necessary does it speak for them. This assumes that they are not already speaking because we do not hear them, because they are not speaking the right languages, or because they are not saying what we demand of them. Finally a praxical pedagogy offers people the skills that would enable them to understand and intervene in their own history as they see fit. But this assumes, not only that they are not already doing so, but also that the teacher understands the right techniques to enable emancipatory and transformative action. If practices define possibilities, all of these elitisms assume that the teacher already understands history, and people's positions within it, better than they do.

Despite an increasing recognition of the complex and contradictory relations, not only between but within economic, political, cultural, and familial practices, the Left has not questioned either its easy interpretations of popular cultural forms or its assumptions about the nature of the masses (as cultural and political dopes). Nor has the recognition that power cannot be reduced to any single essential structure enabled the Left to deal with the concrete realities of people's ongoing struggle to, as Rambo says, "win and survive."

A radical pedagogy for the current times which struggles to move people into a more progressive ideological space is only possible if history is never guaranteed in advance. If social complexity is always organized according to real relations of power, its structuration is never complete. Contradictions are never stitched up into a secure coherent structure. History is the ongoing struggle to disarticulate and rearticulate the connections between social, cultural, economic, and political relations. Although no articulation is necessary, they are always real. Although there are no necessary correspondences between signifying practices, subjective identities, and political positions, history always involves the production of such correspondences. The stronger the links, the more necessary they may appear, but they can always be challenged. Of course, not every articulation involves struggle, not every struggle is won, not every victory is resistance, and not all resistance is progressive. But people do make history even if they have to use what they have been given, within the constraints and tendential forces pushing them in certain directions and limiting their possibilties.

This has significant consequences for our understanding of popular culture, politics, and pedagogy. First, we have to recognize that the meaning and politics of particular discourses are not indelibly and transparently written upon the surfaces of a discourse, never innocently available as the result of the production of a particular discourse, nor even by how a text is consciously appropriated by an audience fraction. Interpretations are always struggles to construct the text and its effects by articulating it into particular relationships. Consequently, not only is the text a site of struggle, but it may have contradictory effects, both within a particular plane (e.g., it may have contradictory ideological effects; it may be implicated in the circuits of capital even while it reclaims a certain productive independence for its audience) and between different planes of effects (it may largely reproduce the dominant ideology while challenging the dominant libidinal economy).

Second, the multiple relations of power are not reducible to a single plane of determination, but their autonomy is always limited by the ways they are linked together in specific relations. For example, although systems of power organized around gender and sexual difference cannot be explained in terms of economic and class relations, their specific historical forms cannot be understood apart from the ways they are articulated into specific economic, class, and race relations. Thus, while the elimination of capitalism does not guarantee the elimination of sexism, the battle against each cannot be entirely separated from the other.

Third, there can be no secure knowledge which predefines people's interests and progressive positions. People are neither unaware nor passive in the face of their own interests, needs, and subordinations; they are not waiting to be told where or how to struggle. Radical interventions must build upon efforts to map the complex and contradictory forces operating at specific sites in the social formation. We have to enter the terrain of everyday life to make sense of the dispersed realities of people's lives. Only then can we prise open already existing contradictions, "thereby renovating and making critical an already existing activity."[2]

This is not a task that teachers can perform for their students; it is a general social struggle over the politics of everyday life. And it is within this ongoing struggle that the possibility of a radical pedagogical practice can be located. If ideological struggles are won and lost in the broad spaces of civil society, where identities are constructed and linked to social positions, cultural practices, and political values, it is here that pedagogy must operate. The task is never to convince a predefined — whether empty or full — subject to adopt a new position, but to win an already positioned subject to a different set of positions. But if the subject is always multiply positioned, fragmented, contradictory, the most powerful ideological appeals are likely to be those which construct a sense of identity, however flawed, for the individual.

The Left has not confronted the increasing power of the mass media and popular culture within civil society. Too often, it has been content to mourn the changes and, thus, has simply abandoned the struggle. The pedagogy of popular culture is not a matter of uncovering or disturbing an interpretation of popular discourses, whether encoded or decoded. Popular culture operates at three levels of civil society: 1. It is intimately implicated in the production of common sense — the multilayered, fragmented collection of meanings, values, and ideas that we both inherit and construct and which largely define our taken-for-granted interpretations of the world. 2. It is arguably the most powerful determinant of our libidinal and affective lives, where desires and pleasures, joys and pains, emotions and moods are rapidly constructed and deconstructed, promised and withdrawn, celebrated and realized. 3. It is precisely where our identities and experiences are produced. Caught between the varieties of discourses we speak and the ultrarapid shifts of moods we inhabit, we are offered possibilities for experiencing the world and locating ourselves within it. Pedagogy rarely confronts totally hostile subjects, and it never has the luxury of dealing with people innocent of all articulations and positions. A radical pedagogy can only begin by locating itself on the complex, contradictory terrain within which those it wishes to speak with are already being articulated and actively struggling.

STRUGGLING WITH YOUTH

Although youth is not the only audience for a radical pedagogy, it is the most problematic in the 1980s. Dick Hebdige has argued that youth only becomes visible when it is a problem.[3] I would give the relation a different inflection: whenever youth becomes visible it is because it is positioned as the site of an already-constructed problem. For the Left, a significant problem is its apparent swing, if not to the political right, then to apolitical forms of selfishness, apathy, and complacency. This assumption defines the pedagogical struggle as a war of maneuvers in which we must do battle with the devil who has colonized the minds of youth. But how have we come to this conclusion: by reading the politics of different youth fractions from their tastes, their emotions, their moods, their "mattering maps." If some youths like Rambo, and Reagan, Madonna, and *Top Gun*, if they felt good when temporary military victories were won, if they want comfort and security for themselves, they have been duped into conservatism.

We need to weaken the confidence of such ascriptions, to destabilize the links that are already being forged between the practices, experiences, and cultural representations of contemporary youth. By absorbing youth's behavior into traditional political categories, we not only assent to the Right's articulations of youth's experiences, we reflect those interpretations back to them, and it becomes increasingly easy, if not reasonable, for youths to see themselves in such terms. The question then is whether there are alternative interpretations of the reality of different fractions of youth which would both make sense of their experiences and offer them viable responses. We need a better description of the gestures, practices, and statements (the "microhabits") of contemporary youths in their everyday lives, and of the ways these are connected to their political positions within the world.

In the effort to rattle the already taken-for-granted connections between their cultural and political practices, their lived experience and already-established political positions, we must not merely substitute a different set of assumed connections, which would similarly reduce the complexity and apparent otherness of this position into already-given phenomenological categories. Appeals to youths' own self-interpretations offer no solution, since the question is precisely the lack of fit between their experiences/behavior and the languages available for representing these to themselves and others. If we want to find the conditions which would enable youth to be articulated to more progressive political positions, we have to consider the specificity of youth's existence in contemporary society. There is, after all, no essence of youth, no essential experiences (e.g., of alienation) necessarily attached to the position. While certain meanings and practices seem to have a greater social and historical reach, they are always inflected differently within different contexts. Thus, a radical pedagogy cannot escape questioning how the position of youth is itself being constructed. Youth is a complex and contradictory formation within which a multiplicity of fragmented and mobile subject-positions are offered. It is not a matter of interpreting already-given experiences and identities but, rather, of rearticulating the structure of relations within which individuals experience and understand themselves as "youth." Only if we begin to understand the cultural and discursive struggles around the social construction of youth and the ways individuals are already implicated in them can we begin to engage their political positions. Only then can we operate on the contradictions within the formations of youth and between those formations and the other social positions individuals occupy.

In fact, it is precisely our inability to define "youth" that signals its status as an increasingly central site of ideological struggle. At the present moment, youth is a battlefield on which adolescents, baby-boomers, parents, and New Rightists are struggling to control its meanings and powers, to articulate and thereby to construct its experiences, identities, and, no doubt, its political positions. Rather than talking about youth, we need to acknowledge the complex, interactive, and often contradictory set of social formations within and around which the struggle is taking place. Its sociological and chronological parameters are difficult to define in advance; there is an increasingly tenuous relationship between age and youth in this culture (where youth has become something to be worked for). David Leavitt captures this ambiguous relation: "The goal seems to be to get to thirty as fast as possible, and stay there. Starting out, we are eager, above all else, to be finished."[4] Youth is a field of diverse and contradictory articulations between practices, experiences, identities, discourses, and social differences.

I propose to enter into this field — slowly — in order to open up the possibility for a radical pedagogy. First, rejecting the assumption that political beliefs can be directly read from cultural tastes, we must deconstruct the claim that the various forms of popular culture and behavior appropriated by various youth fractions clearly define a conservative ideology. This requires us to look at the historical specificity of the formation of youth in contemporary society, at the complex social and cultural apparatuses which articulate this historical context, and at the ways these construct the experiences of youth. I will offer a postmodernist reading of contemporary culture to prise open some of the contradictions of the context of youth's everyday lives (constructed from youth's practices, events, experiences, statements, tastes, and social relations) and to suggest an alternative construction of its cultural tastes. But rather than be reassured by the difference between postmodern nihilism and conservativism, I will offer a second (re)articulation of the particular power of this "nihilism" by identifying at least a part of its empowerment of youth. While the mass media and forms of popular culture play a crucial role in constructing youth's subjectivities, they are not the totality of youth's existence, nor do they exist in isolation. If youth lives in postmodernity, it also lives in many other places and contexts. And our efforts to locate the possibilities for more progressive articulations of youth must recognize the contradictions generated out of this real historical complexity.

LIFE IN THE POSTMODERN WARZONE

Postmodernist interpretations of contemporary culture read a wide range of texts, genres, and practices as a singular formation which directly responds to, if not reflects, the changing historical context of everyday life. We can locate the signs of this formation everywhere: on T-shirts, buttons, records, advertisements, movies, and television, but also in concrete choices, self-accounts, practices, relationships, and commitments. Whether in ironic forms like Madonna and Pee Wee Herman, or fragmented forms like Max Headroom, or neonostalgic forms like Batman and E.T., or the post-Holocaust visions of Mad Max, or cynical visions like *River's Edge* or in forms which celebrate commodification like "Miami Vice," every text is potentially a sign of postmodernity. Such signs are simultaneously ironic, cynical, celebratory, and horrified. The formation includes the pained humor of "life is hard and then you die" and "it's hopeless but not serious" and the humorous pain of Crockett telling Tubbs that they are better than the bad guys...better shots, that is. It includes the paradoxical technique of many contemporary ads, where the the future is depressingly like the worst of the present, and the present is nothing if not depressing. All of its statements exhibit an ironic, knowing distance, coupled with a sense of emotional urgency. The problem is to understand the historical conditions which have enabled and proliferated such statements, and to recognize what is unique in these statements.

Frequently, two apocalyptic transformations are identified after World War II. First, youth has had to confront the possibility of the end of the world, of no future. It has become a part of the taken-for-granted reality that it inhabits. What terrifies older generations defines the only reality of youth; what threatens to drive many crazy has become a strategy of sanity for others. This goes beyond the experience of being "damaged by the recent past and uncertain about the future."[5] History—both past and future—is neither rejected nor challenged; it is simply irrelevant, an unfortunate but inevitable entanglement with the cultural debris of others' lives. As a fictional Vietnam vet says, "You can't learn from the past. The main thing you learn from history is that you can't learn from history. That's what history is."[6] It is the irony of this that is troubling: the vet's claim is both paradoxical and so obviously right.

Second, the familiarization (partly through the familialization) of the mass media, especially television, has created a cultural logic of simulation.[7] It is not that reality has collapsed into its image (the vision of both situationism and deconstructionism), but that the two poles have imploded into each other. What television has destroyed is the very possibility of differences which make a difference and, hence, of any effect which depends upon an economy of difference. Meaning is impossible because all differences have become irrelevant. It is not merely that reality fails to give up its meaning to us, or even that it is meaningless, but that it has *any* meaning we give to it. The difference between reality and image has disappeared. It makes no difference which of the two is operating, each is equally effective. A recent Pepsi commercial offers a clear statement of this collapse. The commercial, for caffeine-free Pepsi, is premised upon the identification of the audience's life with the ad's representation of life in television land. While the commercial says, "Because your life is already stimulating enough," the life it represents is more accurately that of "Magnum P.I." (As Lou Reed sings, "Life is a gamble on videotape.") It is not a question of how the media represent reality (of whether they reflect or shape our interpretations, or of whether they fairly distribute information). The ability to distinguish reality and image has become increasingly difficult but decreasingly functional: think of the common experience of seeing a news report and vaguely remembering having seen it before as a television movie, only to see it again as a television movie and vaguely remember having seen it on the news. Which is the real, the original, event? At best, "You have to make allowances for the fact that everything we see tonight is real."[8] Reality is what works on television, what fits the models of media-tion which, consequently, no longer mediate. Ollie North is a hero because he looks and acts like a hero, despite people's rejection of his beliefs and actions. A spectator at FarmAid complained that it was a P.R. hype. A friend responded, "The whole world's a P.R. hype." The American dream was, first, transformed into suburbia as the media's image of the good life and, now, into a designer label — its own medium, something which is simultaneously available and unavailable to everyone. Television can make the event of television more important than the reality, such as Geraldo Rivera's recent specials; even more significantly, television can become more real. When "Cheers" is offered as a Boston sports bar during the world series, no one is fooled but no one seems to think the technique deceptive or strange.

Similarly, what once was thought of as an identity crisis has become an advertising slogan: "Is there a real me or am I just what you see?" Leavitt defends contemporary youth because "at least we don't pretend we're not wearing costumes. . . . At least [we're] not faking it." What they are not faking is, of course, the fact that they are faking. It is inauthenticity as an authentic stance, as another pose. The only voice allowed is ironic, distant, and indifferent: it doesn't matter what you are but what you are not. Leavitt continues, "If we are without passion or affect, it is because we have decided that passion and affect are simply not worth the trouble. If we stand crouched in the shadows of a history in which we refuse to take part, it is because that's exactly where we've chosen to stand." After all, "characterlessness takes work. It is defiance and defense all at once."[9] Radicalism has become the basis of stardom, and history has become a best-selling game.

Living in this historical condition does not render one passive; it does not deny the need for action or the possibility of commitment, albeit always an individualized, local one (and it does, ironically, stand back from the very idea of commitment). In this postmodern condition, one is neither terrified into, nor of, acting. "Seek small passions. Big ones are too risky."[10] "This is a generation that inherited the cry, 'I can't get no satisfaction.' And they live its contradictions, grabbing at satisfactions while rejecting the possibility itself. It's a punk method, nihilism constructed punishingly with the tools of consumer passion."[11] For example, people have often pointed to the devastating impact of the divorce rate on the experience of contemporary youth. But they fail to distinguish two contexts within which this is experienced: one in which it is nostalgically constructed as a crisis of faith and the other in which it is taken for granted. While the former produces a "magazine of adult dating" called *Futile* (with a touch of both irony and pathos, although it could be appropriated into the second position by simply erasing the pathos of expectations), the latter produces characters like Chloe in *The Big Chill*, who characterizes her relationship with a residual countercultural suicide victim as "wonderful. I had no expectations and he had too many." Such statements are pervasive: in the cult film, *Liquid Sky*, one song defiantly asserts: "Me and my rhythm box. We're both high. Know why? It's preprogrammed, so what. Who of your friends are not?"

Youth's actions often seem to signal a return to more stable, traditional values and practices (e.g., the increasing rates of marriage and childbirth and the common, self-consciously naive, demand for heroes). In fact, it prefers the more traditional forms of behavior where, like retro and new wave fashions, the rules, the stakes, and their artificiality are all the more evident. These images are more ambiguous and less constraining precisely because they are so obviously unreal. Reality is, as one friend put it, "the ultimate constraint on your lifestyle." Youths get married because "they see how their parents followed every desire and got totally disrupted and how the nihilism of 1979 caused nothing but O.D.'s and cancer."[12] They get married against the background of the assumption of divorce as a normal if not likely outcome. They maintain their own individual ability to escape the norm, but they are confident that others will not escape it and, if pressed, are likely to admit the precariousness of their own confidence.

Youth's strategy is defined by ambivalence and irreverence. "Ambivalence toward life is [its] only myth, [its] only dream, the only context in which [it] can find comfort."[13] One always hedges one's bets, holds back a little. Such an attitude produces love songs with titles like "Don't stand so close" and "Dancing with myself" and heroic movies with theme songs that claim "we don't need another hero." It's all right to invest yourself in something as long as you realize that there is nothing really to invest. You play the game for whatever the stakes, without taking either the game or the stakes too seriously (although seriousness is a perfectly acceptable game to play as well). A transfigured notion of your own subjectivity makes originality and authenticity into another act, but no worse for it (e.g., "Putting on the Hits" in which people lip-synch hit records; the first major "new romantic" hit in America was the Human League's "Love Action": "I believe in the truth though I lie a lot. No matter what you put me through, I'll still believe in love"). There is no ultimate investment in them; they do not invest "themselves" in them. "Transcendence may sound silly, but I'm ready to try something new."[14] Transcendence as a new game? Everything can be taken seriously and, simultaneously, made into a joke.

It is here that we can locate youth's oft-noted dedication to fun and pleasure, however temporary and artificial the pleasure may be. In fact, the pleasures of the temporary and the artificial have ironically displaced the reality of pleasure itself. After all, pleasure is a risky business, and the demand for it is ultimately as unreasonable as any other. "To be modern is to be hard-edged, coolly aggressive; to celebrate the synthetic and the artificial; to reject softness and easy intimacy and fuzzy-headed visions of what life has to offer; to feel the pull of polarization in every fiber....Modern youth is showing American how to tighten its sphincter—and like it."[15] Consider these "postmodern" political strategies: "Never deny yourself a pleasure in the name of a cause, an ideology, an abstraction." "Pace yourself wisely, avoid burnout syndrome." "Save breath; don't argue with persons who consider the MacNeil-Lehrer Hour must viewing [i.e., anyone who takes information and politics too seriously]." "Put your best face forward and plot your revenge."[16]

It is a philosophy of life which says, "Don't sweat the small stuff" and "It's all small stuff." It works in a world in which the smallest stuff makes you sweat (e.g., driving to work, eating Girl Scout Cookies, even, growing up), but it works, not by simply escaping from the real but by recognizing that, in reality, it makes no difference. Consider Bill Murray's classic speech in *Meatballs*, when he psychs up the members of his team by acknowledging that all of their efforts, even their possible victory, won't get them what they really want: "It just doesn't matter." The surfaces of life become the site at which reality is collected and pleasures are produced. Reality becomes nothing but a collection of quotations from our collective historical debris, a mobile game of Trivia. The narrative is less important than the images. In "Miami Vice," for example, the cops put on a fashion show (not only of clothes and urban spaces, but also of their own "cool attitudes") to a Top-40 soundtrack. They spend their lives not so much patrolling Miami as cruising it, only to rediscover the narrative as an afterthought in the last few minutes. Narrative closure becomes a convenience of the medium more than a demand of our lives. The programs seem to ignore the spectator as subject, much like dreams.

This construction of the postmodern context enables us to deconstruct the conservative interpretation of the political practices of various youth formations. I will consider two of the more obvious signs of youth's "conservativism": support of Reagan and political apathy. What is often ignored is that many of those who like, and even support, Reagan readily admit that they disagree with many, if not most, of his policies and programs. What then are they supporting? Many who voted for Reagan did not vote for a set of meanings or values that they subscribe to; they voted for the one who acted like a president. They voted, paradoxically, for the more real of the candidates, the less boring, the one entirely defined as a media object, who could negotiate that identity successfully—a real measure of success. Reagan's image as hero and defender of American virtues is entirely played out within the media's terms almost as a caricature of itself. Reagan hides nothing below the surface, as the recent coverage of his health problems demonstrated. Similarly, Mondale's greatest moment of success came when he, too, entered into the media's spaces, appropriating the advertising slogan, "Where's the beef?" Those who are horrified at this reduction of political choices to media images assume that their own choices are more stably grounded, but they, too, are caught in the circuits of our collective media images of history.

Reagan reiterated, within the media's cliches, the experience of being abandoned by reality, the vision that the political values of America have no more reality than media images. We cannot assume that these youths are being misled or manipulated. They often have quite sophisticated understandings of what Reagan is about. As one of my pro-Reagan students said, "Ronald Reagan's America is always moving but never going anywhere." After all, if progress is an illusion, "stagnant progress" is as real as any other. Postmodernism cautions us not to take the vote for Reagan too seriously, as evidence of a conservative political turn, for it is, in some ways, no different from any choice between cultural discourses.

Even so, it would be a mistake to dismiss such choices as matters of personal taste or cultural enjoyment. They are, in fact, the very site at which youth attempts to produce its identity and reality. The choice of Reagan affirms, not a particular set of truths or values, but the necessity—however temporary—of choice, meaning, and value. Need such a choice be seen as selfish or conservative? It certainly cannot be framed by any appeal to an abstract collectivity. Myths of the people as the locus of power appear as little more than another media image (if not a hype); they make no difference in the practices of those who constantly appeal to them. But this does not deny the sense of a generational collectivity defined by its common situation—trapped on the Titanic! The resonance of this image is crucial; there are no identifiable enemies and no grounds for confidence in the possibility of change. Yet one feels threatened, under constant attack, simultaneously antagonistic and powerless. As David Bowie sings, "It's the terror of knowing what this world is about/ Watching some good friends scream, let me out." ("Pressure.")

Consider the very obvious signs of contemporary youth's apathy; what we fail to see is how agressive it is, how actively youth refuses the politicization of reality. After all, what reality can politics have if reality itself has no power? What do such attitudes and actions mean in the context of postmodernity: not that youths do not feel alienated but that they do not make sense of their alienation in ideological terms; not that traditional moral and political categories are wrong but that they are simply inapplicable. Youth's power lies in its ability to appropriate any text, to undermine the distinction between production and consumption and, in this way, to deny the power of ideology and of the commodity. Hardcore musician Binky describes this new form of resistance: "The nature of your oppression is the esthetic of our anger."[17] It affirms one's difference by reaffirming that everything is the same, by becoming even more the same, leaving the present behind by entering into it more fully. There is a kind of postmodern irony, a cynicism, operating within our relations to the dominant ideology: we know what we are doing as we are acceding to it.[18] Becoming an object is a way of resisting the constant demand to reaffirm one's subjectivity (e.g., recent slogans like "Born to Buy" and "When the going gets tough, the tough take a vacation"). Consider again the Titanic: "If you're sailing on the Titanic, go first class." This ambiguous slogan advocates a temporary celebration of comfort, not because it is intrinsically and transcendentally valuable, but because the end is inevitable. It advocates an individual search for victory, but leaves open the possibilities of other victories, and even of one's relations to them. It is the simulacrum of a politics in the image of a struggle, within everyday life, for both survival and victory.

YOUTH AND POPULAR CULTURE

This postmodernist description is, in the end, as inadequate and incomplete as the conservative reading. It renders questions of real global threats and power relations irrelevant. Because it assumes a radical rupture in history, it ignores the distinctions between conservative and progressive political positions. It establishes a space within which politics no longer exists except as "a luxury of the underprivileged."[19] In the end, postmodern nihilism is not simply conservative, it is as pessimistic and elitist as the conservative reading. Moreover, it sees this dissociation of the present from the past/future reflected in every event. It finds postmodernity in cultural texts and projects it onto the experience of the audience, as if the critic had some privileged and innocent access to the truth of history. Paradoxically, its claim of historical specificity ignores all other determinations; its descriptions remain oddly unencumbered by the concrete realities and relations, ambiguities and contradictions, practices and contexts, of youth's everyday life. It totalizes its own descriptions, sliding from a description of a determining structure to the identification of that level with the multiplicity of determining contexts that articulate the historical totality of youth's lived realities. It fails to locate the postmodern cultural formation within broader social and cultural fields of everyday life and the struggles—organized by relations of domination, subordination, and resistance—to articulate the very identities and experiences of youth. Consequently, it is unable to locate the specific way in which this formation operates to position and empower youth. We need to rearticulate the postmodernist interpretation into the broader contexts within which youth and popularity are mutually constitutive, in order to limit the claim of postmodern nihilism and to identify its particular mode of communication.

Consider one of the more controversial events in recent popular culture: the enormous popularity of Bruce Springsteen. His success cannot be explained by pointing to an unequivocally shared meaning nor by appealing to a particular sociologically defined audience-fraction. He clearly appeals to a new heterogeneous alliance, the site of a struggle to construct a broad social formation of youth. Springsteen's success embodies many of our questions about the politics and experiences of youth; the contradictions circulating around him are so stark and his success so striking, neither simply instantaneous nor a constant, incremental accumulation. Springsteen: rebel turned patriot? lyricist turned rocker or, even worse, pop star? a performer who cherished the sense of intimacy with his audience playing to audiences of one hundred thousand? The explanations of the success of the song "Born in the U.S.A." range from those who think it is a patriot's anthem (the *Chicago Tribune* labeled him "the Rambo of Rock"[20]), to those who think that his popularity is the result of a mishearing of Springsteen as a patriot, to those who seem to assume that all of his fans understand and care about his lyrics and his message, to more cynical views of the American myth of authenticity. These interpretations fail to recognize that different audiences may simply interpret his message differently and that his audience has expanded at every age, and across sociological and gender (although not racial) boundaries.

Springsteen is, quintessentially, an American rock-and-roll star. While rock in England has largely depended upon the working-class appropriation of middle-class signs such as fashion, in America the middle-class audience has dominated by appropriating images of working-class styles and aspirations, inflected into scenes of personal mobility and fun. This is not to deny that Springsteen sings of and to working-class experiences, yet his images of unemployment speak to middle-class adolescents; his male expressions of loneliness and sexual desire speak to women across a wide spectrum of ages and classes; and his American imagery strikes a responsive chord across national boundaries. How is one to make sense of the strength and range of these identifications, and of the passion of his fans?

The explanation for Springsteen's popularity cannot be read off of his lyrics, anymore than one can read his politics off of the iconography of the flag that appears on the cover of "Born in the USA": patriotic celebration? rebellious desecration? or is he "studying it, trying to figure out its meaning. It is such a big flag the stars don't even show in the picture."[21] After all, nationalism (and its symbols) is an important part of popular consciousness, and not necessarily conservative: it is, like youth itself, the site of a struggle to articulate popular consciousness to particular political effects. The problem is that critics have attempted to understand fans' relationship to music by looking at the texts, rather than by looking at the contexts within which those relations are enacted and displayed. If we are to begin to understand the complex relations organized around Springsteen's popularity, and the sites where political possibilities are opened, we have to locate Springsteen in the broader contexts within which his music is articulated and his popularity constructed.

First, we need to place Springsteen into the broader context of rock and roll. We need to ask what specific audiences do with it, what it does for them, how they listen to it, how it is articulated to their experiences and practices, how it empowers and disempowers them. But we cannot talk about rock and roll in the singular; we must assume neither its unity nor that of its audiences. Still, it is not a set of isolated genres, each with its own isolated audiences defining particular contents, uses, and gratifications. Rock and roll is comprehensible only in its relations and developments, in the differences between various genres and subcultures, between the mainstreams and the margins, between the commercial and the avant-garde, between the mass-distributed and the independents. And yet, these relations, constitutive of the history of rock and roll, are becoming harder to maintain in the present context.[22]

Second, we have to locate Springsteen in the wider context of popular cultural texts: not only rock and roll, but also film, television, comics, and more. There are few Springsteen fans who are not also fans of other cultural texts, and even fewer who are not constantly exposed to an enormous range: from Bill Cosby to "Moonlighting," from *Rambo* to *Repo Man*, from *Mad Max* to *Blue Velvet*, from James Bond to Buckaroo Banzai. The politics of any of these texts is uncertain; most are suspicious of government and corporations and committed to some idea of individuality, but their specific articulations remain open.

Third, we need to locate Springsteen in the context of the construction of the experiences of being young as an explicit site of struggle which has become increasingly visible since the end of the second world war. There are signs of this not only in the behavior of youth itself—such as the increasing suicide and addiction rates—but also in the changing institutionalized relations between the adult population and youth, in the contradictions between the return of a discourse of innocence and protectionism, the proliferation of practices attempting to both accelerate and control the socialization process, and the gradual erosion if not deconstruction of social apparatuses designed to protect and assist youth.

These struggles around "youth" are being enacted as well on our media screens, in a broad range of contemporary cultural texts that are clearly punctuated by images and relations of youth. We can see these struggles in the different and, in some cases, new ways in which youths—their experiences, practices, and discourses and the relations among these—are represented: youth as embodying all of the (negative) characteristics of adulthood, as in the currently popular horror/slasher movies, as well as in certain recent TV series; youth as radically different from adults, "alien, inherently Other"[23]; youth as the repository of adult fantasies of innocence, as in Spielberg's films, and of irresponsibility (*Animal House, Porky's*); youth as the salvation of the world (*The Last Starfighter, Back to the Future*); youth as the site of victory (*Top Gun*); youth as the last champion of justice (*The Legend of Billie Jean*). This diversity signals, at the very least, the contradictions in our feelings about youth. While youth has become increasingly dominant as both topic and audience for cinema, television seems unable to deal with the problematic relation between youth as part of a peer culture (in school and on the streets) and as part of a domestic culture (in the home).

This veritable explosion of discourses is all the more startling given the failure of such movies, and their stars, in the seventies (*The Wanderers, Over the Edge*). The ease with which the current generation of young movie stars (the "Brat Pack") moves between playing high school students measuring the reality of their lives against the momentary possibility of an almost enforced openness (*The Breakfast Club*) and postcollege yuppies confronting a terrifyingly unromanticized reality (*St. Elmo's Fire*) marks their youthfulness by the undecideability of their ages and class loyalties. These new icons are, in fact, surprising diverse — from nerds to tough guys — and even more surprisingly, articulate. Whatever happened to the inarticulate image of James Dean? Never has youth talked so much, nor had so much expertise and knowledge. The fragmented audience for such movies, as well as their hyper-stereotypical forms, suggests that traditional explanations of the identification between spectators and characters cannot totally explain their popularity. Moreover, the different sources of production of media texts, the different audience fractions of the youth market, and the wide range of generic diversity suggest that we cannot take for granted the relations between the lived reality of youths, their social identities, and particular cultural representations.

This leaves us with a dilemma. If the diversity of audiences, determinations, and interpretations makes a sociology of culture impossible, how do we understand the significance of these cultural texts and practices and their relation to the social body of youth? It cannot be merely a matter of identifying the contexts into which these texts are inserted. The contexts are, themselves, neither passive nor passively given. The texts actively participate in the construction of multiple temporary "apparatuses" which are always more than discursive. These apparatuses cannot be equated with, or read off of, the distribution of exposure or of conscious taste; they are, however, closely related to the distribution of taste. But taste is never phenomenologically available; it is always a dispositional structure. Moreover, the notion of apparatuses denies any *a priori* distinction between the center or mainstream and the margins (in which, somehow, the marginal is always politically and aesthetically better) and the correlative assumption of a necessary correspondence of exposure, taste, and effectivity. The mainstream is not the site of hegemonic identity and homogeneity but of the proliferation of difference. It is a floating configuration of marginality, a social pastiche of codes and icons, an unpredicatable but overdetermined economy of vectors along which audiences and practices are articulated and move, temporarily, closer together and farther apart. There is no stable center here, only different distances and densities.

Apparatuses are maps of the distribution of influence or effects, of the various ways in which texts, practices, relations, and subjectivities are constructed together within temporary, multidimensional networks. The problem of pedagogy is never merely that of allowing students to speak but, rather, of locating their speech—in whatever form—and the structures of their experiences and responses, within the larger historical apparatuses that articulate their identities and effects.

Springsteen's dispersed popularity suggests that he is positioned within an increasingly central, albeit mobile, apparatus. Although it is full of tensions and contradictions, and hence quite fragile, it is also quite strong because it is constantly rearticulated before it collapses under the pressures of those contradictions. Moreover, it is both reinforced and contradicted by other cultural formations and social tendencies. If we are to understand the politics of his popularity, we have to identify the force and focus of the particular statements (in both the Foucauldian and everyday use of "statement") he makes. We have to construct the contours and vectors of the apparatus (or the various overlapping apparatuses) within which both his popularity and his fans' identity are constructed. Different statements will have a variety of effects and will open up different political possibilities, depending upon how the apparatus is constructed and which articulations are foregrounded. In what follows, I shall be concerned with only one vector, one statement, within this apparatus: a statement articulated by the intersection of youth, postmodernity, and popular culture. There are, no doubt, other important articulations that would have to be worked out before a full reading of Springsteen's position could be offered. But the intersection of these three determinants provides an important insight into the possibilities, not only of Springsteen, but also of a great deal of contemporary popular culture.

YOUTH, POPULAR CULTURE, AND POSTMODERNITY

Let me begin by summarizing the reading I will offer: 1. The construction of popularity depends in part upon *affective* relations and modes of communication. 2. The visibly powerful articulation of postmodernity and popular culture locates the "crisis" of everyday life in the relations of affect, ideology, and libido. 3. The insertion of this emergent crisis into the practices of the mass media constructs a communicative logic of "authentic inauthenticity." 4. Looking at the transmedia and intertextual relations within which Springsteen is located, we can identify at least one statement enabled by this logic: "sentimental inauthenticity." 5. Emphasizing Springsteen's articulation of this statement as rock and roll, his popularity appears to be the result of the construction of an "affective alliance" within which the audience is positioned as youth and empowered through the construction of a specific identity: the "mundane exotic"; postmodern nihilism is articulated into a social form of empowerment. In elaborating these claims, I do not mean to suggest any essential priority or order to the various articulations. I am, rather, attempting to add determinations (which can never be as easily separated as my presentation might suggest), moving toward an understanding of the concrete statements offered in popular culture and of the possibilities of their articulation into relations of domination and subordination.[24]

I take it for granted that: 1. Practices can have a variety of effects. 2. Everyday life and social relations are determined, not only by the organization of economic, political, and ideological fields but also of libidinal and affective fields. 3. There are no necessary relations between effects and fields—ideological practices can have economic effects, and economic practices can have libidinal effects. Thus, discourse, while it may normally function ideologically through the production of signifying effects, may also have affective or libidinal effects; moreover, in some instances, the production of such effects may not be mediated by the primary production of meanings. The specificity of *popular* discourses depends upon the powerful affective relations which they establish with their audiences. Struggles over the construction of the popular are, in fact, less economic and ideological than affective. They are fought on the terrain of moods, emotions, passions, and energy. Affect describes the "coloration" of everyday life, the particular "timbre" with which we find ourselves already inserted into the world. Admittedly, the notion of affective communication seems odd; it is not only contentless but contagious. It does not follow a linear vector; it has neither a source nor a goal. It operates without being spoken, outside of the normal disciplines of control.

The intimate connection between postmodernity and popular culture operates not only in terms of the role of the media in constructing postmodernity, but also in terms of the ultrarapid speed with which postmodern statements have become central, if not dominant, in many contemporary formations of popular culture. We can locate one of the most visible appearances of the so-called crisis of postmodernity in a new articulation of affective relations. For those generations that have grown up after the war (as a result of a number of specific conditions, events, and contradictions), the relationship between affect and ideology (and later, between affect and libido) has become increasingly problematic. There has been a growing distance, even a rupture, between these various aspects of everyday life (and their expression in our experiences), between the available meanings and values which socially organise our existence, and the possibilities for investing in or caring about them which are enabled by our moods and emotions. It has become increasingly difficult, if not impossible, in other words, to make sense of our affective experiences and to put any faith in our ideological constructions, even though they still operate as common sense. We do not trust our common sense even as we are compelled to live it. It is a crisis in our ability to locate any meaning as a possible and appropriate source for an empassioned commitment. It is a crisis, not of faith, but of the relationship between faith and common sense. It is not that nothing matters but that it doesn't matter what matters. It is as if one has to live two lives, one defined by the meanings and values available to us to make sense of our lives, and the other defined by the affective sense that life can no longer be made sense of. This new status given to the affective as the unrepresentable defines the postmodern rupture. It is not that youths do not live the ideological values of their parents; rather they find it impossible to represent their mood, their own affective relationship to the world, in those terms and increasingly, to invest themselves seriously in such values. Postmodernity demands that one live schizophrenically, trying on the one hand to live the inherited meanings and, on the other hand, recognizing that such meanings cannot enable them to respond to their affective situation. Their "mattering maps"[25] no longer correspond to the available maps of meanings. Meaning and affect—historically so closely intertwined—have broken apart, each going off in its own direction. Each takes on its own autonomy, even as sanity demands that they be reintegrated. Of course, the gap is never complete and stable; it is always mobile and temporary. As it has extended into and disrupted relations between afffect and libido, we have become increasingly suspicious of any object of desire as well, and even of desire itself.

To illustrate: In a recent "Bloom County" cartoon, Binkley is confronted with the worst of all possible nightmares: the future is made present. His future self shows him the dismal state of what is to come and the pitiful means by which Binkley will attempt to hide it from himself. But Binkley does not ask if this future is inevitable or if it can be changed. He knows that he is condemned. How can he place any faith in that future, or in the meanings and values by which he might attempt to deny the horrifying and depressing future realities? How can he wake up the next morning? That is the question to which I will return: How can Binkley's fate empower its audiences.

Springsteen's fans offer widely divergent interpretations of his songs (indeed, the majority are simply uninterested in the question of their meaning) depending on their different relations to the narratives he constructs. Yet the similarities of their responses suggest that they identify with the narratives on at least one common level. Even though they have not lived the experience, they have shared the particular affective or emotional structure that saturates his entire performance. Putting it simply, they have felt the same way. Since *The River*, Springsteen has been explicitly singing *about* what I have described as the postmodern condition: the contradiction between dreams and reality.[26] Springsteen articulates the sense of being trapped by broken promises, trapped inside his own dreams and someone else's reality, into populist imagery and mainstream marketing ("Is a dream a lie if it don't come true, or is it something worse?"). Recognizing the need to find meaning, and the impossibility of the task, Springsteen often ends up celebrating the very prisons that such appeals prepare for us ("Glory Days," "Growing Up"). If rock and roll has always "wanted it all now," Springsteen can't stop reminding us that there is a price to pay and the price may be higher than we ever imagined.

However, this says little about the specific way in which Springsteen's discourses accomplish this affective work. His success depends in large part on images. Not only do his songs evoke powerful images of emotions, embodied in desperate situations and confrontations, but, even more importantly, he has constructed an image of authenticity for himself. While critics and fans often contrast this with the possibility of co-optation, that difference has been largely eroded or at least rendered suspect by the increasing commodification and politicization of style. In fact, it may always have been less a difference between musics or musicians than a marker of fans' tastes. In Springsteen's case, authenticity itself has become a powerful style; the question of authenticity, while of immediate relevance to any fan, is always displaced. They know his act is rehearsed and repeated, that his authenticity is constructed, although the authentic is not supposed to be. In fact, they want to see his gestures repeated. Springsteen constructs "immediacy" from the "iconography of the screen";[27] he celebrates an artifical authenticity.

This strategy or communicative logic is a particular form of irony — "authentic inauthenticity" — articulated within the postmodern formation. It is not the same as inauthentic authenticity, nor is it simply a matter of nihilism. The postmodern condition signals a shift in the complex economy of everyday life; it points to significant changes in what one might call "the anchoring effects" through which different planes are related to one another. Authentic inauthenticity is one form of the media logic of indifference or simulation which entails an overindulgence of fragmentation and pastiche. Ignoring its concrete determinations, this logic specifies that all images, all realities are equal — equally serious, equally deserving and undeserving of being taken seriously. The familiar becomes stranger than the exotic, and the exotic become tediously familiar. The lines between the comic and the terrifying, the mundane and the fantastic, the boring and the exciting, the natural and the artifical, the ordinary and the extraordinary, disappear. Or more accurately, the production of the line is understood, ironically, as a necessary but ungrounded activity. If everything is equal, then all differences are equally powerless or powerful, take your pick. Difference is not only impossible, it is *apparently* irrelevant. Recall Marlon Brando's classic response to the question, "What are you rebelling against?" "What have you got?" What was, in the fifties, a powerfully charged statement of alienation becomes, in the logic of authentic inauthenticity, an ironic embracing of the totalization of alienation within everyday life.

But this logic never appears outside of its articulation into specific forms of statements. We have still to identify the concrete form of Springsteen's popularity. Locating Springsteen within larger cultural maps of popularity, we can connect his discourse to a powerful emergent structure of "sentimentality" as the overindulgence of the affective. It is the evocation of emotion for its own sake (*Love Story*, *Brian's Song*); such statements renounce their claim to represent reality, and even their meaningfulness is only relevant insofar as it produces a powerful emotional response. Its value is no longer that of imagining the real — whether as fantasy or utopia; it does not provide rules for learning because the question of the credibility of its images is irrelevant. Narratives go nowhere or, at least, where they go is less important than that one suffers and rejoices along the way. The causes of these emotions are also irrelevant. Narratives do not present situations with which we identify, despite the fact that its situations are personalized and that its characters are often presented as if they were just like us. Thus, for example, there is a significant difference between "Father Knows Best" and "The Bill Cosby Show" because we know that our spouses and children will not be that wonderful!

Such sentimental statements become merely the occasion for a constant movement between affective and emotional highs and lows. They need not be located in the possibilities of our own lives or even in the believability of someone else's. Sentimentality celebrates the liberation of affect from any significant anchoring in reality or intelligibility. While we may not be sure if TV is crazier than reality, it is unquestionably more intense and apparently more desirable because of that intensity. It is the site of emotions more real because they are more extreme, more excessive; the fact that the excess is constructed on the unbelievability and even the unintelligibility of the message seems to make it all the more powerful. Sentimentality defines a discursive realm within which we get to live out affective relations which exceed our lives and always will; it not only places affect above meaning, but places intensity — the quality and quantity of affect — above specificity, as if it were necessary to feel something more intensely than is available to us. There is a *democracy* of affect which can only be traversed by an ever-spiralling search for an excessive affect necessarily divorced from the contingencies of everyday life.

But we can specify the form of Springsteen's particular statement even further. At the intersection of sentimentality and authentic inauthenticity, a number of different articulations are possible (the current popularity of soap operas among youth suggests a different statement). One such inflection — "sentimental inauthenticity" — is predicated on the uncertain intrinsic validity of any specific affective investment. While it is necessary to feel something — anything — in excess, it is irrelevant what one feels because no feeling matters in itself. One does not, and cannot, trust the content of any feeling, emotion, or investment. Even the most temporary and ironic one cannot mark any difference. But despite its apparent negation of the possibility of identities and totalities, everyday life requires structures and identities that order, at various levels, the world and our places within it. Differences can never be entirely erased. Sentimental inauthenticity celebrates the magical possibility of making a difference against impossible odds. What enables that possibility is not any specific affective investment but rather the intensity of the investment itself. Such a strategy requires the ordinariness of the subject: the hero's only difference is that something (usually a fairly common activity) matters so much that he or she is reidentified with and empowered by it, regardless of what is. This is a strategy which constructs images of victory, but the site and stake of the battle, or even whether one recognizes the moral rectitude of the subject, is irrelevant. The subject is just like us except for caring so much about something that it is beyond the sense of our own realities. Ordinary skills, when articulated into such intense passions, become magical victories. An image of heroism is constructed on the basis of a belief or commitment so powerful that one becomes more than human, or at least more than what we can expect of our lives.

Bruce Springsteen is arguably the best embodiment of this discursive strategy. His stories and images constantly remind us that he is just like us, quite ordinary. But he cares more about rock-and-roll and his fans than any other performer. He can renounce all of the activities normally associated with rock-and-roll culture, in order to make even better rock and roll. He is willing to pay any price (not, as it turns out, a very discomforting price) in order to win "it," although the terms of the victory are never clear. Springsteen's response to the depressing terror of the postmodern condition is his own image and commitment. Perhaps with an unavoidable, but self-conscious, touch of romanticism, his audience responds to the fact that he has not broken his promise, though it is a small one in the context of global struggles: "So many videos were full of disasters, with everything flying apart, shifting, in the blink of an eye. The random images on the screen were swirling, beyond anyone's control; everything was falling...but Bruce was still dancing in all that darkness, and the heart of rock-and-roll was still beating."[28] Springsteen's performance becomes an image of surviving this shared affective condition: "This is what I do. I work on staying together, one day at a time. There's no room for anything else. It takes all my energy."[29] Not simply equating survival and politics nor acquiescing to despair, he evokes this affective structure and invokes images of empowerment from within it.

This sentimental inauthenticity (which is obviously not inauthentic sentimentality) is further inflected by Springsteen's obvious position within the broad terrain of rock-and-roll culture. This final articulation accounts for the powerful relationship which he establishes with his audiences and for the particular ways in which they are empowered by that relationship. For, unlike other instances of sentimental inauthenticity (*Rambo*, *Top Gun*), Springsteen does not become the focus of a fantastic difference, nor is he the explicit source of social fantasies. His excess is not in something which differentiates him from his audience

(Tom Cruise's good looks, or Rambo's physique) but, in the very relation which he establishes with his fans. The celebration of ordinariness is empowering when it is articulated into the elitism of rock and roll. That elitism is the result of the ongoing struggle to define rock and roll, constantly to inscribe boundaries circumscribing the limits of appropriate musics and responses. Such boundaries, for particular alliances of fans, define what can function as rock and roll. This encapsulation of the music, however uncertain and temporary, offers fans who are articulated within its boundaries a privileged access to specific affective experiences and differences.

This is the site of Springsteen's popularity: to celebrate one's ordinariness and to assert one's fantastic (and even fantasmatic) difference simultaneously—the ordinary becomes extraordinary. Springsteen's performance celebrates the fans' identity within the mainstream. It gives them an identity in their very lack of difference or in the artificiality of a constructed difference—in their common affective lives. Springsteen makes this more real than their social differences and experiences: the articulation of difference into an identity constructed as the mundane exotic. The inflection of sentimental inauthenticity into a rock-and-roll apparatus makes nihilism empowering by offering it as the site of an "affective alliance" within which youth is positioned and constructed. This alliance does not depend on an explicit social identity or ideological subject-position, but on enabling a sense of difference which is effective despite the recognition that difference no longer matters. The particular form of its statement of in-difference articulates new possibilities for surviving and winning (to paraphrase Rambo) in a postmodern world.

A PEDAGOGY FOR THE CONTEMPORARY CONJUNCTURE

A radical pedagogy for the 1990s needs to seek out new voices and vocabularies, new linkages and new projects: "We know that our dreams are not going to come true. Are never going to come true. We have learned that our dreams are important not because they come true, but because they take you places you would never have otherwise gone, and teach you what you never knew was there to learn."[30] It needs to find new ways of describing and understanding the obsession with images, the sense that there are no criteria by which we can judge, or even predict the future. And it needs to develop new moral and political articulations which do not simply deny, condemn, or celebrate real historical and cultural changes. The Left needs to tell a better story, one which is more in touch with the concrete realities of youth's historical realities, one which offers new possibilities for youth to take up viable political positions in the modern world. Springsteen offers a paradoxical site— that of youth itself—from which to live out an impossible relation to the future, from which to respond to their condition of being "doomed to speak about life in structures contrary to...experience."[31]

We need to acknowledge the contradiction inscribed into our own political and cultural practices. It is a contradiction commonly spoken but rarely thematized: liberals find themselves enjoying films that they abhor ideologically (*Rambo* and *ET*) or secretly enjoying Reagan's new optimism: "Reagan...manages to make you feel good about your country, and about the times in which you are living. All those corny feelings that hid inside of you for so long are waved right out in public by Reagan for everyone to see—and even while you're listing all the reasons that you shouldn't fall for it, you're glad that you're falling. If you're a sucker for the act, that's okay."[32] The New Right affectively recharges political cliches which have lost their power, and, in the process, struggles to articulate them into larger ideological structures. It operates within the postmodern condition and logic, reduces complex questions of politics, values, and meanings to individualized images of morality, self-sacrifice, victory, and community. The reality of America is displaced into its media images (thus, youth can adopt it as another surface identity). The New Right reestablishes a necessary sense of difference by using the affective differences generated upon the surface of the media. And by reconnecting these affective differences to the ideological labels which have, until recently, proven so ineffective, it has managed to create a constituency based on affect rather than ideology. The danger is that, if left unchallenged, the two could easily become rearticulated into a new (albeit simulated) historical conjuncture. This possibility, already visible on the horizon, may account for the new political and affective alliances which are being forged. Therefore, we cannot leave the task of articulating youth's political interests and commitments to the mercy of the conservatives and of the commercial languages of the media.

We must intervene as both critics and educators. But first we must allow ourselves to be educated by those we are attempting to understand, by the cultural forms they enjoy, and by the practices they engage with. We must learn how to listen to them if we expect them to listen to us. But the real task is to enter into the ongoing struggle to articulate new historical possibilities, new "imagined futures."[33] We have to recognize contemporary popular culture, not as the representation of conservatism nor as the site of nihilism, but as the contradictory production of forms of empowerment in the face of the reality, and even the rationality, of nihilism. Postmodern statements are not empowering because they are nihilistic nor merely in spite of it; they are both nihilistic and empowering. The task facing us is to identify the strategic sites of empowerment made available in the forms of contemporary culture. If the Left fails to recognize the reality of such empowerment, then it will never comprehend the contemporary political crisis: it is not one of beliefs but of the energy with which to act. Too often, the Left seeks to define new goals, values, and moralities for others. It must seek instead to enter into the ongoing social struggle of the popular and everyday life, a struggle which already involves our students, if not the teachers. The Left must become part of the masses again!

NOTES

1. This chapter draws and expands upon two previous articles: "Rockin' with Reagan, or the Mainstreaming of Postmodernity," *Cultural Critique* (1988); and "Teaching the Popular," in Cary Nelson, ed., *Theory in the Classroom* (Urbana: University of Illinois Press, 1986), pp. 177–200. For an elaboration of the theoretical perspective of cultural studies used here, see my "Critical Theory and the Politics of Empirical Research" in *Mass Communication Review Yearbook*, vol. 6 (1987), Michael Gurevitch and Mark Levy, eds., and "History, Politics and Postmodernism: Stuart Hall and Cultural Studies," *Journal of Communication Inquiry* 10 (Summer 1986): 61–77.

2. Antonio Gramsci, *Selections from the Prison Notebooks*, Q. Hoare and G. Nowell-Smith, eds. (New York: International Publishers, 1971), p. 331.

3. Dick Hebdige, "Posing...Threats, Striking...Poses: Youth, Surveillance and Display," *SubStance*, No. 37/38 (1983): 68–88. The use of the singular "youth" throughout this chapter refers not to a homogeneous collection of people with certain essential characterisics, but to a set of social struggles to articulate particular meanings, values, experiences, images, and social groups together.

4. David Leavitt, "The New Lost Generation," *Esquire* (May 1985): 93.

5. M. Coleman, "New Order's Leap of Faith," *Village Voice* (Jan. 11, 1983): 61.

6. Bobbie Ann Mason, *In Country* (New York: Harper & Row, 1985), p. 226.

7. See Jean Baudrillard, *Simulations*, Paul Foss, Paul Patton, and Philip Bleitchman, trans. (New York: Semiotexte, 1983).

8. Don DeLillo, *White Noise* (New York: Penguin, 1985), p. 12.

9. Leavitt, "The New Lost Generation," 93.

10. Tom Ward, "Sex & Drugs & Ronald Reagan," *Village Voice* (Jan. 29, 1985): 36.

11. Pat Aufderheide, "Sid and Nancy: Just Say No," *In These Times*, 11 (November 19–25, 1986): 14.

12. Kathy Acker, *Great Expectations* (New York: Grove, 1982), p. 78.

13. Philip Moffitt, "R U Hip, sixties people?" *Esquire* (April 1981): 6.

14. Coleman, "New Order's Leap of Faith," 61.

15. Frank Rose, "Welcome to the modern world," *Esquire* (April 1981): 32.

16. Ward, "Sex & Drugs & Ronald Reagan," 36.

17. Cited in Gary Robert, Rob Kulakofsky, and Mike Arrendondo, *Loud 3D.* (San Francisco: IN3D, 1983), p. 23.

18. See my "Postmodernity and Affect: All Dressed Up with No Place to Go," *Communication* 10 (1988), and "Putting the Pop Back into Postmodernism," in Andrew Ross, ed., *Universal Abandon? The Politics of PostModernism* (Minneapolis: University of Minnesota Press, 1988).

19. Peter Schneider, *The Wall Jumper: A Berlin Story.* L. Hafrey, trans. (New York: Random House, 1983), p. 123.

20. "The Rambo of Rock and Roll," *Chicago Tribune* (Aug. 9, 1985)

21. Mason, *In Country* , p. 236.

22. See my "'I'd Rather Feel Bad Than Not Feel Anything At All': Rock and Roll, Pleasure and Power," *Enclitic* 8 (1984): 94–110.

23. Tom Carson, "Head 'em up, move 'em out," *Village Voice* (Nov. 6, 1984).

24. See my "You Still Have to 'Fight for Your Right to Party': Music Television as Billboards of Postmodern Difference," *Popular Music* 7 (1988).

25. Rebecca Goldstein, *The Mind-Body Problem* (New York: Laurel, 1983).

26. Jay Cocks, "'Round the World, a Boss Boom," *Time* (Aug. 26, 1985): 71.

27. Ariel Swartley, "Chief Executive Officer," *Village Voice* (Sept. 3, 1985): 65.

28. Mason, *In Country*, p. 230.

29. Ibid., p. 235.

30. Michael Ventura, *Shadow Dancing in the USA* (Los Angeles: Jeremy Tarcher, 1985), p. 55.

31. Ibid., p. 24.

32. Bob Greene, "It's confession time," *Chicago Tribune* (Dec. ll, 1985).

33. Stuart Hall, "Gramsci and Us," *Marxism Today* (June 1987): 16.

Chapter 6

CURRICULUM POLITICS, HEGEMONY, AND STRATEGIES OF SOCIAL CHANGE

R. W. Connell

♦ I wish to explore a basic social issue in education through its relationship with general problems of social reform and popular politics in the relatively rich, capitalist, patriarchal societies of North America, Western Europe, and the South Pacific. The issue is, broadly, what to do about persistent massive social inequalities in education. Large-scale structural inequality is so basic, it mocks the claim of these societies to be democratic and poses an urgent practical problem to progressive politics as well as to workers in the education industry itself.

EDUCATIONAL INEQUALITY

Inequality in education is a distinctively modern issue. In previous periods of history access to education was limited, a situation that was accepted because it was taken for granted that priests and merchants needed to read and write, but peasants did not. Popular literacy became an issue in the Reformation, already connected with popular politics and critiques of hierarchy. The state-backed mass education systems created in the nineteenth century were designed to bring the majority of workers into basic literacy without giving scope to dangerous agitators. The "3 Rs" was a political program, literacy without radicalism. The intense cultural conservatism of traditional public schools was no accident; they displaced more chaotic but also more organic educational activity within the newly formed industrial working class.[1]

Despite these intentions, the mass education system became the vehicle for new radical demands. Once state-provided education was established, there was no logical reason why it should be limited to basic literacy. The rivalry of different industrial powers fueled an expansion: Germany invested in technical education, the United States in universal secondary education. Poor people's access to the university became an issue as a small minority of working-class children funneled up through the fierce competition of selective schools. By the 1940s, unequal access to education was firmly on the political agenda. Solutions to the problem were a significant part of the "postwar reconstruction" packages—which also included full employment and welfare policies—thrashed out during the struggle against fascism.

At this point, "common learnings" was a radical cry. The core of the democratic program was to break down the *segregation* of the education system. In the United States, which alone at that juncture already had a common secondary school system, attention moved to widening access to higher education. Though the radical wing of the progressive education movement addressed itself to some curriculum issues and early versions of a "core curriculum" were worked out as an alternative to subject-based curricula, the thrust of reform was around access. *Who Shall Be Educated*, to quote the title of a famous American book of the period,[2] not "what does good education consist of?"

Accordingly, the academic curriculum that already existed in institutions constructed to serve ruling-class boys became the framework on which the content of mass secondary and tertiary education was hung. Classics was steadily displaced by science, but academically defined content, teacher-centered pedagogy, individual appropriation as the mode of learning, and individual competition as the form of assessment remained; not only remained, but were now writ large. Common learnings there were: increasingly girls' education was assimilated to boys; working-class education to ruling-class education. The previously excluded were incorporated, on very specific terms.

Thus the democratic and radical upsurge of the 1940s, which gained a definite victory in state commitment to greatly expanded education systems, was undermined by the form in which the victory was realized. Twenty years into the postwar boom it was becoming clear that the competition was somehow rigged. Massive inequalities persisted, though their shape and locus had changed: streaming rather than simple exclusion, for instance. "Equal opportunity" did not in practice turn out to mean equal access.

Why? Research in the 1960s and 1970s turned to the cultural content of the dominant curriculum and began to show how it was connected to the ideologies and practices of dominant social groups. Research on the subcultures of the oppressed showed how the education system failed to value their specific experience, speech, ideas, skills and, more actively, how the interplay with formal education became destructive and divisive for disadvantaged groups, expelling most into the labor market (or into unemployment) while selecting out a minority for the system's rewards. In radical thinking, an image of the education system as a monster of inequality began to displace the earlier confidence in education as a tool of democracy.[3]

The question of democratizing education thus came to center on how these informal mechanisms of exclusion could be broken down or turned to the advantage of the excluded. Teacher activists mostly turned to one form or other of *enclave* strategy. Black experience, women's experience are excluded: we build black studies, women's studies curricula. Working-class access through the system is blocked: we turn away from the blockage and build organic working-class schools, Many groups lose contact with education before adulthood: adult education can be revitalized, conscientized, and expanded by outreach programs.

These strategies are to be distinguished from the ultraindividualist progressive education that developed in the "free schools" movement and had a mainly wealthy clientele. Though the approaches overlap, what is of lasting importance is the attempt to create a relevant pedagogy for the disadvantaged, out of their own experience and on their own terms.

To negate those rules of the game that guarantee unequal competition is possible, just: active and energetic teachers have done it, building an organic relationship between working-class school and community. But the price is high, as this strategy abandons the ground of common learnings. The strategy has been strongly criticized for its tendency to create curriculum ghettos in which better individual learning experiences occur, but the group *as a whole* is confirmed in its exclusion from whatever goods the mainstream education system provides. Since the mainstream education system does produce substantial labor market effects, the short-term consequences of this strategy are not very saleable. The labor movement does not like it, and the democratic movement in education becomes increasingly vulnerable to attacks from the political right.

For the common learnings logic is now inflected toward conservatism. The back-to-basics rhetoric is not seriously intended as a strategy for solving educational inequality. Rather, it is the ideological side of a new power play that became possible with the collapse of the postwar employment boom. Unemployment becomes the means of labor discipline, and with the recently constructed links between schooling and labor markets its effects reach back into the schools. Working-class families are pressured to value schooling for what is immediately salable in the labor market, what will help escape unemployment. In a recession, what is saleable is defined by the employers. A constituency for conservative rhetoric is created by *force majeure*.

There is not, it should be noted, a simultaneous narrowing of the curriculum in *ruling class* schools, They are brought into the argument only to show the supposed advantage of "private" schooling. Both the curricular turn in radical educational thought and the market ideology of the New Right have developed in ways that deflect attention from what the radicals of the 1940s did understand: the existence of educational *advantage* as a material, institutional fact. In most current debate, state-subsidized schools for the children of the rich might be on another planet from the ghetto schools, the disadvantaged schools, the Educational Priority Area schools. But they are at the deepest level intimately connected. Each is the secret of the others' existence. They work the way they do because the others are there.

STRATEGIES OF SOCIAL CHANGE

This course of events has both parallels and direct connections with the history of democratic movements in the more conventionally political sphere.[4] The postwar reconstruction settlements that included expanded education for the working class and for women temporarily stabilized a social order that had seemed on the brink of revolution. Labor and social democratic parties, even communist parties, were incorporated into capitalist regimes and for the most part subordinated there. (In the United States, which has no labor party, the radical unions were likewise incorporated into an increasingly right-wing union confederation.) The social mobilizations that had created them petered out into electoral jockeying. The parallel to the unequal competition created in the education system is not accidental. The cold war and the taming of political labor were the conditions in which the educational policy issues of the 1940s could be resolved around a conservative curriculum.

By the late 1960s the political settlements were coming unstuck, under the pressures of the Vietnam war, urban malaise, and the economic dislocations of the long boom itself. In some contexts this produced a new radicalization within the old party structure (the McGovern campaign in the United States, the Whitlam program in Australia, the 1974 Labor Party platform in the United Kingdom). But its major effect was to stimulate a remarkable growth of new radicalisms outside the old structures: the student movement, the New Left, Black Power, and indigenous people's movements, the counterculture, second-wave feminism, gay liberation.

To the extent that these movements were addressing forms of oppression not recognized, or not emphasized, by traditional parties and unions, their effect was to broaden the scope and deepen the understanding of radicalism. But their image of the social system as a closed, one-dimensional system of oppression commonly led to something different — a definition of radicalism as necessarily *outside* the system.[5] The "great refusal" chose negation because all affirmation could be co-opted. An Australian book on the counterculture in the mid-1970s sums it up in its title: *The Way Out.*[6] The very language of *radical* politics, directed at reform, was displaced by *alternative* politics, *alternative* culture – an option that existed alongside, not a transforming impulse that might shatter and remake.

Once again there is a connection with educational strategy. Notions of alternative culture were an essential support for the free school movement, and for a while at least these schools (and some free universities, too) were among the few successes the alternative movement could point to. The connection with strategy on educational disadvantage is less immediate, but I think important nonetheless. The New Left gave a big push to the notion of community-based politics as the authentic form of democracy, and that gave a much-needed antibureaucratic cast to the thinking of activists in the schools. Centrally imposed reforms would not work democratically unless they were brought alive by local communities. Indeed, local communities would be the key source of genuinely relevant curricula. Beyond these ideas about democratic practice, the notions of cultural alternatives both legitimated the critique of the hegemonic curriculum as irrelevant and, more dubiously, suggested that the building of enclaves was an effective strategy in its own right, part of a cultural transformation.

It is perhaps too easy now to criticize the New Left; since it was formative for me I find it difficult to judge objectively. I think it had a contradictory effect. Its emphases on living one's politics and on recognizing politics in new fields beyond elections and parliaments were important in sustaining radicalism. Those traits are among the New Left's legacy to feminism and have been important in sustaining that movement in the face of reaction. But the drift toward a politics of alternatives carried the immediate danger of separation from the lives of the majority of people. The famous clashes between protesters and hard hats in the antiwar campaigns in the United States were an early warning sign; the very effective media attack on the Left in Britain is a more recent one. An enclave strategy has a real possibility of diminishing a broad popular impulse for change.

In the chill winds of recession a popular radicalism has not been very prominent. Socialism and labor governments have certainly come into office in many parts of Europe and Australia. But, with a couple of exceptions (Greece and Sweden), the flavor of their radicalism has been somewhat between bland and vaporized. The parties have become more centralized and media oriented; their policies more tailored to what multinational capital will stand for. They have taken over from conservative ideology a concern with efficiency in education, adding a concern for access. Generally the financial crisis of the state prevents a major expansion of public education, and the fear of media and electoral backlash from the privileged prevents a major redistribution of the resources already available.

Radicalisms outside the parties and unions have, by common consent, fragmented. The public face of feminism has increasingly been presented by a conscious separatism which sees reforms benefiting men as no part of its business. Extraparliamentary socialism is gradually throwing off the husk of Marxism but has yet to find new organizational forms. Fashionable forms of academic radicalism fiercely criticize the ideas of a "main contradiction," of a common program, or of representation, and insist on the importance of a multiplicity of different do-it-yourself struggles.

The critique of imperialist tendencies in orthodox Marxism is sound, but orthodox Marxism is intellectually dead. The fragmentation of the Left, although protecting against certain forms of manipulation, dangerously risks demobilization in the face of centralized power, for the Foucauldian image of the world — with power and oppression diffused through an entire social and cultural order — does not allow a clear-cut identification of the *beneficiaries* of the system and thus a strategic assessment of who it is up against, what has been gained, what can be done, and what cannot. A very similar problem arises, as Segal points out, in relation to current radical feminism, where male domination is seen as universal and unchanging.[7]

Yet we are seeing considerable evidence of the ability of the holders of power and privilege to mobilize in their own defense. And we are seeing their ability to *connect* issues, from sexual politics through labor market deregulation to curriculum reconstruction. New Right programs are by no means confined to fringe parties; they feed into mainstream conservative and labor agenda setting. And it is no accident that one of their major campaigns has been in education, to discredit democratic public education and impose a freshly narrowed definition of common learnings.

COMMON LEARNINGS AND HEGEMONY

Any curriculum must make a selection from possible knowledges, possible methods, and there is no generalized guarantee of the correctness of that selection. That is the sense in Bourdieu's conception of the "cultural arbitrary" underpinning the politics of the curriculum.[8] But no selection of knowledges or methods is random or neutral with respect to the structure of the society in which it occurs. In that sense the notion of a cultural *arbitrary* is a fiction, and a potentially damaging one, as it implies that a simple epistemological relativism is a sufficient critique of mainstream curricula. A pluralism of alternatives is not a sustainable strategy, as the counterculture outside and inside education has found.

Taking cues from the sociology of knowledge and from fieldwork on schools, we can see a curriculum — meaning by that the ideas (content), the method by which they are appropriated and put to use (form of learning), the social practices in which those ideas and methods are materialized, and, above all, those three things in combination — as *necessarily* intersecting with the processes that constitute social interests, embodying relations of social power. It is not just that there are social bases for particular curricula, which is true enough. A curriculum as an ongoing social organization and distribution of knowledge helps to *constitute* social interests and arbitrate the relations among them. A common learnings program, i.e., a curriculum which seeks to operate across the whole population, embodies and negotiates relations of hegemony among interests in the society it deals with.

Definitions of common learnings cannot arise from abstract, presocial definitions of human need, as if child development could take place in a social vacuum. They exist only as *programs* for the organization and transmission of knowledge, which attempt to constitute the educational process in a particular relationship to social forces. Such programs arise in definite historical circumstances, are promoted by particular interests or alliances, have specific social effects, and have greater or less worldly success.

For example, a particular organization of knowledge and method which was first called "natural history," then "natural science, and increasingly just "science," was institutionalized in schools and universities in the nineteenth and early twentieth centuries. As historical research is now showing, this form of knowledge and method embodied a quite specific set of gender relationships, expressing a form of masculinity and its relation of dominance both to femininity and to the natural world.[9] This masculinity was not preformed; in fact, the rise of natural science and industrial technology was an important part of the historical process by which a rationalized and calculative masculinity displaced forms organized around traditional patriarchal authority as the dominant form of ruling-class masculinity. By the mid-twentieth century the sciences constructed along these lines had become the leading component of the academic curriculum, displacing Latin and literature in a process familiar to all teachers over forty years old. The social consequences of this expansion include the cultural exclusion of women from dominant forms of knowledge, and from careers based on them, that equal opportunity programs in science and technology are now grappling with.

In much the same sense, though through different mechanisms, the definition of common learnings that is institutionalized in the academic curriculum, its language, and its practices of individualized learning and atomistic and competitive assessment, results in a general exclusion of working-class students from the world of higher learning and the resources to which it gives access. The process, as traced out in the recent sociology of education, is complex and subtle, but its effects are powerful. I would include among them not only the statistical exclusion of working-class youth from higher education, but also the cultural intimidation of the labor movement. In many parts of labor politics we have reached the point where leaderships are unable to conceive of any form of working-class educational advancement *except* getting more of the dominant curriculum and its institutions.

To acknowledge these historical facts is not to be committed to a strategy of alternatives or to the relativism that is its epistemological side. The intellectual strength of the currently dominant curriculum is its claim to embody objective knowledge. That claim cannot be effectively contested by denying the idea of objectivity as major currents in the counterculture and in feminism presently do. The radical critiques are correct in pointing out that curriculum as an organization of knowledge has particular social bases and advances particular social interests. But that argument shows that knowledge is inherently *socially constructed*, not that it is inherently subjective or nonobjective.

Objective does not mean abstracted, divorced from a situation, as the rhetoric of positivism would have us believe. Indeed, in the social sciences, abstracted knowledge is likely to be exceptionally distorted and misleading, the opposite of objective. A current example is provided by the controversy in Australia over the cutting of funds for migrant education, such as English as a Second Language programs. These cuts have been justified by studies that purport to show there is no migrant disadvantage in education. The studies are highly abstracted, generalized surveys, typically done by people with no grass-roots experience of ethnic education and no awareness of where in practical experience (and with which specific groups of migrants) the problems are known to be.

People have great trouble in breaking out of the conventional dichotomy that contrasts objective with subjective and neutrality with bias. It is nevertheless essential to do so: to understand that knowledge can be socially constructed *and* objective. Deutscher's argument is a key to this difficulty.[10] Knowledge always has a context, since the knower lives in the world (especially a social world). Being objective, gaining accurate and undistorted knowledge, requires a subjective *commitment* within that context, an *engagement* with the issues. Subjectivity and objectivity are not dichotomous opposites. Objectivity is a characteristic of the process of discovering (or of learning) which is fueled by subjectivity.

Objectivity, we might say, is methodological, subjectivity is relational. Objectivity can equally be a characteristic of quite different relationships to the social world. (If that sounds odd, think of spy novels. In Le Carré's famous series both the British and Russian spymasters, Smiley and Karla, show a high degree of objectivity in reasoning and inquiry, though their purposes are diametrically opposed.[11]) With this perspective on knowledge, it becomes possible to think of common learnings programs which are as objective as the currently dominant curriculum but which are constructed from other social standpoints and prioritize other interests.

The mainstream curriculum is hegemonic within the educational system in the sense that it marginalizes other ways of organizing knowledge, is integrated with the structure of organizational power, and occupies the high cultural ground, defining most people's common-sense ideas about what learning ought to be. Its position in the education system is bolstered by its close connection with teachers' professionalism and self-conceptions, though also undermined to the extent that it comes to be recognized as a major source of teachers' occupational problems in mass schooling.[12] The mainstream curriculum is hegemonic in the society at large in the sense that it is part of the cultural and practical underpinning of the ascendancy of particular social groups—specifically, capitalists and professionals, men, Anglos.

To move beyond relativism and the strategy of alternatives, without buying the definition of knowledge in the dominant curriculum that condemns excluded groups to continuing marginalization is to embark on a strategy of *inverting* hegemony. This strategy accepts the need for a program of common learnings but not the basis on which it is currently constructed. It seeks an organization of content and method which builds on the experience of the disadvantaged (as the organic school argument did) but attempts to generalize it to the whole system, rather than confining it to a section. It thus seeks a practical reconstruction of the system which will yield relative advantage to the groups currently disadvantaged. It attempts to turn a defensive, compensatory strategy into a proactive, universalizing strategy.

In principle, there are many possible common learnings programs, though in a particular historical setting only a few are likely to be of great practical importance. A minimal criterion for choice among them, and a minimal defense of the strategy of inverting hegemony, is the criterion of social justice. We can accept with Rawls that social justice means taking the standpoint of the least advantaged, though we can do without his fantasy that this might occur in ignorance of one's own social position.[13] Indeed, understanding the real relationships and processes that generate advantage and disadvantage is essential in evaluating the practical consequences of any action that claims to embody the interests of the least advantaged. (Note that this is a claim made—albeit falsely—for New Right educational strategies such as voucher systems.) But this is only a minimal defense. There are stronger reasons for seeking an educational program constructed in this way.

Different social standpoints yield different views of the world, and some are more comprehensive and powerful than others. This is a classic proposition in the sociology of knowledge that we owe to Lukacs and Mannheim and a major reason why the classical sociology of knowledge does not lead to relativism in the way notions of cultural difference or the cultural arbitrary do.[14] If you wish to teach about ethnicity and race relations, for instance, a more comprehensive and deeper understanding is possible if you construct your curriculum from the point of view of the subordinated ethnic groups than if you work from the point of view of the dominant one. Racism is a qualitatively better organizing concept than natural inferiority, though each has its roots in a particular experience and embodies a social interest.

The general point here is that the position of those who carry the burdens of social inequality is a better starting point for understanding the totality of the social world than is the position of those who enjoy its advantages. This is a structural argument about bodies of objective knowledge, it should be noted, and not an argument about the quantities of information held by individuals within a particular hegemonic organization of knowledge. On tests and examinations constructed within the paradigm of the competitive academic curriculum, as is well known, on average working-class children do worse, i.e., they appear to have less knowledge. For all the effort that has gone into devising culture-free intelligence tests, no such test has ever gained general acceptance, for good sociological reason: neither intelligence nor information is a culture-free thing.

At its simplest, the standpoint of the least advantaged presents experience and information not normally available to dominant groups, and hence overlooked or marginalized in their constructions of knowledge and in curricula based on those constructions. A familiar example is the criticism of traditional school history curricula centered on the deeds of famous men and the attempt to reconstruct them to include the histories of working-class people and of women. This, however, need do no more than add on some new content to an old framework, as when social history is added to political (= real) history. At best, it would simply parallel curricula for different groups, a position now adopted by one strand of feminism.

This, however, is to miss the larger intellectual significance of the standpoint of the least advantaged. When Lukacs discussed "the point of view of the proletariat," he had in mind the way the structural location of the working class at the point of production revealed to workers in the most concrete possible way the basic mechanism of capital accumulation through the extraction of surplus value. However sophisticated the other points of view which did not have this as a guiding insight, they could not grasp the reality of a capitalist society. In his classic demonstration of the importance of standpoint in constructing knowledge, Lukacs explored with great subtlety the blockages in European philosophy that arose from the philosophers' collective location in the world of capitalist privilege. The standpoint of the proletariat is crucial in overcoming these blockages, not because factory workers are better analysts, but because the insights arising from their experience and action allow a reconfiguration of the whole domain of culture.

What Lukacs argued for the case of class relations applies with surprising precision to the case of gender relations. There has long been a body of information and discourse about the family, women's employment, children's social development, masculinity and femininity. This remained for decades a backwater in social sciences hegemonized by the interests of men and was largely construed in mainstream social science through concepts such as role and modernization.. The standpoint of the least advantaged in gender relations, articulated in feminism, has transformed that. Modern feminism has produced a *qualitatively better* analysis of this large domain of social life. Partly this was by bringing to the fore experiences — such as sex discrimination, sexual harassment, or the experience of mothering — little discussed before. Partly, and I think more importantly, it was by developing new concepts and a new kind of social theory embodied in terms like "sexual politics," "patriarchy," "sexual division of labor." These concepts allowed a massive reconfiguration of the existing domain of knowledge, as well as the addition of experiences not previously included — a conceptual revolution still going on in the social sciences, whose effects are still to be felt across much of the school curriculum.

In both these cases, an understanding of the central mechanisms producing a social structure is accessible through the experience of the groups *subordinated* by those mechanisms and not through the experience of the groups who are advantaged by them. To explain this fact would be to produce a general theory of ideology, which is a little beyond my scope here; all I hope is to register the importance of this fact for questions of curriculum. To say "accessible" is not to say that a generalized understanding is automatically produced, as a matter of fact, among the subordinate groups — an idea that Lukacs firmly, and correctly, denied. It is to say that a kind of knowledge is produced that *can* be generalized. This process requires constructive intellectual work to turn the basic knowledge into an open-ended intellectual program reaching out across a widening field of knowledge. If this work is done, the point of view of the least advantaged becomes the basis of a program for the organization and transmission of knowledge which, I have suggested, is the substance of a definition of common learnings.

It is then possible to construct a generalized educational program, a common learnings program, whose claim to preference over the existing academic curriculum is twofold: it follows the principle of social justice in education by embodying the interests of the least advantaged, and it is intellectually better than other ways of organizing knowledge and thus has an epistemological advantage. This gives a more powerful meaning to the strategy of inverting hegemony. It is not just a matter of changing the beneficiaries but of overcoming the blocks that current power structures offer to intellectual and cultural advance. Along these lines, countersexist curriculum, working-class curriculum, and the like cease to be names for curriculum ghettos and become principles for systemwide democratization and intellectual growth.

MAINSTREAM AND DEMOCRACY

The dilemma of recent radical politics has been not to find a popular base so much as to hold it, to turn democratic impulses that continually well up (from the student movement of the 1960s to the peace movement of the 1980s) into a continuing practical politics with real purchase on the social system.[15] Programs of educational reform must take note of this. A program that contests power structures from a position of continuing weakness will lead more easily to Valium prescriptions than to reform.

To formulate a democratic program in education as an *oppositional* program—acknowledging the large differences between notions of alternative schooling and critical pedagogy that are still the case with most radical thinking in education—is to invite defeat in detail. Democratic programs need the protection of democratic support. Those teacher activists who sought to build a program of parent participation and community control were absolutely right on this point of strategy, and that is one reason such programs are still in existence where most of the free schools have gone.

But the notion of community in the sense of neighborhood is too weak a base for democratizing whole educational systems. Among other things, this style of democratization gives no grip on universities and colleges, whose role in the curriculum politics of the educational system is persistently underestimated.

I don't have a strategy wrapped up in a parcel to offer, but I want to suggest three criteria for strategy in educational reform that are suggested by the recent history of democratic politics.

First, popular politics is about majorities, and a democratic politics should be even more concerned about majorities than the rich and powerful have to be. Majorities do not grow on trees, they have to be constructed, in an immensely complex process of negotiation and alliance. This doesn't always go well—the coalition building may be more successful from the Right, as Reagan and Thatcher illustrate. It is unlikely to go well for any particular part of a potential alliance of democratic forces without the support of others.

Second, democracy is mainstream, not marginal. The New Right has gained its remarkable initiative by making large claims, by occupying ground that was seldom contested. A radical program has to insist on its place in the center of cultural advance, to operate across the board, to be a generalizable program.[16] This does not mean that everyone should put on suits and ties and go and sit quietly in boardrooms: we know from experience that is very unlikely to produce structural change. It does mean that progressive educational politics needs practical means of operating programmatically across the full range of educational issues.

Third, it is important to consider the workers on whom a reform program depends, in this case mainly the teachers. Teachers have a complex relationship to the competitive academic curriculum, with motives both to protect and to change it. A good deal of the argument about change will undoubtedly occur among teachers. It is important on political as well as on industrial grounds that teachers' interests be engaged in democratic curriculum reforms. Teacher professionalism is a real force and by no means wholly integrated into the system; it can, for instance, fuel resistance to deskilling through commercially packaged learning systems and to the domination of curricula by economic pressures. How far it can be mobilized in more positive ways in current circumstances can only be found in practice.

NOTES

1. P. Miller, *Long Division* (Adelaide: Wakefield Press, 1986).

2. W. L. Warner, R. J. Havighurst, and M. B. Loeb, *Who Shall Be Educated?* (New York: Harper, 1944).

3. R. W. Connell, D. J. Ashenden, S. Kessler, and G. W. Dowsett, *Making the Difference* (Sydney: Allen & Unwin, 1982).

4. R. W. Connell, "Socialism: moving on," in *Moving Left*, D. McKnight, ed. (Sydney: Pluto Press, 1986), pp. 9–45.

5. H. Marcuse, *One Dimensional Man* (London: Routledge & Kegan Paul, 1964).

6. M. Smith and D. Crossley, eds., *The Way Out* (Melbourne: Lansdowne, 1975).

7. L. Segal, *Is the Future Feminine?* (London: Virago, 1987).

8. P. Bourdieu and J.-C. Passeron, *Reproduction* (London: Sage, 1977).

9. B. Easlea, *Science and Sexual Oppression* (London: Weidenfeld & Nicolson, 1981).

10. M. Deutscher, *Subjecting and Objecting* (Brisbane: University of Queensland Press, 1983).

11. J. Le Carré, *Tinker Tailor Soldier Spy* (London: Hodder & Stoughton, 1974).

12. R. W. Connell, *Teachers' Work* (Sydney: Allen & Unwin, 1985).

13. J. Rawls, *A Theory of Justice* (Oxford: Oxford University Press, 1972).

14. G. Lukacs, *History and Class Consciousness* (London: Merlin, 1971); K. Mannheim, *Ideology and Utopia* (London: Routledge & Kegan Paul, 1954).

15. D. Altman, *Rehearsals for Change* (Melbourne: Penguin).

16. A notable example is D. Ashenden, J. Blackburn, W. Hannan, and D. White, "Manifesto for a democratic curriculum," *Australian Teacher*, No. 7 (1984): 13–20. For a recent discussion of possible bases in the lives of working-class youth, see B. Wilson and J. Wyn, *Shaping Futures* (Sydney: Allen & Unwin, 1987).

Chapter 7

ART OR CULTURE? AN INQUIRY

Paul Willis

♦ I start from the recognition that most young people see the arts as special, remote and institutional, not part of everyday life. It is what they were forced to do at school and, therefore, don't like. Art is the preserve of art galleries, museums, and concert halls that are "not for us." The image is bad, but so is the reality. Research shows that attendance rates at galleries, museums, concert halls, and theatres are insignificant for the great mass of the young, especially for those without the experience and equipment provided by higher education. For the young unemployed, they are hardly measurable. More damaging, however, is the fact that the formal existence of the arts, in the sense in which the term is commonly used, seems to exhaust everything else of its artistic or cultural content. In other words, because Art is in the art gallery, it can't be anywhere else. It is that which is special and heightened, not common and every day. It does not belong to the lives of normal people.

The commonly attributed purposes of the arts include the reflection and expression in symbol and artifact of important human qualities and values, of human identity. Most young people's lives are not involved with the arts and yet are actually full of expressions, signs, and symbols through which

This is a First Position Paper prepared for an unfolding inquiry funded by the Gulbenkian Foundation. The Project is under the direction of the author and is based at Wolverhampton Polytechnic, Wolverhampton, England.

individuals and groups seek to establish their presence, identity, and meaning. Young people are all the time expressing or attempting to express something about their actual or potential *cultural significance*. This can be the starting point, where the received arts fail to connect or are seen to be irrelevant. The inquiry sets out to recognize creativity wherever it is and whatever its forms. This might be in some of the extended institutions and community arts practices which many have struggled for over recent years, but it may also be in the unseen practices of daily life and in expressions not yet recognized as arts. There is a multitude of ways in which young people humanize, decorate, and invest with meaning their immediate life spaces and social practices—decoration of bedrooms; personal styles and choice of clothes; selective and active use of music, TV, magazines; the rituals of romance and subcultural styles, as well as general styles and attitudes developed in friendship groups and leisure; the widespread informal and local interest in music making and dance. The inquiry, then, assumes that symbolic activity, reflection, and expression are in all young people's lives all of the time, only they have different names. Not arts, they are cultures or cultural activities. The heart of the inquiry is to name these new names, to provide a living guide to the actual cultures and cultural activities of the young today, removed from the shadows of the arts institutions, in which these activities are usually invisible.

In the identification and presentation of these cultures and activities I also hope to identify the conditions under which they exist: the relationships, situations, and processes in which they are possible, develop, and have meaning. This is so that the inquiry is not only able to recognize hidden cultures, but is also able to make realistic recommendations aimed at strengthening the conditions of their possibility—so that cultural activities might grow the better, from their own roots.

These aims can be framed in the following developed terms of reference:

1. The *concrete activity* that is involved or might be involved in what we refer to as arts and culture.

2. The *conditions* under which such activity occurs and which might be open to policy intervention in order to further encourage the cultural and artistic activity associated with them.

The basic parameters of the inquiry, wherein lies its hoped-for distinctiveness, are to test and present the productive results of what happens when both terms (and the possible forms of their inter-relationships) are resolutely extended from their conventional and historically received definitions to explore new areas and to explore that common ground which might be established between the old and the new.

Definitions are not only of academic interest; they also designate what can be placed under them and, therefore, what can be legitimated and promoted. It is difficult to direct recommendations at encouraging what might be, as yet, invisible, unrecognized, or without a name. It follows that the main objective of policy intervention rests on some work on, and demonstration of, redefinition. The two definition poles can be described for each term. For the *concrete activity*, (1) I want to shift (pulling out the very tension of my title) the emphasis from activities related to the received arts to those activities associated with culture, defined as the expressive practices and involvements of the everyday life of the young. For the *conditions* (2) under which such activity takes place, I want to shift the emphasis from the institutions and conventions which support and reproduce the received arts to the life processes of the young, the everyday material context and social practices which frame and order their common experiences – the home, the street, work, college, leisure, the social group, going out, staying in, spending money, the things on which money can be spent, spending time without money.

THE NEED TO MOVE ON FROM ART AND OUT OF THE INSTITUTION

What is the definition of art, the pole of definition that we have inherited, which we start from but want to move on from? It is those practices, artifacts, and texts which universally, autonomously, and creatively embody crucial values and truths about the human condition and whose forms are separate, special, heightened, and distinguished from the everyday by their internal aesthetics (principles of beauty). The conventional list of arts includes: classical music, ballet, opera, drama, poetry, literature, the visual and plastic arts. Within these branches of art are canons, and competing canons, which attempt to place the works into finite hierarchies differentiating greater and lesser value. Of course, these hierarchies are not fixed. In contradiction to the sense of the universal which characterizes great art, new works (by no means always newly created) are admitted over time, just as established ones slip down or out. But at all times there is a limited number only of great works.

The existence, reproduction, and appreciation of the arts depend on their conditions of existence – institutions. Institutions include buildings and organizations, but also systematic and specific social values and practices concerned with the manner of engagement with the arts. Their appreciation (or consumption) further depends on the acquisition of certain kinds of knowledge and therefore on a prior educational process – the taste for art is learned. The creation or production of artistic works depends on these institutions and on the learning of the canon, but also on an unspecifiable creativity which is rare, individual, and the highest of human callings.

There have been, and plainly continue to be, struggles over these institutions – to make them more open and flexible on the one hand, or to save them from the account book philistines on the other. The art market distorts the whole field and sets much of the terrain on which the institutions must stand. Art as commodity admits the influence of market forces into the sacred process of the determination of aesthetic value, introducing the possibility of all kinds of manipulation, from out-and-out fraud to the weight of money determining, for instance, that for the moment Van Gogh's *Irises* stands at the apex of value. But the main arts establishment has been concerned throughout to protect and, where possible, to extend the established institutions and practices, and with reaching extended or new publics. The many strands of the community arts movement have in common the concern to democratize the arts and to try to make them much more a part of common experience. From my perspective, however, the search for new or expanded publics suffers from the implicit assumption that such groups are, in some sense, nonpublics, that they have no forms of their own, no culture, except perhaps a very much debased version of elite culture or mass culture passively consumed. But I maintain that such publics do have their objects, their cultural fields, their own strongly active and participatory symbolic forms — even if made up from preconstituted and common forms. The case studies and commissions described here will test precisely this — that there is a culture already present in their life space which, for most young people, is preferable to the received arts.

It seems that there can also be a final unwillingness and limit in the many forms of a movement towards an arts democracy. These movements may have escaped the physical academy, but not always its conventions — the forms must be kept more or less intact. If they must go, then so, too, does any notion of a specifically artistic practice. What is left is indistinguishable from other activities such as community action or politics itself. Some activists are, indeed, led by his logic to pure community action. But such an approach makes assumptions which presuppose effects which must be free. If it is to be free, creative activity must be allowed to be what it is and to lead where it will, without clapping categories on it to chop it up in advance as art, not art, relevant, not relevant.

There seem to be hidden questions behind some of our arts initiatives and policies to date, not "What are their cultures?" but "Why are their cultures not like ours?" "Why are their cultures not as we think they should be?" We need some way of conceptualizing the field which allows us to ask "What is there?" and to start from the roots of the social whole — without advance specifications from one part of it.

LIFE PROCESSES: A NEW YOUTH STAGE?

The conditions of existence of common expressions — symbols, texts, decorations, communicative activity of all kinds — are not taken as institutional, but as the conditions of everyday life, its economic and social constraints and possibilities in relation to the symbolic and expressive resources commonly at hand.

Recognizing common expressions in relation to the conditions of everyday life may mark the intention of a decisive shift from conventional perspectives but it can also be a laziness. Are we to deal with the whole of life? Is everything equivalent to everything else in the life processes of the young? If not, how are we to begin to specify?

An important point of departure here is the appreciation of some of the overarching changes in the condition of life of the young. In Britain, and in different ways in all Western industrial societies, there is an emerging construction of an imposed youth stage, or youth status. Our older images of youth, from the 1950s and 1960s, concern style, fashion, and consumption: young people comprised a powerful new consumer group with vastly increased disposable income based on early, relatively high, full employment wages and low housing and subsistence costs subsidized by (fully employed) parents. An extension of youth or adolescence seemed to be something of a voluntary choice and celebration. Now this, perhaps originally self-created, space has turned into something of a prison for many. There is now an enforced extended period between the dependency of childhood and the autonomy of adulthood. It is economic power—the possession of the wage and the ability to set up a home independent from parents—which underwrites the transition out of this stage into the autonomies of adulthood. But this stage of wage earning power and independent living is being ever delayed. This is obviously the case for the young unemployed, who account for a third or more of the under-25s in most areas of Great Britain. But it is also true of the many young workers who are increasingly forming a periphery to the core adult labor force. They are in low-paid insecure work or passing through what seems to them an interminable mosaic of short-term, temporary work, often in low-paid service sectors, part-time, temporary schemes, cash work in the "black economy," and unemployment. It is also true of the more privileged working sector of youth where the continuous professionalization of older skill areas, the developing hierarchies of the new tech and new services, and the diminishing chances of joining the closing ranks of key core labor in the older industries have spun out whole new obstacle courses of certification and whole new apprenticeships to be faced before a secure future can be planned.

To be sure, this gathering external structuration of a prolonged adolescence hides a new social stratification based on differential waiting periods and differential certainty about the lengths of waiting periods, expected before assuming the mantle of adulthood and autonomy. Some groups, perhaps especially the elite academic groups, can plan for some certainty of making the transition, but even they pay the price of many years of dependency.

Young working-class women may experience this youth stage in the special form of partial, early, and exploitative transitions (often in an imperceptible extension of childhood domestic chores naturally expected of girls but not of boys) into domestic roles of care and maintenance. This may

seem to be a destination of sorts and a meaningful, useful activity when labor market opportunities are scarce or difficult, but it can often be a specific, unofficial training and subjective preparation for a lifetime's future in part-time, low-paid, insecure, usually dead-end, female service work.

Large sections of black youth face what seems to them a waiting room turned into the whole of foreseeable life, attended only by different kinds of racism, racist harassment, and institutional neglect or indifference or, increasingly, hostility.

To some degree, sometime, all young people, in different combinations and to different strengths, face the contradictory position of becoming adult in chronology, biology, and appetites, while remaining adolescent, through no choice of their own, in their power and autonomy. They all experience aspects of the subjective characteristics of the youth stage: unwilling economic dependence on parents and parental homes; uncertainty regarding future planning; powerlessness and lack of control over immediate circumstances of life; feelings of symbolic as well as material marginality to the main society. We have here one important starting point for understanding the functions and possibilities of their own cultures and cultural forms—how do they understand and react through their cultures to the extended adolescent stage?

These considerations raise another important aspect of the conditions under which the cultures of the young develop. What are the tools and raw materials at hand for the young to come to their own understandings? What are the symbolic resources and reservoirs of meaning which they can adapt, adopt, or combine to produce their own expressions?

Many of the traditional resources of meaning have lost their legitimacy for a good proportion of young people. Organized religion, the monarchy, trade unions, schools, public broadcasting, and public culture itself, no longer supply ready values and models of duty and meaning to help structure the passage into settled adulthood. This is certainly partly a result of much-commented-upon wider processes: secularization, individualization, decollectivization, weakening respect for authority. But it is also the case that these inherited traditions owe their still-continuing and considerable power to the stakes they offer and seem to offer to the individual—some graspable identity within a set of relationships to other identities; some notion of citizenship within a larger whole which offers rights, satisfactions, and loyalties, as well as duty and submission. However, for many young people made to feel marginal to this society and without any material stake in it, these merely symbolic stakes can seem very remote. These public traditions and meanings cannot make good what they offer, undercut at another more basic level by unfulfilled expectations. These things are for parents and adults, for those who have an interest in and make up the civil body. For the young black British they are even more remote, they are for other people's parents. No longer can we be blind to the whiteness of our major traditional public sources of identity.

Alongside the symbolic erosion of traditional public institutions, indeed perhaps in part as response to this diminuition in the sum of public authority, have grown other state-financed, professional, and altogether more directed institutions offering shape, control, and form to the new youth period of amorphousness.

The existence of the extended youth stage proves itself through the arrival of new institutional forms, and the adaptation of old ones, aimed at its regulation. The Youth Training Scheme, the Job Training Scheme, the largest chunk of the Community Program, recent developments in Youth Work Practice and Drop-In Centers for the unemployed, civil disorder and community policing, changes in benefit rules for the under-25s, all are aimed in some way at controlling and filling the time of youth or at maintaining some promise (and discipline) for future transitions or at preventing or pre-empting alternative uses of time and capacity not devoted to preparation for future transitions. There is a set of meanings and identities on offer here — highly restricted, applied, and focused. Whether or not they are or will be really taken up, and to what extent the new institutional developments will be adequate sources of, and frames for, the meanings, hopes, and values of young people, cannot yet be judged. These new developments carry the contradiction and partiality of a redoubled focus on just what has become problematic for so many of the young. There may be new sites here with the potential to become battlegrounds for the shape and direction of time, for how it is used collectively and individually, as well as for what the relevant human capacities are for the passing of what kinds of time.

But these old and new forms are not the only raw materials at hand for the young. They are also surrounded by the commercial productions of, and advertisements for, the cultural and consciousness industries — records, magazines, clothes, and all the visual and audio software for domestic electronic hardware. This generation of young adults is truly the pop generation, in that its whole nurture and growth has been in an encompassing world of consumerism — the world not simply of more and more things as objects, but also of things which attract and sell through their associated ideas and symbols and are often themselves composed of ideas and symbols.

The eruption of mass experience into visible history — the creation of a popular history itself marked through landmark pop songs, entertainment personalities, and social style, as well as great events — has been through the image and products of a commercial culture aimed specifically at youth. Whether we object or not to the manipulations and coercions involved, the cultural industries have produced a new cultural terrain which cannot now be ignored and which constitutes the effective horizon for many young people. The young unemployed may no longer be the leading consumer target groups, but they live with the employed in the cultural world created by postwar, Western consumerism with its ever increasing appetites for signs and symbols as well as for things.

Many of the current problems and uncertainties of public life, not least in the realm of arts policy, come back to the disorientations, conflicts, and confusions of turning and faltering between these three bases of meaning: declining public institutions; newly ascendant regulative institutions; omnipresent commercial forms. Much hypocrisy and self-deception attend how we function in and understand our roles as educators, policy makers, and putative formers of youth opinion and expression, caught and formed ourselves in that last informal world, yet operating and directing youth toward the former ones.

However, for the young, perhaps especially, the commercially produced landscapes of meaning are not only fields of consumption. They are also productive tools to fashion new meanings and expressions, both for the living and understanding of the contradictory and difficult conditions of everyday life and for the making of products for which there are (realistic or not) commercial aspirations. The public and commercial worlds are now thoroughly enmeshed at the cultural level. The recent vertiginous rise of the international art market shows that the world of high art is shot through with commercial relations. Subsidy and public provision of one kind or another have supported popular culture and made possible many movements, performers, and personalities long before they took off in the commercial world.

One important aim is to try to identify the *general* role of public funds in cultural life and then to make recommendations for a rational and explicit policy concerning their role, or possible role, in all kinds of creative activity.

MOVING TO CULTURES: A GROUNDED AESTHETIC?

I have tried to specify more exactly and historically the conditions under which the cultures of the young develop. Can one further specify the expressions and communicative activities of the young? Are all expressions equally interesting?

Some expressions are indeed distinguished from others—by their capacity for, and role in, meanings. Many expressions communicate information or signify intention or presence—they have not to do with making meaning. As the dumb suffering of illiteracy shows us, the world is full of signposts to direct, inform, and control. The very socialness of life in families and peer groups depends upon continuous and mutual communication about needs, feelings, and obligations. Complex organization in the office, school, college, or factory rests on networks of information and expression as rules, procedures, expectations, job descriptions, and objectives. Much of the output of the media and leisure industries consists of information or seeks to place people passively as consumers—to be entertained without engaging reciprocal meanings.

There are clearly overlaps in the functions of communications. No party to a communication is ever totally passive, but the specific interest is in the active use of expressions and communications to make particular meanings in particular contexts—the moment when the tools or raw materials produce new meanings or reset or rediscover the possibilities of what is received, the moment of symbolic production, if you like.

In among the plethora of expressions which constitute the cultural field of the young are some which are made to come alive to some degree. They are symbolically appropriated to produce a critical reading of meaning which not only reflects or repeats, but transforms what exists — received expressions as well as what they represent or are made to represent — in some indentifiable way. This is a making specific, in relation to the social group or individual and its conditions of life, of the ways in which the received natural and social world is made human *to them* and made, to however small a degree (even if finally symbolic), controllable by them. I hypothesize, for this moment, a notion of a "grounded aesthetics" to designate such a possibility.

The aesthetic is in some sense the most specific quality which characterizes the human mind. This is its capacity to be made conscious, through some concrete practice or active mediation, of its own qualities of consciousness of the world. This is to know, as a practical accomplishment, to however small a degree, that control of nature beyond the body is possible and that is the form of knowing our own consciousness.

The possibility of such control is, of course, a collective principle for the possibility of political action on the largest scale. But it also has importance in the individual and collective awareness of the ability to control symbols and their cultural work. In so-called primitive art, for instance, a central theme is the naming of fundamental forces as gods and demons, thereby to reveal them, make them somehow knowable and finally subject to human persuasion or placation. The urban industrial world is much more complex in its organization than are primitive societies, and our apparent technical control over the threatening forces of nature seems greater and different in kind from those. What we seek to control, persuade, or humanize through symbols and expression may be, in part, the force and expression of other human beings rather than forces emanating directly from nature (if you like, the work of culture on culture). Whatever the complexity of working through its applications, the point is essentially a simple one. To be crude: that to know it, and to know ourselves, it is necessary not merely to be in, but to change, however minutely, the cultural world. The appreciation of the arts might embody one side of this — admiration of the formal properties of expressions as things — but misses the heart of it being a practiced capacity. It is this practiced capacity which we wish to hold and highlight as an everyday accomplishment.

By the addition of grounded to the traditional term I hope to signify both irony and substance, to convey some sense of skepticism about the flight of conventional aesthetics. Too often this renders the once socially relevant and serious effects of art into the sublime entertainment of a purely formal aesthetic response to, for instance, religious art now installed in the antiseptic stillness of the museum. Instead, I want to bring aesthetics back to earth, not for a crash landing, but to give it an opportunity to show its quality, if it has it, in the earthiness of the real material conditions of life.

A grounded aesthetics is a view of an aesthetics *not necessarily* enclosed in a single artifact, but one articulated as the creative quality in a process wherever meanings are carried. This also suggests suspension of traditional canons of evaluation and suspension of the notion that artistic activity is *sui generis*, unconnected with other social practices. For the purpose of discussion and development, it is possible to outline some general characteristics and some possible concrete dimensions or types of grounded aesthetics for case study and research to further test and elaborate.

A provisional, short, basic definition will help to anchor the fuller specifications which follow. A grounded aesthetics is the quality of creativity in processes of meaning making which utilizes commonplace materials in concrete, everyday contexts.

Characteristics

The Senses. The received sense of aesthetics emphasizes the cerebral, abstract or or sublimated quality of beauty. At times it seems to verge on the an-aesthetics, the suppression of all senses. I would want to pull the term back (actually onto its original terrain) into some direct relation to the senses and to sensual heightening.

Economy. I would not, however, wish to jettison a sense of formal economy or efficiency in the use of expressive symbols and the articulation of symbols, especially in breaking and disrupting the smooth surface of the banal or the cliched as often the shortest possible or allusive way of penetrating, questioning, or destabilizing the obviousness of received meaning.

Skill. I would want to emphasize the concrete skills involved in the exercise of grounded aesthetics. Such skills are a matter of concrete acquisition rather than natural distinction or gift.

Use. I would see grounded aesthetics as having use rather than having ontological value (Arts for arts' sake). Such use could be concrete and practical, or instrumental, i.e., to produce meanings, explanations, and payoffs in relation to concrete conditions and situations which seem more efficient or adequate, perhaps, than other proffered meanings. Such useful meanings may well have moral dimensions, providing collective and personal principles of action, cooperation, solidarity, distinction, or resistance. Useful meanings may also relate to difficulties and dilemmas in the realms of necessity—school, work, college—as well as to choices in the realms of leisure and free time. Where the traditional view of aesthetics privileges formal questions to the exclusion, often, of all else, we are interested in questions of socially relevant, active, and useful content.

Dimensions

Reception aesthetics. Circumstances change cases. Contexts change texts. The received view of aesthetics suggests that the aesthetic effect is internal to the text, a universal property of its form. This places the creative impulse squarely on the material productions of the creative artist, with the reception or consumption of art wholly determined by its aesthetic form — palely reflecting what is timelessly coded within the text. I want to spread out the possibility of creativity to embrace the conditions of distribution, the consumption, and the decoding of expression. I am interested to explore both how far meanings and effects can change quite decisively, according to the social contexts of consumption. I am also interested in the extent to which viewers, listeners, and readers bring their own work to a text or create their own relationships to technical means of reproduction and transfer (which produces specific situational meanings, and create the possibilities for new kinds of cultural production). Young TV viewers have become (often unconsciously) critical and literate in visual forms, plot conventions, and cutting techniques. They now listen, often highly selectively, to pop music within a whole shared metahistory of pop styles and genres. How do these things mediate the meanings of texts? Does it matter that texts may be classified as banal, contrived, formulaic, if their living reception is the opposite of these things? The inquiry hopes to show the creative elements and implications behind apparently passive reception.

Production aesthetics. The creative reception of, and work on, texts and artifacts can be seen as part of a social process which may include its own productions, either of new forms or of recombinations of existing ones. Perhaps we should see the raw materials of cultural life, of communications and expressions, as always intermediate. They are the products of one process as well as the raw materials for another, whose result are raw materials for successive groups. Why shouldn't bedroom decoration and personal styles as combinations of other's productions, as well as creative writing or song and music composition, be seen as fields of aesthetic realization? Furthermore, the grounded appropriation of new technology and new devices may open new possibilities for expression, or recombinations of old ones, which the dominant culture misses because it does not share the same conditions and contradictory pressures of that which is to be explained or come to terms with.

Dramatic aesthetics. Dramaturgy and poetics occur in everyday life, in social presence, encounter, and event. They may be invisible in the routinized roles of adult life, but the young have much more time, and they face each other with fewer masks. They are the practical existentialists. They sometimes have no choice but to be, too often, absorbed in the moment. For them some features of social life may not be about the regulation and containment of tension, but about its creation and increase. The aimless life of groups and gangs may be about producing something from nothing, from doing nothing. It may be about building tensions, orchestrating and shaping their release and further buildups, so that a final catharsis takes with it or changes other tensions and stresses inherent in the difficulties of their condition. Making a pattern in an induced swirl of events can bring moments of transcendence or transformation, strangely still centers of heightened awareness, the holding of time, control, and insight. It may also be that the reception aesthetics of, for instance, crowds, public spectacle, and sports events may draw on, or parallel, the immanent dramatics of social life itself.

Bodily aesthetics. The shift to the senses is an important emphasis in the notion of a grounded aesthetics. The ways in which the senses are used to control—indeed to be—the body as a medium of expression may be a specific and privileged case. The questions of economy and usefulness and skill all enter into the grounded aesthetics question of how the body is used. Bodily aesthetics would include personal style and presence, certainly dance, and perhaps also large areas of music and performance.

Festive aesthetics. The traditional view of the aesthetic can be profoundly ascetic. Joy, pleasure, and fun can be equated with the common and the vulgar, with a necessary coarseness of form. We are interested to explore the features of pleasure and desire, whether collective or individual, which are fun but also work through aspects of grounded aesthetics to give human meaning and control. Group events, performances, carnivals, parties may all figure here.

Therapeutic aesthetics. These are, perhaps, especially private, symbolic, and expressive therapies for the injuries of life. They work not only because of their musical, literary, or philosophical forms but also because of some associated aesthetic capacity to produce meanings and understandings which were not there before. This may involve internal, imaginative, and spiritual life. It may be in the realm of dream and fantasy; in the realm of heightened awareness of the constructedness and constructiveness of the self; alienation from obvious givens and values; the sense of a future made in the present changing the present; the fear of and fascination for the *terra incognita* of the self. The work of grounded aesthetics may be in the holding and repairing, through some meaning creation and human control even in desperate seas, of the precariousness and fragmentedness of identity whose source of disturbance is outside, structural and beyond the practical scope of individuals to influence.

It is possible to entertain a notion of the artist as one whose full-time work it is to engage with and make explicit grounded aesthetics—making special and further heightening the everyday and practiced sources of creative meaning. But this should not be our starting point. It is, if anything, not at the center but at the periphery of our concerns. It may certainly be argued that the traditional function of the artist and the traditional notion of aesthetic realization are in the production and appreciation of a refined aesthetics in things, texts, and artifacts from the raw materials of grounded aesthetics.

But this is a practice which covers its own roots: the periphery of the field pretending to be at its center, thus disorienting the whole field with respect to its own real cultural practices and functions. Our testing of hypotheses is in trying to uncover and strengthen grounded aesthetics, rather than in the attempt to recover another version of the traditional or classical aesthetics. Besides, it may also be that certain kinds of grounded aesthetics in the expressive and communicative activity of disadvantaged groups exercise their use and economy in *precisely eluding and evading formal recognition*, publicity, and the possible control by others of their own visceral meanings. In this case, the continuous search to identify and systematize grounded aesthetics is, by definition, doomed to endless labor—for the aesthetic will be wherever it isn't.

Nevertheless, a recovery of some conventional aesthetics and of full-time artistic practice might be results of this inquiry. But this recovery would be a critical recovery in the sense that the autonomous, ahistorical, value of art would not be assumed. Such value would have to be made to work and to show its relevance to the grounded concerns of much wider groups without any guarantee, or even likelihood, in advance, of its success.

Perhaps the greatest barrier to be understood and overcome concerns the institutionalization referred to earlier, not just in the physical and organizational separation of art, though this is involved, but in the internal hyperinstitutionalization of art. This is the process whereby the merely formal features of art become the guarantee of its aesthetic, rather than its relevance to, relation to, and total effect on (including its contents as activated meaning by and to receivers) real life processes and concerns.

Indeed, aesthetic effects do rely to some degree on specifiable formal features of an expression or communication, but this has substance and effect only because of its dynamic and creative embeddedness in daily life processes. Cultural practices involve, to be sure, symbolic representations, and part of their creativity is in the critical and creative transformation of these representations. But representational work cannot claim the distinction of a creative aesthetics unless it is in some real productive relationship to what is represented and embedded in a process of consciousness and meaning making—categories which may not be internally coded but are in part a result of, for instance, what we earlier called "reception aesthetics."

In the hyperinstitutionalization of art, this work of aesthetic appreciation is so atrophied as to make culturedness only the knowledge of form, expressions, and artifacts as inert things. Aesthetic communication can become an assembly of clever allusions and of wholly self-contained artistic cross references. Though starting in grounded aesthetics, art ends up as a floating aesthetics without its own associated human processes and transformations. Furthermore the floating aesthetics actually conceals its own social process of appreciation which relies to a considerable extent on the prior institution of a liberal arts education to supply the knowledge of the purely formal and internal history of art. The others, the uncultured, merely lack the code, but they are presented and may sometimes understand themselves as ignorant, insensitive, and without the finer sensibilities of those who really appreciate.

So the hyperinstitutionalization of art is very divisive, but the ultimate danger, it seems, is in the terminal decadence and growing irrelevance of the separated sign—the appreciation of form for form's sake (aesthetics), with no content or associated creative process. The elite may sit at the opera house knowing all the allusions, references, formal differences, and internal histories of what they see and hear—knowing only too well that others do not know these things . But they may simultaneously be bored through and through with the institutional shell emptied of the creative meaning which was once its grounded aesthetics and *raison d'etre*. Apart, perhaps, from some possible immediacy of sensuousness in color and pattern, it is difficult to see that late, modernist avant-gardism has ever enjoyed a grounded aesthetics. The late modernist fine arts may mark the point where aesthetic production itself, never mind its appreciation, has become a wholly formal exercise.

If traditional or conventional aesthetics are to be recovered, it will be in their regeneration of themselves for another generation through the work and social dynamism they offer—respecting what is or may be represented, transformed, or changed, rather than merely the forms of what is represented.

CONCLUSION

The aim of the inquiry can be simply stated. It is to make a provisional reversal in what seems to have become the accepted chain of logic in society—that art produces culture. A comparative or historical view readily grants that different cultures produce different arts. But this awareness has worn very thin in our everyday sense of our own culture. We need to say again: Cultures produce art, only a small part of which is ever recognized.

This prompts questions. What if the cultural forms of everyday existence and identity are made the subject not the object of aesthetics and creative expression? What if we make the working assumption that the young are already engaged in imaginative, expressive, and decorative activities, but they are not recognized? What if the young are seen as already, in some sense, the artists of their own lives?

From the basis of some substantial answers to these questions I hope to make a set of wide-ranging and specific policy recommendations—a platform for discussion and development in the diverse areas of public policies on the cultural industries; training policies, youth policy, and provision; local authority and other provision for the young and for the unemployed; and policies generally for subsidy and support for arts and cultural activities.

The basic policy issue here is this: How is it possible to provide the conditions and the protections which make it more likely that the actual cultural activity of the young is recognized — not least by themselves — and more likely that such activities develop from within, either into new artistic practices or into a confluence with established arts practices. The aim is to inject concern with creative activity — realistic, grounded, and familiar — into *all* youth activity and organizational forms concerned with youth across the board, wherever they may be.

Chapter 8

TELEVANGELISM AS PEDAGOGY AND CULTURAL POLITICS

Peter McLaren and Richard Smith

♦ The emergence of the Christian Right as both a cultural movement and a political force in the United States and in Australia is of immense interest to radical educators. While there has been sporadic debate by left educators about the ways and means of countering the ideological excesses of the Right and its political success, the initiative has been with the Right. The combination of evangelical Christianity with new-style conservative politics has created a formidable educative apparatus that far outstrips the purely religious or the party-political.

Televangelism is in many ways the epitome of the new educative process. Televangelists were the dynamos behind the so-called Born Again politics of the 1980s. Hadden and Swann (1981) maintain that whether or not they directly advocate political involvement, most televangelists remind their audiences on a frequent basis of the collective sins of the nation and the need to repent.

Much of the work dealing critically with the New Christian Right, particularly in education, understandably dwells on the effects of interventions in policy and practice. Christian Right ideology and practice are marked off from the mainstream of liberal/capitalist social practices so that one is seen to effect the other either through agency (Christian state officials) or by implied correspondences (mediated or not). As Bernstein (1986: 205) remarks in another context, such work gives voice to class, race, and gender in various discourses rather than focusing on their media, the structures through which they are communicated.

Our intent in this chapter is to examine televangelism in the United States and Australia as a field of popular cultural relations within a larger social totality that is presently distinguished by a retreat from liberalism and emancipatory social reform. In particular, we are interested in understanding how the appeal of televangelism as a product of the consolidated forces of the New Right, is constituted, both within the text and within the audience.

TELEVANGELISM AS PEDAGOGICAL DISCOURSE

Bernstein (1986) has long been concerned with the production, reproduction, and transformation of culture. In his recent work he addresses the "internal orderings" of the interface between power and knowledge, on the one hand, and forms of consciousness, on the other hand. This interface he calls the pedagogic device which provides an "intrinsic grammar of pedagogic discourse" (Bernstein 1986: 207). Pedagogic discourse and practice are produced by a series of discursive transformations of time, text, and space into acquisition, evaluation, and transmission.

Frow (1986) argues for a conception of discourse which lends itself to this formulation. His position is that two levels of discourse can be distinguished, universes of discourse and genres of discourse. For our purposes, we use pedagogic discourse and genres interchangeably. Frow's first term is coextensive with society, consisting of a number of distinct but general discourses, each with its own modes of authority and relation to the distribution of power. He lists religion, education, family, and others as being relatively autonomous semantic domains, with their own forms of referentiality and figurality (Frow 1986: 67). Subjects, in the most general sense, are constructed in the overlap and contradictions within and between these domains.

The second level is concerned with the normatively structured sets of formal, contextual, and thematic features or rules that are characteristic of ways of speaking in particular situations. As social practices, they produce what is taken to be "proper" meaning, appropriate speech, and action, in particular settings. Rules in this sense are selection principles that govern the content and processes of social settings, the relations of power and solidarity between speakers, and the semantic medium. These Frow refers to as field, tenor, and mode, respectively (1986: 68). In Bernstein's (1986: 209) formulation, distributive rules delimit what is and what is not thinkable and who may transmit "what to whom and under what conditions," while decontextualizing rules provide the mechanism for a genre to appropriate concepts from a discourse and to relocate them in a new setting.

The importance of genre, embedded in universes of discourse, is that every text participates in one or several genres, although not irreducibly identified with any one. What Bernstein and Frow have in mind is the intertextuality of discourse. Thus, pedagogic discourse is fundamentally a set of principles for embedding and relating discourses, a principle of delocating a discourse from its substantive practice and relocating it "according to its own principle of selective re-ordering and focusing" (Bernstein 1986: 210). Speakers (writers) enter discourse by way of the subject positions presupposed by these principles in the structure of the genre. In this metonymic transformation of reordering, the original discourse becomes an imaginary subject, signifying something other than itself, even as pedagogic discourse remains a recontextualizing principle, a genre. But, the kind and degree of the implicit presuppositions given by field and tenor are always connected to other discourses. Thus:

> By establishing the limits of the sayable, genre allows the unsaid to be said without being uttered, that is, without the speakers taking responsibility for the enunciation of the message. (Frow 1986: 78; emphasis added)

Serving as a critical resource in mobilizing the New Christian Right as a major social movement in America and Australia during the last quarter of a century, televangelism continues to play a crucial role in the decontextualization and relocation of the social text, the shaping of ideologies (Hadden 1987). Why has the para-Christian message become such a powerful pedagogical discourse in the service of the New Right's political agenda? To answer this question, it is important to gain some insight into televangelism's ability to appropriate and ideologically inject its morality into the public sphere.

We will attempt to address this issue from the perspective of televangelism's revivalist style that has descended historically from American preaching dating back to the Second Great Awakening (c. 1820–1860) and to its current replacement of dispensational premillennarianism with postmillennarianism (the dominion creation myth). We will also examine the New Christian Right's ability to colonize the cultural space vacated by liberal ideology that attempted to relegate morality to the private sphere (Stahl 1987: 83). To understand fully the effects (i.e., pedagogical effects) of televangelism on its viewers, televangelist communication will also be examined as part of an ideological apparatus in which meanings are both encoded and decoded within a larger social formation.

THE NEW CHRISTIAN RIGHT AS A SOCIAL MOVEMENT

The resurgence of the Christian Right in America and Australia and the emergence of fundamentalist-evangelical television ministers can be seen as a product of the sociohistorical changes in the post-1960s era. Alberoni (1984: 41), in his discussion of social movements, describes the experience which enables people to recognize themselves as having consciousness of kind, and "alternative interpretation of reality" or the "nascent state":

The nascent state is an exploration of the limits of the possible within a given type of social system, in order to maximize the portion of experiences and solidarity which is realizable for oneself and for others at a specific historical moment. (emphasis in the original)

Alberoni argues that the nascent state emerges because of the coincidence of certain structural preconditions and the deliberate intervention of "missionaries, agents, or agitators." The former are those circumstances where single persons and collectivities experience *sui generis* authentic contradictions between what they desire in everyday and institutional life and what is, so that the latter becomes intolerable.

This is the "fundamental experience," which, in Alberoni's view, is more likely to occur in persons and groups whose social location lies between the privileged and the exploited, a condition which fits Berger's (1967) depiction of Christian fundamentalists, evangelicals, and pentacostals. In 1970, such a a view was probably justified. They had shut themselves off from the mainstream of American and Australian society by their negation of the Other, defined as empty, futile, or apostate (Knight 1978). To this extent, the fundamentalist end of the Christian religious spectrum existed as a "religious mentality" with an essentially negative view of the surrounding society and was perceived by mainstream religions as being on the edge of ecclesiastical tradition and, in Cardwell's 1985 assessment, of doubtful social respectability.

The concept of the nascent state is simultaneously personal and collective, so that its emergence is connected to fundamental social changes. In broad terms, such change can be identified in America and Australia as the collapse of the liberal settlements of the 1960s and 1970s within an historically contested national identity. In Australia, particular constructions of the British heritage and its concomitant cultural values and political arrangements have been challenged so that there have been enduring contradictions between a "conservative and comprehensive assent to the prevailing historical conditions," and an accelerating pace of change in "dominant structures" (Turner 1986: 143). Similarly, in America, the shifting trade balances and the role of Superpower have emphasized the notion of the nation.

The potential for challenges to lifestyles and traditions arose from the conjuncture of certain major social, cultural, and economic changes. First, the impact of the cultural revolution of the 1960s and after, with its permissive lifestyles and civil disobedience, was particularly marked in both countries. At the same time, culminating in the Whitlam era in Australia, the state was used to secure liberal reforms around demands for equality by women, blacks, Aborigines, and other disadvantaged sectors through legislation and the provision of resources. By the late 1970s, the welfare state and its liberal cultural politics had sparked an increasingly well-organized reaction from political conservatives and fundamentalist Christians who were able in some cases to have school courses and textbooks banned from public schools and have waged an unceasing campaign against the permissiveness engendered by the modest reforms of the 1970s (Smith and Knight 1978, 1981).

Second, in the 1970s, due to a convergence of world economic recession, the growth of transnational capital, and the availability of cheaper or more disciplined labor elsewhere, Australia's industrial-manufacturing sector diminished (Knight, Smith, and Chant 1987). High youth unemployment was the surface symptom of economic restructuring, and its consequences included sustained attacks on the social wage (education, health and welfare, programs for the disadvantaged) by right-wing political forces. At the same time, the alliance of capital, the state, and the labor movement (epitomized in the Australian federal government's corporatist settlement with big unions and big business) failed to incorporate farmers, mining interests, the old petty bourgeoisie, land developers, and the new entrepreneurs (the "white-shoe brigade"). These groups fit uncomfortably with transnational and corporate capital and an interventionist state, asserting instead the virtues of individualism, the free market, voluntarism, and self-interest.

The concern for societal cohesion and stability in a period of transition and conflict come not only from the state, in the form of supply-side economics, but also from the common sense of ordinary Americans and Australians. Lasch (1986) argues that the populist appeal of the political Right is to a large extent a reaction to the academic liberal and social democratic programs of the 1970s which were achieved in the courts rather than through legislative processes. In this scenario, the real social crises which we have briefly outlined are concealed by progressive rhetoric that presents the consequences of capitalist organizational forms, family breakdown, for example, as alternative lifestyles. In Alberoni's schema, such issues form authentic contradictions at the level of common sense and, under these conditions, it is likely that regions of subjectivity are changed so that previously disconnected elements of knowledge and emotions are (re)synthesized while some existing connections disintegrate. Hadden and Swann (1981) point to the formation in the late 1970s and early 1980s of a coalition between diverse fragments of antiabortion, profamily, anti-ERA, and other positions. These individuals and groups found affinity in their anger about what was happening in the United States and Australia, focused particularly on abortion, pornography, and a weariness with being labeled the "lunatic fringe."

It is not surprising, then, that in both America and Australia the overall project of the Christian Right is restoration — of morality, of the dignity of the family, of the fear of God and Jesus's Second Coming to all sinners, and of the nation's past (Hadden and Swann 1981: 85). The nation, founded by God to carry out His purposes in defeating the anti-Christ in the form of secular humanism, socialism, communism, and a host of other social, cultural, and political evils, is mythologized in both America and Australia as the "traditional way of life." The restructuring of fields of experience oriented to the new ends of liberation from liberalism, enlightenment through God's word, and self-determination to live according to these ends is the basis of a shared affinity on the part of millions of Americans and Australians and which, in their view, sets them apart from liberal academics and other conspiratorial forces intent on destroying all that is Good, Beautiful, and True.

As such, the New Christian Right serves as a structuring agent related in varying degrees to the felt need of protecting a distinct lifestyle and set of values, based on its interpretation of the teachings of Jesus, from what appears to be the impending threats of secular humanism, the centralization of "big" government, an increase in moral decadence, and a lack of Christian leadership in society at-large.

Citing recent work by Randall Collins, Hadden (1987: 7) maintains that the relatively high level of structural differentiation between "religion and regime" in the United States reveals that the "greater the degree to which modern states legitimate their existence in secular rather than religious foundations, the greater the autonomy of religious institutions to pursue their own interests vis-a-vis the state." As an alternative to secularization theory, Hadden proposes that the "resource mobilization theory" of social movements holds much greater promise for understanding present-day workings of religion in the modern world. Religion, in this view, becomes a resource both to legitimate and to repress social movements which are engaged in the process of social reform, rebellion, or revolution.

The New Christian Right, as a social movement within the United States and Australia, focuses not only on the nature of the moral and political discontent felt by fundamentalist and other religious groups toward the larger society, but also on the resources that facilitated their mobilization from the 1970s onwards.

As Hadden notes, the roots of the New Christian Right as a social movement are buried deep in the tradition of early American religious revivalism. Mid-century religious revivalism, which began as a religious movement aimed at Christianizing the "unwashed masses" and thereby transforming their social character, came closer to resembling the character of a social movement when the revival invaded urban centers. It eventually evolved into a discrete institutional form, differentiated from the denominational structures of American Protestantism. These quasi-autonomous structures, now partially freed from entrapment within any particular Protestant denomination or ecclesiastical authority, developed into private or parachurch structures such as Bible institutes, conferences, and independent missionary societies. Hadden argues that these parachurch structures can be shown to have directly influenced, in both form and content, the organizational model for the contemporary electric church (Frankl 1984; Hadden 1987).

We have described the New Christian Right as a social movement. In the United States, this movement involves organizations such as the Moral Majority, Christian Voice, Religious Roundtable, and the Institute of Religion and Democracy (a neoconservative think tank supported by the American Enterprise Institute); in Australia, the Festival of Light, the League of Rights, the Queensland National Party, STOP and CARE, and the Moral Majority are well known. These organizations frequently attempt to rally conservative fundamentalists to take political action on issues important to them (Johnson et al. 1986: 1). It is certainly the case that the New Christian Right has been vigorous in its promulgation of a public philosophy whose moral charter celebrates the virtues of the nuclear family, defends at all costs the nation's God-fearing cultural tradition, and interprets world events according to a selective, literal reading of the Gospels, yet we do not wish to make the claim that it is a unified political movement.

We do, however, distinguish the New Christian Right from secular New Right groups. The political baptism of the New Christian Right in the 1970s, which saw activist groups target school boards, state administrative offices, abortion clinics, adult bookstores, and adult theaters, was not centrally organized. Nevertheless, such experiences certainly "involved a fusion of religion and politics as the principal matrix of existential commitment" (Hughes 1986: 74), and, broadly speaking, the discursive fields of both televangelism and the New Christian Right are mutually compatible and in some ways mutually constitutive.

THE MOBILIZATION OF RESOURCES

We take the rise of the New Christian Right to be an imposing structuring agent in the making of American and Australian consciousness and society. We identify the ideological aspects of televangelism's discursive field as being constituted not only through theological criteria, such as belief in the literal truthfulness of the Bible, but also through the various related allegiances: to right-wing civil religion; to the notion that the United States and in turn its protectorates (such as Australia and South Africa) are God's instruments in the fight against communism; to untrammeled and unhindered entrepreneurial activity and monopoly capitalist development; and to an adherence to social traditionalism.

Ideological Origins

Rallying around the symbol of the Babylonian Exile (the Soviet Union in particular is identified with Babylon and the anti-Christ), the New Christian Right has secured its ideological link to the secular New Right: "Manifest destiny and America as the New Israel conjoined in a project of renewed capital expansionism, a vigorous anticommunism, a rigid and legalistic social order of purity, and a religion steeped in nationalistic fervor" (Wildman 1986: 115).

To a large extent, the ideological origins of the New Christian Right are deeply grounded in the revivalist view of America as a New Israel. This mythical interpretation of the birth of America adheres to the conviction that the United States has been providentially endowed by God with a special mission in world history (Hadden 1987: 1). This new America, a "light to the nations" (Cherry 1971: vii), is presumed to be guided by a host of saintly men such as Jerry Falwell and Pat Robertson who are saving Americans by constantly directing them to turn to the past in order to embrace the presumed biblical morality of the founding fathers. Jerry Falwell (1980: 25) puts it thus:

> I believe America has reached the pinnacle of greatness unlike any nation in human history because our founding fathers established America's laws and precepts on the principles recorded in the laws of God, including the Ten Commandments. The religious foundations of American find their roots in the Bible.

The New Christian Right is fundamentally concerned with serving as the moral conscience of the country and protecting its biblical roots—which it sees as prominent in American charter documents. This, coupled with an unflinching concern for the protection of family mores, constitutes a reaction to what is sometimes called "a crisis of dominion" (Hadden 1987: 7).

America's special place in God's plan is now apparently in peril as a result of its "unfaithfulness to stewardship, the call for repentance, and the promise of redemption" (Hadden 1987: 7). Thus, Jerry Falwell proclaimed in *Listen America!*, "I cannot keep silent about the sins that are destroying the moral fiber of our nation. As a minister of the gospel, I have seen the grim statistics on divorce, broken homes, abortion, juvenile delinquency, promiscuity, and drug addiction" (1980: 101). This perceived moral crisis in the United States—the dissolution of the morally autonomous ego—gives a specific form to the political culture articulated by the televangelists (Hughes 1986: 78–79. Similar stances can be found in the polemics of the *Queensland Premier* and other New Christian Right publications in Australia.

Fundamentalists hold to the doctrine of premillennialism, which maintains that only Christ's return can save humankind from Satan and his minions. Yet it is an eschatology of defeat and despair (Hadden 1987: 17). In the 1970s, it was obvious that premillennialism was running in sharp contradiction to the dominion creation myth, the postmillennial belief that God has a special providential plan for the United States. The dominion creation myth was reinforced throughout the nineteenth century by the doctrine of free will, which encourages individuals to take up the struggle against Satan. Strains of both premillennialism (which emphasizes individual salvation before it is too late) and the dominion creation myth (which stresses social transformation), which exist in the preaching of Falwell and other evangelicals, have caused a tension in the New Christian Right. As Hadden notes, "The tension between engagement and disengagement (in the problems of society) is a struggle that goes on not only between groups within the fundamentalist and evangelical sectors, but also involves a personal struggle to discern God's will" (1987: 18).

As exemplified by Falwell, the New Christian Right views all of America's military and industrial endeavors as an extension of the message of Jesus. In this regard, it also bears an ideological affiliation with some Catholic New Right groups (see Sullivan 1987: 62). The New Christian Right's real, as distinct from mythical, agenda—especially as manifested in its critique of the interventionist state, its attempts to revitalize a politically active citizenry, and its view of mass consumption and communication as the dissolution of the autonomous ego—can be compared in some ways to the current political project of the Left (Hughes 1986: 72). Yet once we move past these broad critical generalities, such a comparison rapidly breaks down. But the New Right has certainly been more successful on a national scale in mobilizing bias towards its own ends.

Marketing the Word of God

While we agree that the impact of the New Christian Right on voting behavior during the 1980 and 1984 presidential elections was greatly exaggerated by the media and by the New Christian Right itself (Johnson and Tamney 1982; Johnson and Shibley 1985), we nevertheless acknowledge that the current political strength of the New Christian Right is felt most acutely in its ability to set a political agenda and in its capacity to "create a new social construction of reality" (Stahl 1987: 82; Knight, Smith, and Chant 1987).

The New Christian Right possesses the power *to nominate the agenda for contemporary political discourse*, a power manifest most strongly in the electronic church, whose call for salvation is effectively backed up by direct mail techniques and telephone banks—what Hadden (1987) refers to as the "living room social movement." The political agenda for the New Christian Right grows out of what Hughes calls a "double strategy for cultural space" (1986: 86) involving the mass media and the legislation for personal morality for the purposes of creating a "disciplined citizen" (1986: 86). In Hughes's (1986: 86) words, "This will reconstruct the Nation of America as a political unity which can once again be strong and disciplinarian (paternal) at home and in relations with the rest of the world."

The political agenda of the New Christian Right is especially evident in such political efforts as introducing the Family Protection Act of 1981 (S. 1801 and H. R. 6028). Numerous sections of this act trivialize complex issues over which experts disagree and research evidence is inconclusive. These include: parental notifications of minors receiving contraceptive devices or abortion-related services; restricting federal involvement and funding for child-abuse prevention; restricting federal involvement and funding for spouse-abuse prevention; tax exemptions for married couples for childbirth or adoption, but not for single parents, even for adoption; prohibiting busing for racial quotas or desegregation purposes; and free exercise of religion, expressly school prayer (Goettsch 1986: 451). This legislation is but one of many instruments of purity designed to establish a patriarchal society that reduces children's and women's control over their physical and reproductive lives.

Of more immediate concern to educators is, of course, the New Christian Right's ongoing challenge to the public schools; this has a significant impact on pedagogical practices, ranging all the way from the textbooks that teachers are permitted to use in their classrooms to how, in science classes, they must account for the origins of humankind.

Colonizing the Moral Void

The New Christian Right has taken advantage of the moral void in the public sphere left by the retreat of interest-based, marketplace liberalism and pluralist pragmatism, which relegates morality to the private sphere and abandons the common good for free choice in the marketplace. Morality that has been reduced to freedom of choice within marketplace ideology means that the freedom to choose among various beliefs, values, ideas, and morals is privileged over the moral basis of what is being chosen.

According to Stahl (1987), there are four basic contradictions in the New Christian Right's moral teachings which make it inadequate for the teaching of the common good or for replacing the moral vacuum exacerbated by the retreat of liberalism. The first contradiction is the way in which the New Christian Right bases its authority on the Bible at the same time as its teachings are not biblical; the preachers are often cavalier as they frequently engage in "prooftexting" – hunting through the Bible to find a passage which they take out of context in order to fit their preconceived notions. Stahl offers the example of feminism. While New Christian Right spokespersons like Falwell can argue that "many women have never accepted their God-given roles. They live in disobedience to God's laws and have promoted their godless philosophy throughout our society" (1980: 30), the scriptural warrant for such a position is often taken from the "household codes" incorporated from popular Stoicism into several of the late epistles. Predictably, the tradition of women prophets (Stahl 1987: 84) – Miriam, Deborah, or Esther – is completely ignored. When Falwell claims that the free-enterprise system is clearly outlined in the Book of Proverbs, Stahl claims that he is lying and quotes Callum (1985: 15) as arguing that "the primary standard the Bible gives us for judging any economic issue is the priority of the poor. The righteousness of a people is to be seen in how they treat the weakest member of society."

The second contradiction is that the New Christian Right actually supports the causes of many of the social problems it publicly opposes. Televangelists exhort against child abuse, family breakdown, drug addiction, alcoholism, and suicide, but they offer no explanations for the dynamics of modern social change because to do so would reveal the oppressive workings of the capitalist industrial system; it would mean examining inflation, interest rates, and unemployment and their effects on family income and stability. This is particularly evident in the agendas of political pressure groups such as the Australian Free Enterprise Foundation.

The third contradiction can be found in the New Christian Right's condemnation of individualism. In its approach to individualism, the New Christian Right returns a good portion of the ideological baggage it purports to overturn. In reality, the New Christian Right's morality is built on individualism. But, as Pankhurst and Houseknecht (1983: 6) make clear, it is an old-style individualism stressing adult male prerogatives which, in its clash with a more inclusive new individualism, reveals a struggle between patriarchy and egalitarianism. Morality in this view consists of individuals refraining from vice. Thus, the moral issues targeted by the New Christian Right are abortion, homosexuality, pornography, and drugs; poverty, environmental protection, and social and economic justice – which fall outside the bounds of refraining from temptation – are rarely, if ever, addressed. By far the greatest omission in the moral discourse of the New Christian Right is a recognition that sin must be understood in more than personal terms. Sin has both personal *and* social, historical, and structural dimensions; individuals do not simply fall victim to their sinful nature but are also the victims of larger social sins involving the exploitative relations brought about by late monopoly capitalism as well as sexism, racism, ecological destruction, and political and economic repression (McLaren 1987). Redemption, too, has both private and socially transformative dimensions. It does not simply speak to personal salvation or to a privileged community of "the saved," but also implies the transformation of existing conditions of oppression at work in larger sociocultural contexts (Ibid.).

The fourth contradiction cited by Stahl involves a morality that is depoliticized and invasive and a willingness among members of the New Christian Right to impose its moral authority. This can be readily seen in its paranoid dualism. On the side of good is the "moral majority" and on the side of evil is communism or anything else the New Christian Right chooses to disagree with. Within the logic of this moral teleology of apocalyptic thought, liberals, feminists, and the peace movement all suffer damnation by association. Such moral extremism forecloses the concept of moral prudence and creates a climate ripe for fanaticism and terror. Here we enter the practice of what Michael Rogin (1987: 284) refers to as "political demonology," a countersubversive territory in which the foes of the New Christian Right are transformed into the alien, the baleful Other.

David Wildman (1986: 115–16) links the moral vision of the New Christian Right to an attempt to restore a priestly part to American politics based on the lessons of the Babylonian Exile. While the American Catholic bishops in their critique of capitalism have also drawn upon themes that emerged from the Babylonian Exile, such as those of liberation and reform, the New Christian Right emphasizes its legalistic, hierarchical, puritanical, and nationalistic aspects. The New Christian Right's attempt to restore purity to society rests on the moral claim that God's will must be theocratically imposed, since in doing God's will there is no need for the democratic process. At its heart lie two idols: the national security state and capitalist economic relations.

In fact, capitalist economic relations and the logic of the commodity most inform the model of morality embraced by the New Christian Right. It is a morality reduced to a form of exchange, one that has evolved from the immediacy of irrational emotional responses in a commodified culture devoid of transcendence and rational thought. Hughes describes such a morality as "based on a market objectification of the ego" (1986: 82). Thus Robert Schuller, in his Christmas 1986 "Hour of Power" show, asked, "What should be the Christian attitude to money?" He dismissed the claims that money is "intrinsically evil and in fact the pursuit of money is a most un-Christian motive" and "contradictory to the essentials of Christian faith." His position is: "I can't subscribe to that." Instead, he argues that money makes charitable acts possible. The screen caption was "The poor cannot help the poor," while Schuller proclaimed, "Christians should make all the money you can. I like that." He drew on the words of John Wesley to add that a Christian should "save and invest wisely all the money you can" and "give all the money you can." The body of this argument is then secured:

> You and your money—if you have nothing you can be happy but I encourage you at Christmas time to pick the kind of faith that can help you to believe in a God who believes in you and unless a commitment on your part to a career or to people or to other values leaves you with no time to manage your own finances toward accumulating greater wealth, I would say "Boy!...try to make more money than you are...try to take what you've got and make it go further...." [screen caption: "The pride of earnership is even greater than the pride of ownership"].

TELEVANGELISM AS DEATH WISH

A particularly disturbing characteristic of the New Christian Right, one that informs the direction of its pedagogy, is that many key figures in the Republican Party—including high-ranking government and military personnel—use the Bible as a chronometer of history and subcribe to a variation of "immanent rapture/holocaust," in which the "purifying violence" of nuclear war is perceived as part of God's plan. Of course, true believers will be instantly teleported to heaven by Jesus, just prior to the apocalyptic showdown (Jones and Sheppard 1986). Martin Gardner (1987: 23) captures the logic of this position in the following expression: "The war is inevitable, so let's get it over with and maybe we shall be among those who escape death by being levitated above the clouds." Public sentiment like this, when expressed by the leader of the most powerful nation on earth, can be unnerving—and potentially fatal. Consider the following remarks made by Ronald Reagan at a 1971 dinner:

> Everything is falling into place. It can't be too long now. Ezekiel says that fire and brimstone will be rained upon the enemies of God's people. That must mean that they'll be destroyed by nuclear weapons. They exist now, and they never did in the past. Ezekiel tells us that Gog, the nation that will lead all of the other powers of darkness against Israel, will come out of the north. Biblical scholars have been saying for generations that Gog must be Russia. What other powerful nation is to the north of Israel? None. But it didn't seem to make sense before the Russian revolution, when Russia was a Christian country. Now it does, now that Russia has become communistic and atheistic, now that Russia has set itself against God. Now it fits the description of Gog perfectly. (Cited in Gardner 1987: 23)

TELEVANGELISM AS POPULAR CULTURE

As a popular culture text, televangelism resonates with the lived experiences of groups by offering the promise of new forms of sociality which celebrate hard-driving entrepreneurial values, an ethos of competitive individualism, and a fervent anticommunism. The popular positionality of televangelism grants it the identity of the "people's religion."

The aspect of popular culture relations that is most linked to televangelism's appeal to its viewers is its ability to speak in a language and tradition that is familiar, that resonates with "an informal knowledge of the everyday, based on the sensory, the immediate, the pleasurable and the concrete" (O'Shea and Schwartz 1987: 104). Many of the viewers who attend the electronic church in the chapel of their living rooms are undoubtedly already familiar with the revivalist style of preaching—its emotionally charged restricted code, its familiar political language, its domestic ideology, its expropriation of personal experience, its appeal to a false sense of human agency, and its standard format as both a religious and an entertainment "spectacle"—from their own past as churchgoers. Martin notes that the audience for religious broadcasts is composed overwhelmingly of people who are already Christians, and repeated studies such as the recent Annenberg/Gallup poll (Gerbner 1984) revealed that a high proportion of those who claim to have been converted by a media minister later acknowledge that they were, in fact, already Christians and attending church on a regular basis at the time of their conversion. Televangelism as a popular genre is thus constructed out of the cultural histories of its viewers.

As Ann Gray (1987: 31) notes:

> The cultural resources which are available to individuals and from which their

particular cultural competencies are gained can be seen as major determining factors in the choices of popular genres which people make.

Televangelism secures its hegemony as a popular religion through a ritual condensation of its basic messages and through a particular restricted code used by evangelical preachers and known by many of its viewers. The telecast becomes a means of representing the audience to itself in a highly traditionalist form; the roots of the message are linked to the language of the underdog—the alcoholic, the unemployed, the adulterer, the sinner. The essentially restricted code of television, in which a wide range of signifiers is used to represent a limited range of signifieds, works well because it resonates with the semiotic universe of the viewer's past and present life circumstances. Grossberg (1987: 41) states that "the 'popular,' whatever its economic and ideological effects may be, seems to work at yet another level (the affective) and, in fact, the very notion of popularity (which entails certain kinds of investment of energy, e.g., enjoyment) seems to signal the unequal—and perhaps even unusual—weight of the affective."

To the extent that the telecast is able to create an affective alliance with the lived culture of a constituency of its viewers, we can discuss televangelism as a form of popular culture, although it is safe to say that televangelism often elides the distinction between popular and mass culture.

Popular culture, in this view, becomes an arena of exchange between the culture and ideology of dominant and subordinate social groups. The various cultural and ideological exchanges that take place do so through cultural forms that include articulations of mass media—radio and television in particular—and constitute "points of confluence" between oppositional and dominant cultures (Bennett 1986: 19). The effects of popular culture formations are hardly nominal; they necessarily account for "the changing balance and relations of social forces" throughout the history of popular classes (Hall 1981: 227).

The power of the electronic church not only resides in its claim to familiarity, i.e., its ability to resonate with the popular lived sentiments of its audience, but also in its complex articulations, i.e., its sophisticated technological infrastructure. Possibly, without the support of the telephone and computer, televangelism could not support itself. As Derrick de Kerckhove (1982: 259) notes:

It is the conjunction of all these related technologies which must be examined as the total ground from which grows televangelism. In short, the television set presents the evangelist, the telephone enables his organization to mount a "call-in" and "telecounselling" operation, and the computers provide the facility for a "direct mailing" system which makes person-to-person appeals for donations. This quasi-organic process supplies the evangelist's organization with the funds necessary to ensure the whole operation's survival and growth.

The medium of television allows televangelists to establish innovative communication feedback loops with their audiences and to master parapersonal communication by directly talking into the camera and acting as though viewers were part of the minister's own family (see Hadden 1987). In fact, the "wiring" of the Church has created a new type of intimacy and affective structure. Over a decade ago Marshall McLuhan pointed out that the introduction of the public address system in the Catholic Church played a significant role in the replacement of the Latin mass with the vernacular because it forced the celebrant to turn around and face the audience – a turning away, so to speak, from the dead letter to the living audience, from "reading" the word to communicating with the congregation (de Kerckhove 1982: 258–59). The new electronic media that now wire the evangelistic telecasts have literally reprocessed their viewers as spectators, which is what McLuhan meant when he claimed that the real content of any medium was its user (De Kerckhove 1982: 260). It should come as little surprise that televangelists have greater unrestrained access to media than any other interest group in American (see Hadden and Swann 1981).

Televangelism: Exoticizing the Mundane

One common rhetorical device used by televangelists in their broadcasts is popular appeal to everyday miracles. Several centuries ago, philosopher David Hume argued that one can only accept an event as a miracle if the likelihood of the event proving true is greater than the likelihood of the claimant's account proving false. If it is more likely that the claimant is lying, deceived, deluded, or mistaken than it is that the laws of nature have been violated, then one has a good cause for rejecting the claim that a given occurrence is indeed a miracle. Hume's argument, it must be emphasized, was directed against the traditional notion of the miraculous as supernatural intervention in the normal actions of nature. Many of today's televangelists, however, argue that the miraculous may have nothing to do with the notion of nature deviating from its regular patterns; rather, televangelistic miracles involve personal salvation, athletic victories, successful business ventures, and reunions with lost pets (McCarron, in press).

According to Gary McCarron, if a Christian athlete claims a miracle in the success of his team, there is no point in putting Hume's formula to the test, for it is not more likely that the claimant is lying or in error than it is that the event took place. McCarron writes that "televangelistic miracles escape the sting of Hume's critique by simply being so ordinary." He calls these miracles "contingency miracles." Contingency miracles, in which no law of nature is said to have been breached, can be contrasted with violation miracles, those which refer to the transgression of a natural law, such as the parting of the Red Sea. Whereas violation miracles are event oriented, contingency miracles are interpretation oriented and describe events which defy probability or seem too remarkable to explain as coincidences.

As McCarron makes clear, contingency miracles are miraculous only because the believer interprets them that way. For instance, a couple in financial difficulties write a check to the 700 Club and mail it away, trusting to Pat Robertson's Kingdom Principles that there exists a law of reciprocity by which those who tithe regularly will be blessed *by God* with rewards that exceed the extent of their donation. A week later they discover that the IRS has mailed them a check for tenfold what they sent to Pat Robertson and claim this to be a miracle. In the minds of the couple, they did not send a donation to Pat Robertson and then receive a check in the mail; they received a check in the mail *because* they sent a donation to Pat Robertson. In McCarron's view, this represents a contingency miracle with a very plain and discernible cause, and there is no way the secular critic can dissuade the couple from the causal analysis they have decided on. To evoke contingency miracles constitutes for the televangelist a powerful means to acquire both financial and emotional currency from their viewers. It is another way to make the mundane events of lived meaning miraculous and exotic; it inflates the everyday and platitudinous to apocalyptic significance.

Televangelism as Pleasure

In classical film narrative, the spectator is positioned as a subject within the fictional world. Identification is established by the spectator's desire to submit others (people and objects) to a "controlling gaze" (scopophilia). The gaze of a character within this fictional space displaces the spectator's identification from camera gaze to character gaze and intensifies our scopophilic viewing pleasure by the continual relocation of our look within the fictional world as we participate in the changing point of view of the characters (Mulvey 1975). Caughie (1981: 28) writes that in the process of watching television, the spectator is freed from the type of fictional space that is created in the classical film narrative. Rather, "the spectator *watches* television (in a way quite different from the *look* in cinema) without being lost in it" (quoted in Corcoran 1984: 149). Voyeuristic pleasure associated with watching classical film narrative (the social voyeurism or "look of power") can thus be contrasted with the emphasis within TV viewing on the perspective of the writer, the script, and the performer—a process which privileges the point of view of the author or the director of the telecast.

Signification and signifying possibilities invade the textual territory of the televangelistic telecast and are controlled by its semiotic coding. The semic codes—those which operate as an agency for inscribing power relations—act as *epistemological strategies* which repetitively express themselves as binary oppositions: good/evil, heaven/hell, secular/religious, secular humanism/word of God. In the mouth of televangelists such as Swaggart and Schuller, the truth gets reduced to trite, fallacious either/or distinctions which are used as weapons to undermine the potency of denial or refutation. More than anything else, the televangelist fears the indeterminate text.

Religious meanings are most often anchored to a transcendental signified, and the televangelist often encourages master symbols (e.g., Christ)
to bleed their meanings into other, less potent symbols. Christ becomes the
secular banker ("Send us your support") or the patriot ("Love America") or
the good Republican (vote for Judge Bork, "John for PM," fight "ungodly
communists") – or all of these mixed together. There is always a centrifuging
force, an overdetermination, among the multiple symbols and their various
meanings produced by the moral authority of the televangelist which encourages the viewer to choose good over evil, the soul over the body,
salvation over damnation, patriarchy over equality, humility over pride, Christ
over anti-Christ, love over hate, the symbolic over the imaginary, and free
enterprise over communism.

In other words, when televangelism interpolates its listeners as God-
fearing Americans, traces of other discourses, such as patriotism, the
sanctity of the family, and private property, are connoted. Consequently,
televangelism is able to yoke often contradictory ideologies through the
construction of equivalent meanings tied to both religious articulations and
the concrete specificity of capitalist productive relations. There often occurs
a curious confluence of biblical and market objectifications. Moral choice
becomes linked with free choice within the capitalist marketplace, and the
good Christian life becomes embodied in the patriarchal family. These
distinctions, the meanings of which interpenetrate each other, become
blurred, leveled, or naturalized. In this way, televangelism is able to associate
the symbols of salvation with those of democratic capitalism.

Reality in the televangelistic telecast is arranged according to certain
discursive conventions which position the viewers so that they can readily
identify themselves in the performance. They see their own lives scripted
into Swaggart's or Schuller's text. He is really just one of them, speaking to
others "just like themselves." Thus, televangelism fills out the sovereign
category of the individual through the particular codes and conventions
which govern the broadcast.

Getting Macho with the Devil

Although somewhat subdued since the revelations of his sexual relations
with a prostitute, Jimmy Swaggart has a way of strutting on the stage like a
raging bull, flailing his arms, railing against Satan and the nonfundamentalist
denominations, breaking into tears, tickling the piano keys, and stomping
his right leg to the Nashville beat of a band pounding out a gospel hymn. It
is a saucy, machismo-style display of "takin' on" the devil. But at just the
right moments, the pulpit pounding is tempered by an emotional display of
tears running down Swaggart's substantial cheeks. From a maudlin wail, he
will instantly shift gears and work himself into a fever pitch while the audience
screams "Hallelujah! Praise the Lord!" followed by another abrupt discursive
shift. "Let me get my composure [tears streaming down his cheeks]....

God's coming back on silver clouds of glory!" An impassioned face turns and looks directly at the camera, followed by a swirling torso and a finger pointed directly at the lens. "Do I upset you? Do I trouble you?"

Swaggart is particularly adept at repeating phrases, at pointing his finger in the air, jabbing the ceiling, and then swooping his finger down and thrusting it at the audience. He will take off his eye glasses, hold them aloft in his hand, and gesture with the frame. Repetitive gestures and phrases, combined with the show's standard format, tend to stabilize the semiotic field of the performance: signified becomes anchored. Swaggart will often switch moods rapidly, also part of the repetitive and pleasure-producing nature of the performance. During one telecast (before his own sexual relations with Debra Murphree were disclosed to the public) he made a joke about asking for money (the Jim and Tammy Bakker scandal then providing the context for such jokes), after which he shed tears over the thought of those who were going to go to hell if they didn't accept Jesus as their savior: "If you do not warn them they will die in their iniquity!"

At this moment, Jimmy Swaggart becomes a Prime Knower, the ordained one who protects the viewer from having to make sense of the divine news from heaven; he serves as a unifying subjectivity for his message, which can range anywhere from a damnation of desire and the flesh to a gushy celebration of the power of holy love. It is important to recognize that Swaggart's popularity is not produced in the manner of the movie star, a process which is based on "the distanced, the exceptional, the idealized, the archetypal, to be contemplated and revered, standing outside the realm of the familiar and the routinized" (Corcoran 1984: 137). Rather, Swaggart's popularity is based on the systematic tendency of the television personality to construct and to foreground intimacy and immediacy; it is grounded in the ordinary, the everyday character who is "part of life," not larger than life (Corcoran 1984: 137). (This is why Swaggart and Bakker are likely to make a comeback.)

Similarly, "Hour of Power" produces complicitious participation among the teacher, the viewer/live audience, and knowledge. The presentation of self perfected by Schuller, including "a smile that can sparkle off the glass walls of his Crystal Cathedral" (Cardwell 1984: 111–12), his use of personal anecdotes and common language forms, and his fatherly appearance, creates an image of neighborliness and evokes the small community. At the same time, his priestly-cum-academic attire and his gesture/bodily movement forms plagiarize cliché movie depictions of the High Priest and learned Guru. His very presence is the intertext of a range of discourses about religion, learning, and Western popular culture.

In this way, televangelists are able to present themselves as "down home, good ol' boys," "nice men." The propensity of television for direct address, eye contact with the spectator, and a reliance on the close-up shot — all optimal conditions for disclosing the inner characteristics of the TV personality — helps Swaggart, Schuller, and others reduce the distance between their message and their image. In Langer's terms, television helps to construct a "pseudo-gemeinschaft" (Corcoran 1984: 137).

The television medium is able to create intimacy through shifting the gaze of the camera from the congregation (the symbolic viewer) to Swaggart (who speaks both to the congregation and directly into the camera). While voyeuristic (scopophilic) pleasure is not as heightened as it would be in a classical narrative film, a qualitatively different kind of pleasure is produced through the structure of the televangelistic format, i.e., through its emphasis on the familiar and already domesticized routine of a church sermon with its reliance on oral and gestural codes familiar to many of the viewers of the televangelistic broadcast (codes which are perfectly suited to the television medium). If Corcoran is correct in the distinction he makes between the gaze of the spectator watching a film and the spectator watching a television production, then it could help us to explain the positioning of the viewer (outside the classical narrative frame) as one of the primary characteristics of the ideological structuring of the televangelistic telecast.

Televangelism transmits its meanings not from some fixed essence or point of origin but through a cluster of complementary and competing discourses — its discursive field — which we earlier argued is produced by the transformation of other available discourses according to the conventions of a particular genre. The authorial voice of televangelism's text, while it may be provisionally challenged by alien subtexts, such as situational ethics, secular humanism, evolutionism, or democratic socialism, is usually subtended by the moral authority, discursive alignments, and power/knowledge configurations structured into televangelism's particular genre.

Corcoran conjectures that the process of television viewing may also produce a different type of hegemonic function from the familiar "active engagement" or "active consensus" of individuals with the dominant sectors of society (articulated by Gramsci in his 1971 *Selections from the Prison Notebooks*) by reducing the audience to a state of passive acquiescence. By minimizing the possibilities for spectator engagement in fictional space, the television broadcast undercuts the potential for empathetic involvement such as that found in the classical cinematic narrative. This reduction of engagement is heightened by the fact that viewers can change channels at will and confront various news telecasts, comedies, or dramas, which tends to create the impression that everything on the screen is of equal importance. This, apparently, positions the viewer as a passive participant in the TV event. Hegemony, in this case, operates as a televised narcotic, creating a society of viewers too disinterested and too emotionally detached to challenge the status quo. He suggests that the rise of the New Right in the United States, with its combination of sexual repression and right-wing authoritarianism, has been helped by the polemical vocabulary of television.

This perspective all too readily underestimates the power of television to create affective alliances with its viewers.

TELEVANGELISM: AFFINITIES AND HEGEMONY

Fredric Jameson has argued that mass cultural texts such as television both release and manage utopian impulses within "a complex strategy of rhetorical persuasion in which substantial incentives are offered for ideological adherence" (quoted in Corcoran 1985: 142). This raises the question of how to conceptualize the nature of the incentives offered by these texts. The crucial issue here is the one posed by Gramsci and deals with the issue of consent. What are the productive and persuasive dimensions of culture in which consent is manufactured? Colin Mercer (1986: 51) frames the question in this way: How has the agenda for consent been organized quite distinctively around ways of *including* (rather than repressing or excluding) people and their pleasures in a common national culture? Following Mercer, we would frame our question thus: What is the nature of our contract—the complex nature of our complicity—with cultural forms such as televangelism? This, of course, points us in the direction of the contradictory *play* of ideology (Mercer 1986: 54). This also raises the question of understanding the nature of the appeal—the "affective nature" —of televangelism through the way in which subjectivities are produced "not just 'in the head' but across the space of the body too" (Mercer 1986: 66). Corcoran's suggestion that television watching produces "passive acquiescence" in its viewers is, in our opinion, mistaken. Such a perspective fails, among other things, to account for the active ways in which complicity and pleasure are mobilized in the electronic church. Such affective investment in televangelism may indeed produce ideological passivity, but this is not necessarily the case.

We feel that a partial explanation can be found in the writings of Lawrence Grossberg that deal with the political economy of affective investment. Though not unproblematic, Grossberg's work allows for the recognition that discursive fields are organized affectively (within a "politics of feeling") as well as ideologically (Grossberg 1986b). According to Grossberg, affect is a resource that can be mobilized. More specifically, he argues that

> affect points to the (relatively autonomous) production of what is experienced as moods and emotions by an asignifying effectivity. It refers to a dimension or plane of our lives that involves the enabling distribution of energies. While it is easy to conceptualize it as the originary (causal) libidinal economy postulated by psychoanalysis, one must avoid the temptation to go beyond its existence as a plane of effectivity. Moreover, affect is not the Freudian notion of disruptive (or repressed) pulsions of pleasure breaking through the organized surfaces of power; rather it is an articulated plane whose organization defines its own relations of power and sites of struggle. (1986a: 73)

Grossberg (1987: 41) is quick to point out that affective economies ("mattering maps") are not equivalent to discourses of pleasure which function as the alibis for sexual deployment. Nor are affective formations which deal with structures of feeling and the texture of lived experience confined to cultural activities such as leisure or romance. Rather, all affective relations, according to Grossberg, are shaped by the materiality and negativity of everyday life. It is important not to confuse affect with the possibility of enablement (e.g., pleasure and excitement) because it may also include boredom and compulsion. It is important, too, to recognize that institutions such as the home and work shape affectivity; affectivity depends on ideological articulations of both the general cultural activities in which affectivity is produced and the specific activity in question. Articulating affect in this way can help to bridge the historical relations between ideological and affective struggles, between resistance and empowerment, that surround mass media and contemporary social struggles.

To use Grossberg's (in press) terminology, we can argue that televangelism mobilizes viewer sentiment by setting up an "affective boundary." This refers to televangelism's relation to the dominant culture, for example, in the way it constructs itself as an enemy of atheism and secular humanism. It also may serve as an "affective alliance," the various ways in which the viewers invest their energy in a vision and experience of *what ultimately matters*. In other words, televangelism may offer its message as a vision and experience of an ultimate telos (e.g., achieving the Kingdom of God on earth), as an experience to be celebrated (e.g., being born again), or as a rejection of the dominant culture to be reiterated (e.g., an attack on premarital sex or abortion). As an "affective structure," televangelism constructs possibilities for emotional intensity which the broadcast can generate through the charisma of the televangelist, the structural format of the show, or the television medium itself.

The affective appeal produced by the televangelistic broadcast is constructed around an affective economy, the axes of which are a condemnation of the Other (the unsaved, or other misguided denominations such as the Catholics), a celebration of sameness, and the emotional intensity produced by the feeling of having been "touched" by the presence of God. During the program, we can literally see and feel the affective investment of the audience as the televangelist celebrates the identity of the congregation and viewing audience as God's Chosen. Such emotional intensity, such affective investments, are not spontaneous and natural but are socially structured, the products of a complex amalgam of discourses and structures which position viewers in particular ways in relation to the telecast.

Part of the pleasure of viewing televangelist performances is related to their emphasis on rhetoric over rationality. De Kerckhove argues that religious broadcasting basically assembles the mainstreams of two distant cultures, the religious mental setting of the preliterate tribe and the mental processing of postliterate culture. He further argues that the viewers of televangelistic shows need little substance and variety to fulfill their mental needs because these needs are basically emotional. He comments that,

in a religious broadcast, no matter how onimous or seductive, the semantic content of a statement has hardly any emotional impact compared with the slightest intonation in the voice of the preacher. In the days when our whole world was translated into books, emotions were under the control of the semantic line of print. A person had to know the meaning of the words before he could have the experience they implied. With radio and television, the experience comes first and the meaning later. (1982: 262)

Grossberg makes clear that good pedagogy produces strong affective investment on the part of the participant. Understanding the pedagogical efficacy of the televangelistic apparatus involves analyzing the contexts within which the relations between the viewers and the televangelist acquire affective, ideological, and political functions. Televangelism, considered in this way, represents as affective difference inscribed in an attempt to abolish the obscenity of secular values. Moreover, it becomes a vehicle for recontextualizing the secular world and at the same time celebrating a relocation of temporal life into the binary oppositions of good and evil. This is not to suggest that contradictions do not exist between contemporary affective organizations and the ideological appeals which attempt to articulate them (Grossberg 1987: 44). For Grossberg, television's most powerful enunciation is its emotionalism, "the fact that it is structured by a series of movements between extreme highs and extreme lows" (p. 43). This could not be more true of the televangelistic broadcast, which often moves from an unbounded celebration of God's glory to acknowledging the eternal damnation of all those who are not saved. An affective economy, marked by such extremes, resonates well with the ideological messages which help to constitute it. The emotional extremes also resonate with the ideological production of equivalences of oppositions such as goodness = Christian = profamily = conservative *versus* evil = homosexuality = feminism = secular humanism = liberal.

Within the discourse of televangelism, lines of affect are constructed around a cosmic battle, whose combatants include God, Satan, angels, and demons—and the viewer. Its power resides in the transcendental signifieds that stabilize its ideological structure, a structure that confers certainty, meaning, and a sense of ultimate purpose. For the viewer, the affective economy of televangelism provides a medium through which multiple subjectivities (the decentered subject) can be collapsed into an unambiguous, *though temporarily unified*, subject. In this way the spectacle of televangelism becomes a cathedral of our desires, invested in affect, in which the mundane external world becomes arrayed with importance and substantiality; after all, televangelism makes viewers prime actors in the drama of good and evil, life and death.

It is inevitable, however, that the affective structurations which give rise to the temporarily totalized subject become contested – ruptured – by the intertextuality of television discourse, that is, by the unbounded nature of the television medium itself. The boundary of a television show is always malleable, always tentative, can always be shattered by the flick of a dial, which can result in other affective structurations becoming mobilized. Not only is television intertextually mediated by other programs, its effects are also determined by multiple subject-positionings (i.e., articulations) and differentially distributed viewer identities – which means that television meanings are constantly being contested. The site at which such an ideological struggle is waged is not the television monitor or the televised image, but the space that exists between the text and its meaning: the interdiscursive space of the viewing subject. It is a space that is only partially autonomous, one which bears the traces of past struggles. It is a colonized space, a structured absence, into which necessity has already been inscribed by the broader field of political, economic, and cultural relations. But it is also a space in which new meanings can emerge.

Generic Forms, Social Texts, and the Public Sphere

Any attempt to understand televangelism as a form of pedagogy must attend not only to its discursive function in the production of meaning, but also to its characteristics as a Christian Right genre which structures the *encounter* between text and reader. Such an encounter cannot be seen as external to the social practice of television viewing, nor can it be seen as removed from power/knowledge configurations in which preferred discourses and readings are constructed. This analysis must attend to the way in which meanings and subject positions are constructed for the viewer, the contradictions inherent in this process, and its political implications, both in its historical sense and in the present act of viewing.

In the 1980s, the dominant ideological principles of Reagan's America and Hawke's Australia are neoliberal. Liberal values, ideas, and practices have been discursively recontextualized so that boundaries are constructed between the people and their adversaries: the young, permissives, feminists, blacks, and so on (Laclau and Mouffe 1985: 170). These years have seen the emergence of a populism based on self-interest, competitive individualism, a reliance on markets, and growth rather than on equity, combined with renewed fervor for nation, family, duty, standards, and "traditional" values. Educational institutions have geared up for the new vocationally oriented students, intent on careers in business and technology and aspiring to entrepreneurship and the property and wealth of private-enterprise heroes (Lekachman 1987). These new values and practices overlap with traditional frontier individualism and enterprise while creating antagonisms around personal life-style issues between older and younger cohorts.

These populist categories and practices provide a further clue to the productivity of televangelism and New Christian Right discourse. It will be recalled that the mode and register of televangelist address are self-consciously that of the "common" *man*. Further, the authority of the text lies in its apparent even-handedness when dealing simultaneously with discursively dangerous issues such as Christian morality, money, and Christmas, or the rich and the poor and wealth. The reality that is finally constructed in the resolution of such issues takes on a strong moral overtone of being theologically appropriate (God approves of this view), while at the same time it is recognizable as being the common-sense experience of the congregation in church and in their (electronic) living rooms. Thus, rather than being a cognitive minority, the congregation is discursively produced and positioned as individual and group exemplars of the majority, as being conventional, right, and proper. The world that lies beyond the performance and the television screen is thereby naturalized and terms relating to the nation, lifestyles, morality, work, and so on become ideological in their effects (Urry 1981: 60–61).

In the final analysis, televangelism must be understood as a form of pedagogy and read with respect to the multiplicity of positions assumed by readers and generated by texts; its meaning can never be reduced to a single level of determination. Rather, the meaning of televangelism can only be grasped by understanding how meanings are produced through an interactive process between viewer and telecast; in this interaction new meanings are generated, struggled over, and constantly reformulated in the historical and contextual specificity of the performance. In effect, it is in this interdiscursive space that televangelism employs a semantic and affective pedagogy that both mobilizes and reconstructs the terrain of ideology and desire. At the same time, viewers operate out of a pedagogy that provides the basis for how they see, learn, and accommodate their own desires and needs. As educators, we need to understand, deconstruct, and reformulate the interests that structure the meaning and possibilities inherent in the desire for community and struggle that televangelism mobilizes. This is not simply a political task, but a pedagogical one as well.

REFERENCES

Alberoni, F.
  (1984)   *Movement and Institution*. New York: Columbia University Press.
Bennett, Tony
  (1986)   "The Politics of the Popular." In T. Bennett, C. Mercer, and J. Woollacott, eds., *Popular Culture and Social Relations*. Milton Keynes: Open University Press.
Berger, Peter
  (1967)   *The Sacred Canopy*. New York: Doubleday.
Bernstein, Basil
  (1986)   "On Pedagogic Discourse." In J. G. Richardson, ed., *Handbook of*

Theory and Research for the Sociology of Education. New York: Greenwood.

Callum, Danny
   (1985)   "The Way America Does Business." *Sojourners* 14 (10).

Cardwell, J. D.
   (1985)   *A Rumor of Trumpets: The Return of God to Secular Society.* Lanham, Md.: University Press of America.
   (1984)   *Mass Media Christianity: Televangelism and the Great Commission.* Lanham, Md.: University Press of America.

Caughie, J.
   (1981)   "Rhetoric, Pleasure and Art TV—Dreams of Leaving." *Screen* 22: 9–31.

Cherry, Conrad, ed.
   (1971)   *God's New Israel: Religious Interpretations of American Destiny.* Englewood Cliffs, N.J.: Prentice Hall.

Collins, Randall
   (1986)   "Historical Perspectives on Religion and Regime: Some Sociological Comparisons of Buddhism and Christianity." In J. K. Hadden and A. Shupe, eds., *Prophetic Religions and Politics.* New York: Paragon House.

Corcoran, Farrell
   (1984)   "Television as Ideological Apparatus: The Power and the Pleasure." *Critical Studies in Mass Communication* 1: 131–45.

de Kerckhove, Derrick
   (1982)   "Televangelism: A Theology for the Central Nervous System." *Communio* (Fall): 258–65.

Falwell, Jerry
   (1980)   *Listen, America!* New York: Bantam.

Frankl, Razelle
   (1985)   "The Historical Antecedent of the Electric Church." Paper presented at the annual meeting of the Society for the Scientific Study of Religion (SSSR), Savannah, Ga.
   (1984)   "Popular Religion and the Imperatives of Television: A Study of the Electric Church." Ph.D. diss., Bryn Mawr College.

Frow, J.
   (1986)   *Marxism and Literary Criticism.* Oxford: Blackwell.

Gardner, Martin
   (1987)   "Giving God a Hand." *New York Review of Books.* August 13, pp. 17–23.

Gerbner, George, et al.
   (1984)   Religion and Television. Summary report of the Annenberg/Gallup Study.

Goettsch, Stephen L.
   (1986)   "The New Christian Right and the Social Sciences: A Response to McNamara." *Journal of Marriage and the Family* 48: 447–54.

Gramsci, Antonio
   (1971)   *Selections from the Prison Notebooks.* Q. Hoare and G. Nowell-Smith, trans. New York: International Publishers.

Gray, Ann
   (1987)   "Reading the Audience." *Screen* 28 (3): 24–35.

Grossberg, Lawrence
(in press) "Rock and Roll in Search of an Audience."
(1987) "The Indifference of Television." *Screen* 28 (2): 28–45.
(1986a) "History, Politics and Postmodernism: Stuart Hall and Cultural Studies." *Journal of Communication Inquiry* 10 (2): 61–77.
(1986b) "Teaching the Popular." In C. Nelson, ed., *Theory in the Classroom*. Urbana and Chicago: University of Illinois Press.

Hadden, Jeffrey K.
(1987) "Religious Broadcasting and the New Christian Right." *Journal for the Scientific Study of Religion* 26 (1): 1–37.
(1984) "Televangelism and the Future of American Politics." In D. G. Bromley and A. Sharpe, eds., *New Christian Politics*. Macon, Ga.: Mercer University Press.

Hadden Jeffrey K., and C. E. Swann
(1981) *Prime Time Preachers: The Rising Power of Televangelism*. Reading, Mass.: Addison-Wesley.

Hall, Stuart
(1981) "Notes on Deconstructing the Popular." In R. Samuel, ed., *People's History and Socialist Theory*. London: Routledge & Kegan Paul.

Hughes, Patrick M.
(1986) "The Contemporary American Crisis in Morality and the New Christian Right." *Old Westbury Review* 2: 71–89.

Johnson, Benton, and M. Shibley
(1985) "How New Is the New Christian Right? A Study of Three Presidential Elections." Paper presented at the annual meeting of SSSR, Savannah, Ga.

Johnson, S. D., and J. B. Tamney
(1982) "The Christian Right and the 1980 Presidential Election." *Journal for the Scientific Study of Religion* 2 (2): 123–31.

Johnson, S. D., J. B. Tamney, and S. Halebsky
(1986) "Christianity, Social Traditionalism and Economic Conservatism." *Sociological Focus* 19 (3): 299–314.

Jones, L., and G. Sheppard
(1986) "On Reagan, Prophecy and Nuclear War." *Old Westbury Review* 2: 9–22.

Knight, J. W.
(1985) "Fundamentalism and Education: A Case Study in Social Ambiguity." *Discourse* 5 (2): 19–38.
(1978) "The World Not Turned Upside Down." Ph.D. diss. Brisbane: University of Queensland.

Knight, J. W., R. Smith, and D. Chant
(1987) "Australian New Right Discourse: The Dominant Ideology Revisited." Paper presented at Sociological Association of Australia and New Zealand Annual Conference, Sydney.

Laclau, E., and C. Mouffe
(1985) *Hegemony and Social Strategy: Towards a Radical Democratic Politics*. London: Verso.

Lasch, Christopher
(1986) "What's Wrong With the Right?" *Tikkun* 1 (1): 23–29.

Lekachman, Robert
(1987)   "Yuppies, Technocrats and Neoliberals." *Dissent* (Winter): 34–45.

McCarron, Gary
(in press) "Lost Dogs and Financial Healing: Deconstructing Televangelist Miracles." *Journal of Popular Culture*.
(1985)   "Literal Truth: A Study of Creationism in American Culture." M. A. thesis. York University, Ontario, Canada.

McLaren, Peter.
(1987)   "Schooling for Salvation: Christian Fundamentalism's Ideological Weapons of Death." *Boston University Journal of Education* 169 (2): 132–39.

Martin, William
(in press) "Mass Communications." *Encyclopedia of Religion in America*.

Mercer, Colin
(1986)   "Complicit Pleasures." In T. Bennett, C. Mercer, and J. Woollacott, eds., *Popular Culture and Social Relations*. Milton Keynes: Open University Press.

Miller, Wesley E., Jr.
(1985)   "The New Christian Right and Fundamentalist Discontent: The Politics of Lifestyle Concern Hypothesis Revisited." *Sociological Focus* 18 (4): 325–36.

Mulvey, Laura
(1975)   "Visual Pleasure and Narrative Cinema." *Screen* 16: 45–60.

O'Shea, A., and A. Schwartz
(1987)   "Reconsidering Popular Culture." *Screen* 28 (3): 104–9.

Pankurst, J. G., and S. K. Houseknecht
(1983)   "The Family, Politics, and Religion in the 1980s." *Journal of Family Issues* 4 (1): 5–34.

Rogin, Michael
(1987)   *Ronald Reagan, the Movie, and Other Episodes in Political Demonology*. Berkeley: University of California Press.

Smith, R. A., and Knight, J. W.
(1981)   "Political Censorship in the Teaching of Social Sciences: Queensland Scenarios." *Australian Journal of Education* 25 (1): 3–23.
(1978)   "MACOS in Queensland: The Politics of Educational Knowledge." *Australian Journal of Education* 22 (1): 225–48.

Stahl, William
(1987)   "The New Christian Right." *The Ecumenist* 25 (6): 81–87.

Sullivan, Edward V.
(1987)   "Critical Pedagogy and Television." In David Livingstone, ed., *Critical Pedagogy and Cultural Power*. South Hadley, Mass.: Bergin & Garvey.

Turner, G.
(1986)   *National Fictions*. Sydney: Allen & Unwin.

Urry, J.
(1981)   *The Anatomy of Capitalist Societies: The Economy, Civil Society and the State*. London: Methuen.

Wildman, David
(1986)   "Resisting Empire: Ethics for Exile in a Latter-Day Babylon." *Old Westbury Review* 2: 107–20.

Chapter 9

ENGENDERING COUPLES: THE SUBJECT OF DAYTIME TELEVISION

Mimi White

Q. Is there one "ultimately right" person for us?
A. No. This is one of the great fallacies surrounding romantic love.

♦ The quotation can be appropriated as a figure for a broader range of sociocultural discourse. The exchange comes from *The Romantic Love Question and Answer Book*,[1] one of dozens — even hundreds — of books dealing with romance, love, intimacy, and marriage and published in the last decade for a mass reading public. In a condensed formulation, this citation expresses many of the assumptions informing the contemporary production of interpersonal relations — especially "the couple" and "the nuclear family" — as an object of investigation. This particular book situates romantic love as an important topic and an organizing theme, even as it purports to demystify and update our understanding of romantic love in line with the demands of modern life.

THE RELATIONSHIP MONSTER[2] AND POPULAR MEDIA

The book casts its investigation in the form of a dialogue, moving between two positions, one speaker expressing a general curiosity, the other expert authority. The familiar tone of conversation, along with the constant shifts in the focus of discussion, encourage the possibility of mobile identificatory positions. Of course, this is only a simulated dialogue. Both the question and the answer are scripted by the book's authors. Through rhetorical sleight-of-hand they give the impression that their answers are not preformulated dogmas, but uncalculated responses to unforeseen questions that someone else raised in the first place. Here, hegemonic expert injunction masquerades as familiar and spontaneous interchange. As a result, the interest in romantic love as an organizing preoccupation, and in the relationship, the couple, and the work required of everyone who participates in these social constructions, is represented as ubiquitous, even natural.

All of this is in turn situated in the larger context of mass-mediated consumer culture. The book is not intended for experts, but for the public at large. It promotes itself in the marketplace by promoting relationships. It sells itself as a product, one among many similar books, which carries potential productive results, helping you (the reader, any reader) to better understand and control romantic affect in your own life. It is also self-reproducing in the sense that it defines a model of interpersonal relations that relies on advice. The expert, the therapist, the analyst, and the professional interlocutor are hereby instated as the preeminent agency of commodified mediations, whether in an office, a newspaper column, a magazine, a book, on radio, or on television.

While the formation and maintenance of personal relations through therapeutic modes of discourse pervades contemporary mass culture, this chapter focuses on television. This emphasis is at once strategic and historical. For television is certainly the pervasive, if not also the dominant, apparatus of popular media in the United States, occupying a position of hegemonic centrality in the habits of everyday life. It is also the most overdetermined cultural apparatus, negotiating a complex range of economic, institutional, social, and cultural practices and interests. As such, a comprehensive understanding of the medium enables — even requires — an examination of how the production of ideological positions and subjectivity(ies) is imbricated with the workings of consumer culture. By the same token this ideological production cannot simply be equated with the production of functional consumer subjects. Moreover, current television programming includes a variety of nonfiction genres and formats in which the couple as a body is produced, probed, and provoked through mediated strategies of confessional and therapeutic discourse. A close analysis of these programs will encourage a more thorough recognition of the complexities and contradictions of this process as an ideological problematic within contemporary television culture.[3] It also provides a context for understanding how variable viewing positions are authorized and circumscribed. For these programs include distanced, derisory, and superior attitudes as acceptable forms of spectatorship, along with the more conventionally imputed positions of involvement, identification, and sympathy. The possibilities for a politics of oppositional viewing are thereby considerably complicated, if not necessarily obviated.

The production of subjectivities and of particular ways of life offers a point of intersection between cultural studies and critical pedagogy. The analysis which follows contributes to an understanding of the function of the popular media in what might be called the pedagogy of everyday life. In these terms it is crucial to account for television's particular modes of meaning and subject production, while recognizing that this production occurs in a broader context of sociocultural activity. In other words, the field of possibilities offered by television intersects with, and is cut across by, other domains of practice and experience in variable and unpredictable ways. The central focus of the analysis is the couple as a common ideological problematic within daytime, nonfiction television. The couple is produced as both the subject and the object of sociocultural currency and is identified as a split body situated in networks of communication. This emphasis is subtended by theoretical perspectives on television and its modes of ideological production. For example, the very networks of communication which situate the couple as a social identity address the viewer as an interlocutor, as a subject of communication, and not simply as a subject of consumption.

ONCE UPON A TIME. . . .

On "The All New Dating Game," "attractive singles"[4] pick a dating partner from a pool of three contestants and are sent on a date by the program. On "Love Connection," couples who have gone out together — one chosen by the other from a preselected videotape pool — discuss their date with host Chuck Woolery. "The New Newlywed Game" and "Perfect Match" are game shows for married couples, who are asked questions about one another and their relationship and win points when one spouse matches the other's

response. "Couples" is a counseling show offering thirty-minute versions of consultation sessions for "real people" with psychiatrist and family therapist Dr. Walter Brackelmanns. "Divorce Court" uses actors in dramatized reenactments of divorce trials based on real cases.

All of these programs are syndicated or air on cable stations across the United States. They are shown on different channels in different markets at different times of day, usually positioned in fringe time, around network programming. They do not comfortably or easily share a genre. The list includes game shows, but also the counseling show (an emergent genre)[5] and the reality courtroom drama (a genre hybrid). Yet each program stages the couple as a social body, a unit in division, comprised of two individuals — two bodies — submitted to networks of exchange and communication. This body is put into play and under analysis, variably mediated through the family, community, medicine (psychiatry), law, economics, and the television apparatus itself.

Together these programs trace a narrative trajectory, marking various stages in the life of the couple as a social body. The story is in one sense absolutely predictable and familiar: the couple meet, date, wed, and divorce. Yet the very repetition of this narrative fixed on these nodal states of being indicates that a couple is neither a natural nor a stable identity. Rather, a couple is constructed as a social identity through elaborate discursive mediations distributed through time, in a sequence of formation, maintenance, and dissolution which is never finalized.

However apparently frivolous or trivial, these programs produce the couple as a body and a site of social currency. The very familiarity of the couple produced through these shows can be related to the uncanny effects of television's modes of production and distribution. "The All New Dating Game," "The New Newlywed Game," and "Divorce Court" are revivals of programs that are strongly identified with the 1960s — before the sexual revolution, the rise of feminism, gay liberation, and the increase in no-fault divorce, concomitant with the growing divorce rate and other social trends that would seem to contravene a fascination with the traditional rituals of courtship and marriage.

These programs now return to us bolstered by the appearance of new shows demonstrating similar strategies and concerns. Yet this resurgence is not a simple reassertion of conservative values, for the programs return, inevitably, with a difference. "The All New Dating Game" still has its chaperones accompany the couples on dates. But all dates are exciting holidays: no more dinners or nights-on-the-town, only vacations, cruises, and long weekends at resort hotels. "Divorce Court" no longer announces that its purpose is "to help stem the rising tide of divorces."[6] Taken together, these programs can be seen as attempts to (re)instate the couple as a stable social referent even as they endlessly rehearse the couple as a body constituted in unstable mobility. On the one hand, they evoke a nostalgic desire; at the same time, they provoke a recognition of the impossibility of the (nostalgic) media fantasies — and of the historic media programs — which are their point of departure.

Heterosexual pairs are the à *priori* condition of narrativization for these programs, the necessary precondition for playing their games and telling their stories.[7] The pair becomes a couple through a process of discursive elaboration; the couple is not a natural body, but a product of confession and analysis, of a therapeutic procedure. The couple is naturalized in social relations as the linchpin between public and private identity. As the foundation of the traditional nuclear family, the couple is a site of legalized sexual and economic relations, subject to the dictates of secular and religious law.[8] Thus a couple is never strictly a personal affair, even when it is bolstered by a mythical and mystical ideology of love defined in terms of ineffable individuality. A couple is also a fluid and variable body, a moment of affiliation which is not necessarily permanent. Indeed, the very existence of these shows repeatedly demonstrates that — and how — the pair becomes a couple through participation in certain discursive practices and how a couple reverts to a pair in the absence of communication.

According to these shows the very recognition and self-identification of the couple require a willingness to submit to specific testing procedures and to participate in a confessional mode of discourse.[9] The participants in this process are enjoined to speak "freely" and to exercise "free choice," but only within the contours of discursive control defined by the show. With the exception of "Divorce Court," with its dramatized reconstructions of actual court cases, one chooses to go on these programs in the first place, a choice encouraged by appeals to participate aired during the shows. "If you want to try out for 'The New Newlywed Game' and are married less than two years, and you're going to be in the Los Angeles area, call us...." "If you'd like to talk about a problem in your relationship and you live in or plan to visit Southern California, send your name and telephone number to 'Couples.' We might be able to help you. And in sharing your difficulties, you might help other viewers in a similar situation." On the dating shows, you are free to select the person you want to go out with, within the pool of three people preselected by the producers. And within the various shows, you are encouraged to speak openly and to respond to questions as quickly and honestly as possible, whether it has to do with inventing a wild, adventurous scenario to thrill a jungle girl on a date on "The All New Dating Game"; how you enjoyed your dinner with your "love connection"; which of your friends your wife would like to see in an underwear commercial on "The New Newlywed Game"; or expressing your emotions to your partner on "Couples."

STAGING THE COUPLE

The narrativized body produced through the sequence of these programs is in many ways a familiar construction. The initial formation of the couple is exciting, glamorous, and fun and involves a particular emphasis on first impressions.[10] After the first date, however, the real work begins: frivolous communication is replaced by honest communication, and whimsical fantasy construction gives way to the banality of everyday life. Along these same lines, the game of attractions that precedes the formation of the couple is for beautiful bodies—a restricted field of the conventional consumer images of good looks—while the couple, once constituted as a body, admits the idiosyncratic variety of ordinary physiques. This, at least, is the impression one gets if one follows "The All New Dating Game," "Love Connection," "The New Newlywed Game," "Perfect Match," and "Couples" as a protonarrative sequence. ("Divorce Court" initiates the logical reversal of this process with its use of actors, rather than ordinary people. The program involves the dissolution of the couple, the redefinition of the pair as two individuals, as the codes of attractiveness that impinge on singles begins to reemerge.)

On "The All New Dating Game," the public appeal for contestants is literally addressed to attractive singles. The program self-consciously styles itself in terms of frivolity and superficiality, as the first impression is broken down into discrete stages of contact. The contestant who chooses a date is initially barred from seeing the choice pool, identified to her only as Bachelors Number One, Two, and Three, nor can the bachelors see the woman who may choose them for a date.[11] Instead she must rely on their voices and their responses to her questions—which are obviously prescripted and designed to elicit the minimal possible substantive information about the individuals in the bachelor pool. "I'm a DJ at an L.A. rock station. Pretend you're a DJ, and in your best DJ voice rattle off song titles that will describe our first date together." "I find intellectuals very sexy. In your sexiest voice, convince me you're an intellectual."

With questions of this order, the program presents the pairing-off process in terms of make-believe, a simulation in regress, where everyone is asked to pretend over and over again as the basis for purportedly assessing potential congeniality and appeal. The bachelors have to be ready to assume any conceivable mood, attitude, identity, or accent. From time to time the chooser will actually show up with little hats, masks, or other costume paraphernalia that the three bachelors will be asked to wear as part of this masquerade (even though the chooser cannot actually see them in their disguises).

To select a date in this way suggests at once that we must, and do, make choices, but that they are inevitably—even structurally—made on the basis of something other than logic and rationality. The importance of appearance as a part of this process is played out in terms of anticipatory suspense after the chooser has made her selection. One by one, the three bachelors are brought out and introduced, starting with the ones who were not chosen for the culminating date. During this sequence of introductions one inevitably watches for signs of reaction on the part of the participants—the looks of relief, disappointment, even apprehension. The television viewers who have followed the whole selection process are in a position to anticipate these responses and to play their own impressions off against the reactions of the participants. How one looks—at others and to others—is thus a crucial factor in the overall structure of anticipation and narrative engagement. The participants initially rely on verbal rather than visual cues, but the confirmation of their impressions, and the climax of the show, have everything to do with looking good (which also, of course, contributes to the visual spectacle of the program for viewers).

The couple is thereby constituted, having been produced through the mediated stages of first impressions and simulated exchange required by the show. This whole process is reconfirmed by the intercession of host Elaine Joyce, who consolidates the identity of the pair as a couple with a concluding comment. "Perfect! This is what you call instant chemistry. I love it!" "Aren't they a cute couple? They're so cool and lovable. I love 'em." "Those two don't seem too sure about one another." As host and moderator, she speaks as an authority whose regular contact with newly formed couples confers on her particular sensitivity and insight, proclaiming her first impression of the couple as a definitive expert judgment. The reward for participating in this process is always a vacation. One may be sent to a wide range of places, including Encinada, Tahiti, New York City, Bangkok, Jamaica, Anchorage, or the Bahamas, to name a few. Thus the initiation of the couple in terms of frivolity, fun, and out-of-the-ordinary experience is extended in the very prize that caps the process and confirms the formation of the pair as a couple.

The rules of the game shift once one is already defined as a couple, however provisionally. On "Love Connection," the selection process and the first date precede the program itself. The focus of each episode is the retrospective reconstruction of the date, through discussion with host Chuck Woolery. But having already happened, the date itself is far less exotic than the anticipatory fantasy projected by "The All New Dating Game." Thrown squarely into the everyday world of ordinary activity, the couples who have already gone out have usually been to dinner, the beach, a bar, dancing, the zoo, or a concert. Moreover, "Love Connection" does not require "attractive" singles, but only singles, as prospective participants. Having already gone out in order even to appear on the show,[12] the couple is returned to the banality of the imperfect, everyday world.

First impressions do count here, as Chuck Woolery almost always inquires what the couple first thought of one another. But they are hardly definitive or final, having already been supplanted by contact that goes beyond an initial moment of encounter. Dates often start well and end in hostility, or vice versa. Sometimes the individuals like each other well enough, but do not want to date, asserting a difference between the heterosexual pair and the couple. The couple is not just anyone, or rather, any two — it is something else. And in case we are unclear as to just what that is, these programs offer a continual series of examples. The couple is any two who choose to go out and to put their relationship into discourse, mediated through program structures, host's remarks, and audience opinion.

Between "The All New Dating Game" and "Love Connection" there is a significant shift in the use of competition as a strategy of narrative engagement. On "The All New Dating Game" the process of selection — from a pool of three potential object choices — structures the show as a whole, reaching a dénouement with the revelation of the chooser's decision. Within this context, overt competition is emphasized, with the regular posing of questions that force the members of the choice pool to comment on one another. "I just won a Linda Evans look-alike contest. Bachelor #3, look at #2 and tell me what look-alike contest he could win." "I'm overdue for a vacation, but I'm picky about who I go out with. Number 2, look at #1 and tell me what a Scandinavian would say if I went to Scandinavia with him. And sound like a Scandinavian." At the end of the question-and-answer period, the program dissolves between the chooser and each member of the choice pool, specifying the potential couples that could result from the process, constructing a formal paradigm with a restricted range of substitutions. Only after a commercial break do we learn who is chosen, initiating the formation of the couple.

"Love Connection" operates according to a different logic, incorporating studio audience opinion to produce anticipatory suspense as a strategy of viewer engagement. We are introduced to the chooser and then see clips from the three videotapes which were the chooser's initial selection pool. But the choice has already been made, and the date has already occurred. However, before we are introduced to the object-choice, the studio audience votes for the one they feel would have been the most appropriate choice. This vote is later invoked for consideration when the chooser is deciding whether to go out again, and with whom.[13] The audience vote essentially functions as a straw poll to infuse the program itself with a sense of suspense: Who did the audience vote for? Was it the same person initially chosen by the chooser-subject? Was the initial date good or bad? Will the audience vote give the chooser another choice? Will it prove to be better or worse? At the same time it introduces a simulated community voice into the process of couple formation. The studio audience stands in as a measure of public opinion and common sense for both the chooser-subject and the television viewer.

It is not incidental that this voice is introduced when a provisional couple has been identified, that is, the two who have already gone out once. Rather, it demonstrates the shift in the terms of identifying the couple, from two individual bodies who operate independently as a pair to a newly consolidated body-in-division that must function socially in relation to a larger community. The studio vote, however indeterminate and unfinal, represents the consolidation of the couple as a social body. Crucially, social regulation is not represented as prescriptive authority, but as the balance of, and willingness to acknowledge, an array of voices: interested individuals and disinterested communal good will. The structure of the show marks the stages at which it is useful to rethink the process of dating and the formation of the (any specific) couple as a unit of social identification.

A KISS IS (NOT) JUST A KISS

The myth that sustains the dating shows as fantasy is marriage. The programs themselves end in the date, whether a romantic holiday or just another night on the town. The participants are identified as social to the extent that they readily represent themselves as actors within this process. One does not have to win, but only to put oneself in circulation. Indeed, on "The All New Dating Game" alumni shows feature members of previous choice pools who were not selected for a date the first time around, but are given a second chance; former rejects are thus extended the possibility of becoming chosen objects. The more you are willing to situate yourself in this circuit, speaking the language of the desiring other, the greater your chances of being identified in a couple.

Marriage as a possible goal is implicated by the dating programs with the periodic appearance of couples who met through the show and are now married. But it is also an alibi to confirm the need for coupling through mediated discourse in the first place. As a mythic projected end it naturalizes the need to submit to the questions and confessional procedures offered by the dating programs as a guarantee of sociality. Many of the participants on "Love Connection" are identified as formerly married, sometimes more than once, underscoring the relativity of marriage as a narrative telos. Marriage is not necessarily the end of the story—the "happily ever after" of fairy tales—but a shift in terrain, initiating a new kind of testing through confession. The married couple is a body with relative fixity within the law, ultimately no more permanent than the dating couple.

In the context of game shows, "The New Newlywed Game" and "Perfect Match" validate the couple through dual confessions, as married couples are asked questions of a personal nature and awarded points when they give matching answers. The couple with the most points at the end of the game is rewarded with a prize. For the contestants, matching confessions are the measure of the prize-winning couple in literal and metaphoric terms. At the same time the questions are designed to provoke divisiveness on the part of the couples. They are forced, for example, to insult their in-laws and friends, to say demeaning things about one another, or to reveal their attraction to someone other than their spouse. "When it comes to romance last night, which food will your husband say came closest to how he behaves: hot cakes, cold cuts, or leftovers?" "How will your husband say you would complete this sentence: My husband thinks he's a *real man*. So he probably thinks I'd never tell about the time I caught him doing [*what*]. But I will." "How will your wife say you will complete this sentence: If I could redistribute my wife's weight, I would take from her [*blank*] and fill in her [*what*]."

Couples will fight over mismatched answers no matter how silly or banal the topic, even if it has to do, for example, with the kinds of food they buy, a favorite piece of furniture, or the directional orientation of their living room. But they will kiss enthusiastically to reward one another for matching answers, even when they reveal an embarrassing event or personal habit, such as the way one of them picks their nose, or that the first time they made love was in a bedroom closet in their parents' house. On "Perfect Match," contestants are supplied with pillows for the express purpose of beating one another when they give wrong answers. The married couple is represented as a body-in-division on a sliding scale of relative consonance and dissonance. These games require confession as part of the process for judging and understanding the couple as a social unit. But simply participating in the show guarantees one's identity as a couple. You do not have to match all your answers or win, but have only to confess.

In the process these shows enact scenarios of marital discord as well as marital bliss, agreement and disagreement over big and little issues, as the natural structuring parameters of the life of a couple. The reasons for engaging in social life as a body-in-division and the desires motivating such engagement remain uninterrogated. They are, precisely, beside the point, naturalized by the tacit assumption that everyone is interesting not only in participating, but also in having access to what goes on behind others' closed doors. The shows themselves are mutually supporting in sustaining this logic. Indeed, "The All New Dating Game" and "The New Newlywed Game" are both Chuck Barris productions, and often air back-to-back in syndicated markets.[14]

JUST GAMING

Through the course of these shows the couple as a body is produced, examined, challenged, and probed all in good fun. These are, after all, game shows. And the programs deploy an array of visual and narrative strategies to insist that this is all just play, based in the flimsy illusionistic electronic signals of television with no substance beyond their simulated surfaces. The set of "The New Newlywed Game" features silhouette figures of couples facing one another across tables in various poses. At the start of each program the live couples seated in front of this stylized decor are also posed and lit in silhouette, so that they blend into the decorative backdrop and its shadowy couples. On "The All New Dating Game" transitions from program segments to commercials involve transforming the image of the chooser or the couple into an abstract digitalized image of squares of color that seem to dematerialize before our very eyes.

"Love Connection" offers an extreme version of this impulse to announce its own mediated fictionality. The date is defined from the outset as a process staged for, and to be aired on, television. Participants often acknowledge their status as figures in a ritual performed for a public show. In one case a couple attended a party, and the friends of the chooser — who knew this was a "Love Connection" alliance — kept asking her date "if it was love yet." Another participant, also an object-choice, described taking his date to the drug store where he worked to show her off, because his co-workers had insisted that no attractive woman would ever pick him from a choice pool.

This recognition of the mediated, playful nature of participation is reproduced and extended in the very presentational strategies of the show. The distinctions between videotape, video monitor, and on-stage generate a series of relative levels of presence/absence within the confines of the program based on the master opposition between being on television and being on a television screen on television. Only one of the videotape pool of object-choices gets to appear live on a video monitor, though her/his presence backstage is acknowledged. Then, only if and when agreeing to a second date is the chosen one invited to join Chuck and the chooser-subject on stage. In this context, procedures of social modeling and regula-tion of the couple are represented through a complex, internally generated structure of mediation/differentiation of levels of reality, based on how one is situated in relation to this schema of relative presence and absence within the world of video technology.

These strategies represent a marketing tactic, the use of new video technology to sweeten the image, injecting a sense of pizzazz and contem-poraneity. They also demonstrate clearly the simulacral order of postmodernism, a process of extended duplication and reduplication with minimal difference described by Jean Baudrillard as the mode of significa-tion characteristic of contemporary society.

> Reality no longer has the time to take on the appearance of reality. It no longer even surpasses fiction; it captures every dream even before it takes on the appearance of a dream. Schizophrenic vertigo of these serial signs, for which no counterfeit, no sublimation is possible, immanent in their repetition—who could say what the reality is that these signs simulate?[15]

Yet even if we are no longer in the world of representation — if there is no longer any referent beyond the appearance of the sign that declares the absence of any reference beyond itself within the order of simulations — we are, as Donna Haraway has noted, squarely situated in networks of informa-tion, power, discourse, transmission, and domination. "We are living through a movement from an organic, industrial society to a polymorphous, information system—from all work to all play, a deadly game."[16] In other words, Haraway suggests that the logic of simulation does not finally dissolve networks of power and domination (as Baudrillard would have it). Instead, it becomes increasingly difficult to recognize power because it is multiply decentered, always expressed in terms of systemic dispersal and regress.

The stakes in these television games are evident in the conjoining of the injunction to confess with the setting in place of circuits of consumerism. The simultaneous circulation of commodities and of couples as bodies of communication delineates networks of exchange which become mutually interdependent in the course of their repeated (daily) deployments. "Perfect Match" literalizes the question of stakes as each couple begins the game with the same number of points and decides how much to wager on each question. Thus the economy of the couple's confessional discourse is imbricated with an economy of competitive consumption. Through the course of these shows, the body of the couple is produced as a subject and object of consuming interest. It competes for the rewards of winning the game—a financed date, new bedroom furniture, or a camper family vacations.

Consumer culture thus impinges on our very recognition of the couple as the social unit most likely to avail itself of the widest range of consumer products. The couple as a body-in-division is in turn sold to the audience along with the products advertised during the course of these shows. The viewers' time in front of the television is sold to advertisers in the competitive market of commercial television. The couple as a confessional body is thus inscribed in multiple, simultaneous circuits of exchange whose perpetuation through repetition secures the functioning of consumer culture. We (viewers) consume confession as the agency of our own insertion into these circuits of exchange.

A SPECTACLE OF CONFESSION

The ideological efficacy of these programs is activated in the movements through, and convergences among, these circuits of exchange. At the same time—and to further complicate the questions of who is speaking is whose interests—confession as a discourse of truth undergoes a fundamental reconstruction. It is useful, in this context, to recall Michel Foucault's discussion of confession as a particular mode of discourse.

> The confession is a ritual of discourse in which the speaking subject is also the subject of the statement; it is also a ritual that unfolds within a power relationship, for one does not confess without the presence (or virtual presence) of a partner who is not simply the interlocutor, but the authority who requires the confession, prescribes and appreciates it, and intervenes in order to judge, punish, forgive, console, and reconcile....[17]

What happens when the procedures of confession are relayed through the public, commercial, and highly mediated structures of the television game show? Confession is hereby rewritten as a dialogic process, even before an interlocutor is identified. In the terms of the rules of these games, the problem of how to speak is acute. One might say too much, or perhaps not enough. As a constituent member of a couple, it is impossible to judge for *oneself* because in every case another voice has to be taken into account—the other who will complete the identity of the couple as a body-in-division. One must confess all, but the final truth of the couple as a body requires that it speak with two voices. On "The All New Dating Game" the concern from the perspective of the choice pool is to say just enough to make yourself attractive to the chooser (as a contender for the position of second voice) and no more than that: the game is to produce the confession that will be perceived as consonant and appropriate. Even on "Love Connection," where the real decisions about whether to go out again are pretty much settled in advance, how to speak becomes an issue. To reveal too much may prove embarrassing, although these revelations are provoked by the host's questions about the extent and quality of romantic activity. To attack the other half of the couple will cast you in the role of a villain. On "The New Newlywed Game" and "Perfect Match" any answer may provoke dissension, as one spouse questions the sanity, memory, or propriety of the other for giving the response they did.

The body of the couple, produced and tested through the division of confession, is thus a body in anxiety-provoking communication with itself. The discourse one must engage to secure one's identity is concomitantly, and necessarily, a source of stress. In the game shows discussed thus far, this may be exacerbated by the interventions of the hosts as the primary interlocutors. This is particularly striking in "The New Newlywed Game," where the slightest disagreements can motivate Bob Eubanks to challenge one spouse in relation to the other. "Who's the boss?" and "Who's right?" are frequent questions he asks, with the expectation that each spouse will answer, "I am," fully exposing the divided body of the couple speaking in contradiction as a spectacle for the viewer.

The couple as a body experiencing a breakdown in communications is taken up by, and fully developed in, "Couples" and "Divorce Court." These programs exist on a continuum with the game shows insofar as they probe and define the couple as a confessional body. The avowed focus of attention in these programs, however, is the couple as a confessing body under stress. In most cases, the problems that lead couples to seek counseling or a divorce in the first place are represented as a breakdown in communications between the two individuals who together constitute the couple. This retrospective diagnosis itself depends on the perpetuation of confessional communication. In other words, the process of the cure or the dissolution of the couple is the same as the process of its formation and testing. To the extent that the couple no longer confesses with ease, the injunction to confess must be enforced through the agency of the law—in the case of "Couples," the institution of psychiatry, and in the case of "Divorce Court," the legal system. The host of "Couples" is Dr. Walter Brackelmanns, identified as a psychiatrist and a family therapist; Judge William Keene is the star of "Divorce Court," and his credentials as a real judge in the California court system are announced in every episode.

"Couples" at once enacts and thematizes communications as the key to relationships. Dr. Brackelmanns's sessions with his clients have three distinct segments, as he speaks with each spouse individually, and then with the couple together. In the process he repeatedly insists that the members of the couple must talk to one another and express their feelings, a process which he facilitates. The point of all couples is to speak together; and in successful (enduring) couples, each one will take his/her own feelings and those of the other seriously without confusing one for the other. The good couple is defined as a body in harmonious and sympathetic division. At the end of each session, Dr. Brackelmanns sums up the lessons one might learn (as viewers) about relationships based on what we have just seen.

> One powerful point: if a member of a family is detached and angry, he is usually in emotional pain and doesn't know what to do. Be sensitive and caring, and the walls will come down.

> There is an important principle of communication here. If your mate tells you about their feelings, *this must be respected*. If you use those feelings against someone, you're not trustworthy.

> In your relationship, don't be demanding. It evokes negative feelings and hardens your mate to his or her position. Don't take responsibility for the feelings of the person you love. You can't change or fix them. If you try, it won't work and it will prevent you from remaining a caring, supportive listener.

Dr. Brackelmanns is a therapist who aggressively intervenes in the course of counseling, repeating the same messages over and over again. We are responsible for ourselves, but have to communicate with—confess to—the other in the couple.

> You don't throw away a relationship of six years. And you don't throw away a love relationship. You try to make it work. I don't know any other way. And you've got to take a chance. That's what's tough about good relationships: we stick our psychological necks right out there and somebody can chop it off! On the other hand, you can then have a close, warm, caring, intimate, meaningful relationship with another human being. And it's worth it.[18]

Dr. Brackelmanns promotes the value and the risks of being part of a couple, insisting his clients take the gamble necessary to sustain themselves as a couple. Central to this is a labor of loving communication and divided confession. In the course of sessions he will order the participants to tell each another how they feel, that they love the other, to hug, kiss, or hold hands. The participants are rewarded for confessing feelings, but chastised or cut short if they try to analyze, accuse, or describe the facts. "Don't tell him what he did. He knows what he did. Tell him how you feel." One *has* to confess one's feelings and hope that one's mate will be sensitive and sympathetic in response.

This emphasis is reinforced in the very structure of the sessions as they are presented on television. The sessions are edited to fit into a thirty-minute programming slot (minus commercial interruptions) and feature the moments of emotional revelation by the participants and the directive injunctions offered by Dr. Brackelmanns at the expense of detailed case histories. We are given just enough contextualizing narrative to make sense of the particular case, but little more background than that. The logic of elision becomes clear when Dr. Brackelmanns, talking with the couple, refers to something discussed previously (during the individual consultations) that was not included on the show. Thus, for example, he might assert, "We already heard about your difficult childhood," although no such discussion was presented to the viewing audience. Dr. Brackelmanns's reference is the first time we have any idea that one of the participants had a troubled youth. But the point is that the coherence and continuity of the stories of the individuals are less important than the recognition of the couple as a body through the emotional, confessional confrontations provoked by Dr. Brackelmanns.

In the chronological narrative of the couple, "Divorce Court" is the final appeal to the couple as a dialogical confessing body, as each member speaks in the interest of finally dissolving (or, in rare cases, conserving) the married couple. The legal contract that binds the two and defines their obligations, unacknowledged until this point, fully emerges in the process of divorce, retrospectively defining the contractual nature of the couple as a social body. The judge who presides over the divorce court decides who is at fault—which of the spouses has behaved in a manner transgressing the terms of a contract that were not specified at the outset—and how the property will be divided, whether spousal support is indicated, and, when pertinent, which spouse will have custody of the children. Fault and material rewards are directly linked, as the spouse who proves to be the guilty party suffers for abrogating the marriage contract, awarded the smaller share of the couple's assets. And this is decided — unsurprisingly — through a judicial proceeding that evaluates a confessional form of testimony, as spouses and their witnesses attempt to convince the court of the truth of their charges. The courtroom drama is cast in the terms of confessional melodrama, as the members of the couple describe purported acts of adultery, mental and physical cruelty, or alienating affections committed by the other.

The process of divorce, represented on "Divorce Court" as a dialogic confession, does not necessarily or always culminate in the dissolution of the couple. Rather, the presiding judge is the only one with the power and authority to dissolve the married couple. Indeed he may even function like the family therapist on "Couples," suggesting that there is hope that a marriage may be saved, overseeing a reconciliation in court, or declaring a ninety-day delay until the divorce decree is final to encourage the possibility of reconciliation. The couple itself, formed through stages of mediated confession, cannot simply dissolve itself, but must continue to participate in the very processes and structures that informed its formation in the first place, at least in the terms of television's representations.

The signs of staging deployed in the couples game shows are equally apparent in these reality dramas. The multiple mediations of fictionality on "Divorce Court" are as elaborate as the relative degrees of presence/absence produced on "Love Connection." The audience is carefully instructed in how to watch the show, with a verbal title, read by a voice-over narrator, explaining that the cases are *real*, based on divorce cases from across the country, but that the judgments are based on "a combination" of state laws, and thus might not specifically apply in all cases. In other words, the program says, "This is real and not real, actual law but not actual law." This interplay is extended when we learn that actors play the roles of spouses, while real lawyers argue the cases, based on a script. But the judge — a real judge — makes his decisions independently, and none of the participants in the drama knows his decision prior to the taping. Thus the actor's responses are real and spontaneous, even though they are only actors playing the part of litigants in a divorce proceeding and are only pretending to have a stake in the outcome. To underscore this moment of acting, the program uses a split screen, showing the two prime litigants as the judge reads his final decision.

To further extend the fiction of reality, and the reality of the fiction, the judge's decision — purportedly unknown even by the producers until the moment when it is read during the process of taping — inevitably includes rather playful puns and analogies based on the details of the case, consciously styled in the terms of a witty script. For example, when one case focused on a wife's obsessive relationship with a pet dog, Judge Keene suggests that it "certainly adds a new dimension to the concept of man's best friend." In a case in which a father was purposefully involving his children in accidents to collect insurance money, an outburst by the father compelled the judge to threaten him with contempt and a jail sentence. When the man kept yelling, the judge invoked the familiar expression of Clint Eastwood's Dirty Harry character, "Go ahead. Do it [keep up the complaining] — and make my day!"[19]

FIELDS OF SUBJECTIVITY

With the reconstruction of confession as a dialogic procedure of discourse — dividing positions of confessor and interlocutor — along with the repetitive, self-conscious strategies of mediation and simulation, television's staging of the couple through the course of these programs asserts the importance of confessional and therapeutic processes in which positions of authority and hierarchy are relativized, especially when it comes to specifying the place of the spectator. For these programs offer multiple and simultaneous potential positions of identification, carefully sustaining a balance between engagement and detachment, proximity and distance. The very thematics of the programs imply voyeurism, as we are offered elaborately mediated revelations of a personal nature. The devices of fictionality keep us at a safe distance as we hear confessions of an intimate, even sordid, nature.

By the same token, the possibilities of multiple identification authorize our pleasure in listening to strangers discuss their personal lives. As interlocutors, our presence, along with that of the program hosts, is necessary to the confession. We may assume an imaginary position as the therapist-authority to whom the confession is addressed. This may in turn imply sympathetic authority, but equally can involve smug superiority. A range of attitudes is conveyed by the behavior of the hosts-authorities within the programs who support and promote confession, but also respond to the confession variably — with concern, interest, surprise, or even ridicule. At the same time, the viewer can assume the position of one instructed: one has to listen if one hopes to understand the various permutations and combinations of the couple as a social body. Here the audience is subject to the program's mastery — consuming strategies of social regulation. In between these two extremes, viewers may identify — provisionally and unpredictably — with the participants (contestants) in the process, recognizing themselves and their own problems in the course of others' confessions.

The ideological work of these programs does not result in the construction of a single ideal subjectivity or mode of reception. For they produce couples and address viewers in terms of circulation and division. A viewer may find moments of mis/recognition and dis/engagement from any number of positions within the multiple discourses deployed by these programs. These popular media texts contribute to the production of subjectivity(ies) that is (are) contradictory and decentered. The process is not per se specific to these programs, but rather a confirmation of how they operate in a medium whose popular appeal, i.e., its ability to draw and hold large numbers of viewers, can be traced in its inscription of heterogeneous terms of address, a recognition of the mass audience as a heterogeneous mass.

The particular fascination of the programs — and their specificity in relation to the larger process of subject construction — lies in their play on the borders of romantic fantasy and middle-class decorum and propriety. Singularly and collectively, these programs threaten to undermine the conventional gender roles and middle-class values which they simultaneously uphold as terms of reference. By playing with hegemonic social identity they invoke fantasy scenarios in terms that are fundamentally ambivalent. They activate aspirations of fulfillment in conventional terms (marriage, family, middle-class lifestyles) at the same time that they hint at the anxiety, even the impossibility, of its achievement.

In terms of romantic fantasy, these programs invoke and rework contemporary cultural myths of true love, love at first sight, and marital bliss already in place. While they flirt with the possibility of a happily every after, they also dramatize the limits of these myths in practice. In the process they draw on the eternal battle between the sexes. The couple—man and woman, male and female, husband and wife—is shown to work together by being pitted one against the other. The body-in-division of the couple is confirmed in disunity because it is also always, in these shows, comprised of two sexes. And to sustain the gender roles that allow the myths to function (the difference between the sexes that supports the magic of true love) guarantees the divisive body of the couple, promoting the stress and anxiety that will undo it in the long run. The struggle for true love and perfect union (according to the terms of romantic myth) is constant, but essentially undecidable. The programs are unable finally to confirm or deny the truth of the myths, even as they are mobilized as key terms of reference. The pleasure of viewing lies, in part, in the possibility of investing in the myth of true love *and* in the concomitant recognition of its long-term impossibility.

Moreover, the ambivalence of romantic fantasies is dramatized through a confessional mode of discourse that itself transgresses the limits of proper middle-class decorum. For the injunction to tell all can lead to saying too much, the revelation of intimate habits and private affairs. We are not properly expected to discuss sex, or our feelings about close friends and relative, in public, in front of strangers, much less in front of the impersonal mass of the television audience. Yet this is precisely what these programs promote. There is an undeniable fascination and pleasure to be derived from overstepping the bounds of middle-class propriety. The subjects of this process (the couples who agree to participate) are models of transgression at the same time that they implicate themselves as potential objects of derision, because they do not represent themselves as proper, conventionally self-restrained middle-class subjects.

The very existence of these shows signals a blurring of the distinction between personal and social, private and public, individual and mass. But this blurring of previously distinct domains may be taken in several ways. It can be understood in terms of transgression, as the subjects who confess break the bounds of a middle-class morality that prescribes what can be spoken, by whom, in what contexts. On the other hand, these shows delineate the ways in which public and private experience are equally permeated by institutional and impersonal strategies of power—including the community, law, and psychiatry—while requiring the involvement and complicity of subjects who will speak for themselves in their capacity as free, private individuals. Here, the difference between the private and the public is effaced in the interests of the consuming social body. But the relation between the individual subjects and the institutional imperatives remains unstable.

These programs consolidate the couple as the social body whose circulation as simulation secures the repetition and displacement of consuming interests and passions, where the social is always personal and vice versa. This body is constructed as unstable and decentered; it is always already in division and under stress. At the same time these shows engage viewers in terms of confessional and therapeutic modes of discourse, encouraging participation in a process whereby one's personal affairs have currency in the public sphere. They even suggest that personal identity within the social can best be secured by participating in the discursive networks they repeatedly deploy. The couple shows function as social regulation to the extent that they channel free speech in the terms of a therapeutic problematic with the power to diagnose social identity. In this context, the inclusion—even the promotion—of transgressive speech serves as a strategy of containment, confining it within the networks of confessional discourse and consumerism at the center of these programs. We can become good subjects, and good citizens, by consenting to participate in the appropriate channels of discourse and of consumer behavior.

But the production of meaning and of subjectivity is constantly renegotiated, a process exacerbated by the daily repetitions of these shows. The very strategies of discourse that work to secure and regulate subjectivity are also the means for expressing and recognizing social transgression. These programs signal the anxiety of hegemony, including voices that threaten the logic and the interests of bourgeois social control and that cannot always finally be contained. Thus it is by no means clear that social control wins out all of the time, for all viewers, or that everyone will even identify social control in the same terms.

This, of course, considerably complicates the task of cultural studies, and of critical pedagogy, when it comes to understanding television's production of ideology and subjectivity. For it suggests that sometimes complicity with the hegemonic forces of consumer culture can provide the means whereby individuals discover their own (counterhegemonic) power and that the expression of transgression can be readily consumed by hegemonic interests. This means that we must constantly engage in a process of critical reading, without mistaking our own intellectual conclusions or consuming passions for the final word.

NOTES

1. Nathaniel Branden and E. Devers Branden, *The Romantic Love Question and Answer Book* (Los Angeles: J. P. Tarcher, 1982), p. 30.

2. "The relationship monster has truly exceeded all expectations," Rosalind Coward, *Female Desires* (New York: Grove, 1985), p. 131.

3. The ideological problematic refers to the field of representational possibilities a text offers. "The problematic is importantly defined in the negative—as those questions or issues which cannot (easily) be put within a particular problematic—and in the positive as that set of questions or issues which constitute the dominant or preferred 'themes' of a programme." David Morley, *The "Nationwide" Audience: Structure and Decoding* (London: British Film Institute, 1980), p. 139.

4. This phrase comes from the program itself, in its solicitations for contestants.

5. It is not that this genre is "original" to the 1980s, but rather that it is becoming far more common. Thus, for example, in the first four months of 1987, *Broadcasting* included ads for, or brief articles about, four new shows in this genre that were being promoted for the fall season.

6. Alex McNeil, entry on "Divorce Court," *Total Television* (New York: Penguin Books, 2nd ed., 1984), p. 171.

7. This is not strictly the case with "Couples." The "pair" in analysis on this program is usually a heterosexual romantic couple, but may also include siblings, parents and their children, and the like.

8. For critical perspectives on the family and gender, and on the construction of gender in relation to the family as a symbolic force, see Zillah Eisenstein, "The Sexual Politics of the New Right: Understanding the 'Crisis of Liberalism' for the 1980s," *Signs* 7 (Spring 1982): 567–88; Susan Harding, "Family Reform Movements: Recent Feminism and Its Opposition," *Feminist Studies* 7 (Spring 1981): 57–75; Mary McIntosh, "The Family in Socialist-Feminist Politics," *Feminist, Culture, and Politics*, Rosalind Brunt and Caroline Rowan, eds. (London: Lawrence & Wishart, 1982), pp. 109–29; and Gayle Rubin, "The Traffic in Women: Notes on the 'Political Economy' of Sex," in *Toward an Anthropology of Women*, Rayna R. Reiter, ed. (New York: Monthly Review Press, 1975).

9. I am adapting the concept of confession from Michel Foucault, as elaborated in *The History of Sexuality*, vol. 1, Robert Hurley, trans. (New York: Pantheon Books, 1978), esp. pp. 58–65.

10. It can be argued that the "first impression" as a kind of superficial recognition has been a crucial construction in the development and operation of consumer culture. Most advertising relies on the immediacy of brand name recognition, and television commercials emphasize the efficacy of products in unforeseen and spontaneous narrative contexts. Thus, for example, if you use the spray cologne Impulse, a stranger may suddenly give you flowers; it will, in other words, generate a flamboyant and desirable first impression, instant igniting romance and passion.

11. The choosers on the show are not always female, though they are dispropor-tionately so; thus in my description I designate the chooser "she" and choice pool as male. This is to avoid contortions in the writing, not to simplify the show or the implications for its assumptions about gender.

12. Again, this is not strictly true, but has been simplified for sake of description. The show does include people who agree to go out with someone selected from videotape pool by the studio audience with the expectation that they will come back after the date to discuss it on show. This is done on rare occasions with celebrities, and also at the end of the week, to close off the process of the production of suspense as we wait to learn who the chooser selected from the choice pool, or who the audience voted for.

13. If after appearing on the show the chooser elects to go out with whomever the

audience plurality supports, the program will pay for a second date. But s/he is not constrained to follow their advice. Thus, if the date was a success, but the studio audience voted for someone else from the choice pool, it is unlikely (but not impossible) that the chooser will reject the original choice to follow the audience's advice. Similarly, if the date was a failure and the audience voted for the initial object-choice, the chooser is unlikely to follow the recommendation. Even in cases where the first date was unsuccessful and the audience selects a different object-choice, the chooser is free to reject their suggestion. (This occurs, for example, when the chooser feels the audience choice is unacceptable based on having previously seen the whole tape.)

14. There is even a commercial campaign featuring show hosts Elaine Joyce and Bob Eubanks together, promoting the idea that the flow from dating to newlywed is seamless, a continuity sustained through the repeated injunction to confess.

15. Jean Baudrillard, *Simulations*, Paul Foss, Paul Patton, and Philip Beitchman, trans. (New York: Semiotext(e), 1983), p. 152.

16. Donna Haraway, "A Manifesto for Cyborgs: Science, Technology, and Socialist Feminism in the 1980s," *Socialist Review* No. 80 (March-April 1985): 80. See also Baudrillard, *Simulations*.

17. Michel Foucault, *The History of Sexuality*, pp. 61–62.

18. All quotes from the program were transcribed by the author from off-the-air videotapes (air checks) of the program.

19. These particular examples come from Robert Levine, *Divorce Court* (New York: Dell, 1986) which offers narrative summaries of "25 actual cases" from the TV show.

Chapter 10

WORKING-CLASS IDENTITY AND CELLULOID FANTASIES IN THE ELECTRONIC AGE

Stanley Aronowitz

♦ Individual and collective identities are constructed on three sites: 1. the biologically given characteristics which we bring to every social interaction; 2. givens that are often covered over by social relations, family, school; and 3. the technological sensorium that we call mass or popular culture. In Western culture these givens assume meaning over which individuals have some control, but they are often beyond our powers to reverse. Our race and sex confer boundaries as well as possibilities in various relations, particularly the kind of friends we can make, work we can do, mates who are available to us. Surely, the meanings of race and sex, like those of class, are socially constituted; there is no inherent significance to these identities as social signs. However, we are born into these identities, given the social arrangements. The second crucial social site is our interaction with family, school, the workplace, and other conventional institutions such as the church. These relationships are often conceived as self-determining, that is, free of biological givens. Obviously, parents and teachers differentiate between boys and girls. Boys and girls are treated differently; we might say they enjoy/suffer a different moral development regardless of class membership or race. As many writers have argued, the family remains perhaps the crucial site for reproducing gender difference. Schools are crucial secondary institutions in this regard; they play a major part in the reproduction of racial difference, the forms of which remain to be fully explored. It is enough here to point out that schools are the first places children experience as racially segregated, since modernism ended gender segregation. It is in school that children experience themselves as white or black; needless to say, textbooks make clear to blacks their subordinate status, apart from any overt content. Images of blacks even when they appear, are tokens of the power of the civil rights movement over the past thirty years, but black history and culture remain absent, a silence which signifies relations of domination.

Of course, there are less subtle signs of difference. The failure of racial integration since the 1954 Supreme Court decision outlawing school segregation is an overwhelming feature of public schooling. White kids learn that they are of a specific race simply by the absence of blacks in their classrooms; blacks understand this by parental instruction, but also realize that race means subordination by virtue of second-class education, inferior resources made available to them, and finally come to know that their individual and collective life chances were decided long before they entered the work world, a realization only white working-class kids have by secondary school.

Class representations are largely constructed by mass-mediated culture, especially since the working-class community, like the urban-based mass production industries that created it, passed into history. I do not want to devalue the importance of the school for determining "how working-class kids get working-class jobs" (in Paul Willis's account, mostly by rebelling against middle-class curriculum). This process still occurs in schools, but the working-class kids' culture, at least among whites, is acutely marginalized in an era when, in the older cities of industrial capitalism, the traditional working class is being wiped out.

In this chapter I want to trace the historical displacement of representations of the working class in mass-mediated culture. There are, for instance, no longer direct representations of the interactions among workers in American television, but these have been refracted through the police shows that still dominate prime time television in the United States and have, increasingly, become important, even crucial, in British and French television as well. In this connection it may be argued that television shows that are made in the USA have become important exports. As American-made durable goods no longer dominate world markets for these products, the penetration of American culture in world communications markets has grown. This inverse ratio can be seen in new films in Paris, for example. In any given week, of the dozen new films opening in that city, between four and six are American imports. "Miami Vice," "Hill Street Blues," "LA Law" are among the top twenty shows on English and French television; as far as I can tell, only advertising remains truly national, but signs of Americanization are appearing in French commercial videos, including ads.

Here I will focus on media representations and claim that they can no longer be grouped under institutional socializations which include the family, peer interactions, and schools. The media are unique sites precisely because of the specific space of technology in the production of culture. More to the point, mass-mediated visual culture occupies the "objective" space of the dream work and constitutes its double. If Althusser claims that the school is the chief ideological state apparatus, this may hold for the production of the symbolic system, the constellation of signs and codes of which what counts as reliable knowledge is constructed; but the mass media construct the social imaginary, the place where kids situate themselves in their emotional life, where the future appears as a narration of possibilities as well as limits.

I also want to argue that what we call "popular culture" has become technologically mediated, even as the acoustic guitar (formerly a vehicle for the expression of popular sentiment) is now an instrument for the production of high or esoteric music. The popular is still produced by the people, but can no longer be appropriated directly, just as the biologically given returns in a subsumed form, social construction. We can no longer, if we ever could, distinguish what really counts as a popular form from the electronically produced culture that is consumed as records, television programs, or movies. (I exclude "film" from this list because of the market distinction made between the art film and movies in the last two decades, e.g., the cinema of Erich Rohmer, Louis Malle, Yvonne Rainer, Agnes Varda, and the late John Huston, compared with Steven Spielberg, Sidney Lumet, whose position is a bit ambiguous, and Oliver Stone, whose location is not.) Television is not just a manipulation of popular culture, it constitutes a crucial element in the construction of imaginary life and is appropriated, just like rock music for young people, as popular culture, in the same manner as songs and dances for rural populations in the preindustrial era. Thus, a further claim. The electronic media can determine, to some degree, how social life is represented – their autonomous field of action consists in modes of representation – but not whether a social category will be represented. Therefore, it is literally not possible to exclude working-class representation, but it is equally improbable that these representations would remain directly under conditions where the cultural traditions of workers disappear or occupy smaller social spaces. Moreover, modes of representation are themselves refracted narratives of working-class history. So, if we find representations of working-class life assuming the configuration of police shows or, in the case of Bruce Springsteen, nostalgia for the absent subject, we can take these forms as social knowledge subject to critical deciphering like all fictions.

One of the crucial functions performed by schools since the turn of the twentieth century has been to erase the memory of a self representing popular culture. Concomitantly, schools, at all levels, are constituted to devalue popular culture including its electronically mediated forms. Just as science occupies a space of privileged knowledge even if the student never succeeds in learning any, so high art, including the literary canon, especially of the national culture, displaces the popular as valid aesthetics. The objective, conscious or not, of schooling is, among other things, to strip away what belongs to the student, to reconstitute his/her formation in terms of the boundaries imposed by hegemonic intellectuals acting for the prevailing social order. The students who succeed in these terms must be stripped of their ethnicity, race, and sex; if they are of working-class origin, their submission to the curriculum already signifies probable social mobility. Those who fail or otherwise rebel must recognize that their own subculture is not the real thing, even if they own it. I want to insist that central to the ownership of images are the products of electronically mediated art which, for all intents and purposes, must be treated by school authorities as much as by the producers of dominant ideologies, as illegitimate. Cultural histories could be written about this process of erasure in the United States and other late industrial societies. They would chronicle the degree to which English became a cultural ideal for immigrant generations in the first half of the twentieth century and how the American language was imposed on the whole world in the second half. These studies would focus on the induction of whole populations into this language and would also narrate the emergence of the representations in electronic media as the new aesthetic norm against which their own forms—both those inherited from earlier high and popular aesthetics—and those that developed out of these aesthetic forms in the earlier years of film. For it is evident that European film makers—East and West—modeled their art on their literary traditions which, in turn, emanated from popular peasant and working-class cultures as well as from bourgeois appropriations and transformations of these in that unique bourgeois cultural form, the novel. One of the great twice-told tales of film history is the revolution made by D. W. Griffith and Charlie Chaplin, a revolution in image that paralleled those initiated by Henry Ford and Fredric Taylor.

The great forgetting of these transformations remains the debt they owe to American popular cultural forms such as vaudeville, the birthplace of a dozen or more major film comedians, and, in the case of Griffith, the American pageant, itself derived from a Catholic Church spectacle. Under the extreme pressure produced by avant-garde critics and the audience itself, film became a proper object of academic study. A canon has been proposed that distinguishes art from spectacle, authors have been made directors, notwithstanding the fact that film is crucially a collective process of production, and even the critical community is divided between those charged with the task of providing a consumer guide and those whose ruminations count as literature or even science as in the case of semioticians.

But TV and rock music, forms which remain the chief repositories of contemporary popular culture, await their true co-optations and institutional legitimacy. After all, there are no departments of rock-and-roll music in the academies, especially no provision for the study of this form in music departments. Nor, except in some newly founded media studies programs, is television accorded the status of an art form. Its claim to legitimacy is clearly contested on the Right as well as on the Left, and, in the midst of the current ideological offensive by conservatives who aggressively assert their counterclaim as Keepers of the Faith of High Art, the chances for a breakthrough remain dim.

Clearly, for those who want to generate an emancipatory pedagogy the task has changed since the days when the judgments of the Frankfurt School dominated their thinking about mass culture. It is not a question of unmasking TV or rock music as forms of domination that reproduce the prevailing set-up. Instead, we are engaged in a program of reclamation, to rescue these forms as the authentic expressions of generations for whom traditional culture is not available. Certainly one cannot be unambiguously enthusiastic about television or popular music since they are, after all, highly mediated and presented to their audiences as objects of consumption rather than spheres of participation. Nevertheless, the notions of deconstruction do not apply in the usual way. Rather, critical work should uncover the utopian, popular elements of what are considered debased expressions, to invent a different set of aesthetic criteria by which to comprehend electronically mediated products, inventions that necessarily cannot be performed by teachers alone, not only because it is bad pedagogy, but also because teachers have been culturally cleansed of the popular elements of their own cultural formation and must, therefore, reflexively recover them. This process becomes a necessary prelude to reforging collective identities which, in any case, are not on the surfaces, at least for the last decade in rock and even longer in TV.

Appropriation entails production as well as critical analysis. For the real innovation in teaching popular culture is to reintroduce a theme raised in the midst of '60s political and educational movements, the idea that we are all authors of the text and that art should be popularly produced. This aspect of the work involves the struggle for resources; video production costs money (but not as much as it did before miniaturization), and musical training is a formidable regimen. The point is that critical work without an effort to produce popular art forms remains a peculiarly intellectual take on cultural life which is already distant from the experience of students. What I am saying is this: There can be no cultural pedagogy without a cultural practice that both explores the possibilities of the form and brings out students' talents. Otherwise, the statement that the artifacts of electronically mediated art are forms of popular culture descends to rhetorical flourish, or worse, reproduces criticism as high art behind the backs of the critics.

Rock and roll and TV work because they reach down to the erotic dimension of human character, the depth of which marks them as antagonistic to the precepts that control high art. As cultural forms they are neither consonant with the old model of art as subversive activity, according to which the utopian dimension of aesthetic experience consists precisely in its distance from the grubbiness of everyday life in consumer society, nor Brecht's proposal that theatre disengage the mind from emotions. Rather, popular culture both reconciles us to the social order and threatens it because it puts us in touch with pleasure, even when we have to buy it. So, critical pedagogy is, among other virtues, a *discourse on pleasure*. And school is an activity, from the point of view of all of its participants, that systematically denies pleasure; in fact, one of its most valuable features from the view of the dominant anticulture is its regime of discipline and the conversion of play into labor. Together with the effort to purge children of their own culture, to recreate the vain old dream of capitalist production, humans as *tabulae rasae*, the respect for the sovereign authority of the state as represented by school officials forms the place of the school in the division of labor. School offers a reward as the price for the surrender of the underground culture of the youth community, an exchange which substitutes work and consumption for the pleasures associated with subcultures. Since television and rock music both reinforce these values but also undermine them with the dreams of communal life and sexual pleasure, their reproductive functions are not sufficiently reliable to warrant authoritative approbation. Thus a pedagogy of popular culture finds itself in the interstices of the contradictory elements that constitute the forms of the wider society.

One of the crucial moves of the more recent versions of a critical theory of culture was to group all electronically mediated popular culture under the rubric of the "culture industry." Having determined that none of the products of this industry merits its characterization as art, critical theory thereby frees itself of the obligation to read popular culture not merely in terms of aesthetic problems, but even as ideology/critique. One can refuse to listen to rock and roll or watch television without cost, since these do not qualify for cultural analysis. In stark contrast to its critique of Marxist orthodoxy's tendency to reduce art to its so-called social determinations, the major writers in the critical theory tradition simply dismissed popular culture as just another kind of commodity production. However, it is not enough to assert the value of popular culture.

Before looking at specific representations it is necessary to recognize that television and film portray class, race, and sex in a differentiated way. These forms are constructed, to some extent, by the location of these social categories within the discursive formations in a specific space/time. These representations correspond to patterns that have been established both in the medium's own discourse and the social formation of which it is a part; the two are not always in sync, as the differences between television and rock and roll illustrate. With the important exception of recent interventions by women in rock music, this form and its various genres are marked historically by the absence of women as subjects. Unlike television in which this tendency is contested, at least at present (by "Cagney and Lacey," notably), rock music has presented songs of working-class male life and, of course, black popular music in this idiom and is intimately intertwined with black proletarian culture in many variations. Although it can be argued that rock's assertion of male worker as subject is largely nostalgic, as in the case of Bruce Springsteen, or signifies the growing marginality of workers in late capitalist societies illustrated in the bitter, sardonic songs of Clash and the Gang of Four as well as American Heavy Metal, these are all examples of male, white worker as signifier while, in contrast, in the past decade, television has systematically displaced direct working-class representation, whatever the particular ideological content.

So, the first task is to open the discussion by refusing the simple, characterization of popular culture as culture industry and delineating difference.

I want to discuss briefly the representations of women and blacks in the media. Despite their marginality, the existence of recent movements for sexual and racial equality have made a difference in the ways these categories are treated. Even in a relatively dismal era, the late seventies and eighties, blacks and women occupy visible, and, relatively speaking, direct space in media representations. The race and gender "questions" have by no means been resolved in US society and culture; indeed, there is considerable evidence that, in the absence of powerful protest and contestation around these issues, racism and sexism have reinserted themselves into public discourse in the last decade. Nevertheless, even if residual, it is virtually impossible for television to present blacks as racially skewed comic figures (although their subordination is once more asserted) and since the revival of the genre of docudramas about social "problems" where the position of women is a constant topic for both documentary and fiction treatment, women have emerged as moral agents, albeit ambiguously. This ambiguity is expressed in the absence of women's voice even when they become the subject of the film or the television genre.

As feminist analysts of film have shown, women are presented in this medium as objects of the male gaze, that is, their subjectivity is simply absent. This lack is exemplified by the rarity of women as protagonists in films, by the standpoint of both enunciation and utterances (male) from which the *mise en scene* emanates. The male voice is heard; that of the women is not, if by voice we mean not simply speech but the declaration of a standpoint; women appear but the camera gaze is from above, whereas, in contrast, male power is presented by the angle shot which magnifies the male image.

One can argue that the absence of the female voice in popular cultural representations does not apply to images. There are female cultural images but most of them exclude woman from historical and moral agency, that is, from the role of world maker. This situation is egregious, but is not the same as the problem facing black and working-class people. Blacks are rarely, if ever, represented, and when they are, they are typically devoid of agency, even in the cop television shows where they often are given the position of sidekick to an agent. Although the brief period — 1965 to 1970 — witnessed a partial reversal of the tendency of media corporations to revise the agencyless presentation of blacks, the fate of workers' representation in film and television is somewhat different. For until the early 1960s a small number of films and TV offered direct representations of white workers (usually in a comic or pathetic mode), but the mode of this presentation changed in the next decades. Workers became the object of liberal scorn; they were portrayed as defenders of the status quo, racist and sexist, and equally important, politically and socially conservative. Archie Bunker ("All in the Family") was not only a comic character, as were Chester Riley ("Life of Riley") and Ralph Cramden ("The Honeymooners"), he was also a moral agent suffused with evil, a direct violation of the code according to which the working class, however scarce in his media image, was invariably a hero. In contrast to Marlon Brando's 1955 portrayal of a benighted but brave longshoreman who, in the last analysis, comes down for truth and justice, Bunker is a troglodyte, a "hard hat" whose wrath is aimed at the young, the poor, and blacks.

It was hard for working-class kids to identify with Archie in "All in the Family," but he was, as late as the mid-1970s, a palpable working-class figure, recognizable by his syntax, his body language, his gruff, semi-articulate speech that parodied the results of working-class culture. As I shall argue in this chapter, Archie proved to be a rear-guard character. After his demise (or, as I shall show, his good fortune to have moved up the social ladder), specifically working-class representations disappear with him. Today, working-class kids may still look forward to getting working-class jobs, but forging a class identity is more difficult than ever. They confront a media complex that consistently denies their existence or displaces working-class male identity to other, upwardly mobile occupations, for example, police, football players, and other sites where conventional masculine roles are ubiquitous.

The message is clear: working-class identity, always problematic in American mass culture, is no longer an option in media representations. We live in a postindustrial service society in which the traditional markers of working-class culture survive — especially, the barroom, where waves of male industrial workers have congregated to share their grievances against the boss, their private troubles, their dreams of collective power and individual escape, their visions of women, their power displacements to the sports arena. But working-class men do not inhabit these television or movie precincts; they are the watering holes of off-duty cops, of derelicts, of miscellaneous white-collar administrators. The working class is absent among these signifiers, even as the sites and the forms of conviviality correspond to typical working-class culture.

Electronically mediated culture forms play an enlarged role in the formation of cultural identities. Of course, the claim that media are so hegemonic that they may exclude the influence of family, peers, and school appears excessive. But it would be a serious error to conclude that it is an even match. I claim that electronically mediated cultural forms have the upper hand because they carry the authority of a society that, over the last half century, has displaced patriarchal authority. For the discourse of social authority promises what family and friends can't deliver: a qualitatively better life, consumption on an expanded scale, a chance to move beyond the limits of traditional working-class life.

No institution represents the promise of this type of transcendence more than the school. Its curriculum is widely understood as a ticket to class mobility. But the content of that alternative is offered working-class kids by the situation comedies of television, the celluloid dreams of the movies, and, especially, the advertisements which evoke lifestyles considered worthy of emulation. The relationship between schooling and media representations of vocational and cultural aspirations has become symbiotic, to the extent that the curriculum is almost entirely geared to presumed occupational requirements of modern corporations and the state. The dependence of what counts as education on the collective cultural ideal is almost total. These occupational requirements, especially in large parts of the service sector, are not so much technical as they are ideological. That is, just as many advertisements sell not products but capitalism, so school learning is organized around behaviors required by types of bureaucratic work as well as the rewards offered by consumer society for performance according to established corporate norms. Students are no longer (if they ever were) enthusiastic about discovering new things to know, much less Truth; rather they want to find out how the real world works, especially what it takes to achieve a certain level of consumption. And the high school is the major site in which the "real" world of work is discovered. Students retain little or nothing of the content of knowledge (facts of history, how to perform algebraic equations, the story line of *Silas Marner*) but remember how to succeed in receiving good grades, gaining admission to a decent college or university, and how to curry favor with authorities, teachers, counselors, and employers.

Working-class kids often fail to get the message right. As Paul Willis tells us in *Learning to Labor*, their rebellion against school authority, manifested as the refusal to internalize the two parts of the curriculum—its "knowledge-based" content and its latent demand for discipline and respect for authority—insures that they will get working-class jobs rather than make it up the ladder of economic and social mobility. But, as I have argued elsewhere, while assembly-line, construction, and other heavy industrial

labor was available for school leavers until the early 1970s in the United States and United Kingdom, these options are today largely foreclosed by the restructured world economy. Parents, especially fathers, can no longer serve as substitute representations of viable occupational alternatives to those imposed by school and the media. And, this ideal erases working-class representations — the class sensorium has disappeared.

We see this problematic replayed in the film *Dirty Dancing*. An upper-middle-class family in the early 1960s goes to a Borscht Belt Catskill resort for a short vacation. Two daughters are immediately plunged into the social life, mostly with waiters and entertainers. The waiter chosen by one of the daughters is a Yale law school student; he turns out to be a philanderer. The other daughter commits the transgression that provides the dramatic grist for the narrative: she falls in love with the resort's star attraction, a working-class youth who has succeeded in learning Latin, ballet, and other "exotic" dances. He gives lessons, performs, and fools around with the women who work as entertainers or in the kitchen, similarly of lower-class background. Unlike other films of this developing genre of class indiscretion (working-class men and upper-class women), the film has a happy ending because the young woman chooses to become a dancer — she exercises her option to downward mobility, to be declassed. The working-class man has become a professional; he may be working in the Catskills but he certainly is talented. And these qualities have already separated him from his roots, so the relationship is acceptable.

I shall amplify on the theme of displacement later in this chapter. For now, it is enough to ask how to engage in a pedagogy among working-class students concerning their social identity. Indeed, if identification is a basis for the forging of a personal identity, school and media consort to persuade, cajole, and by the absence of representations force working-class kids to accept middle-class identities as the only legitimate option available to them. However, it is obvious that many will choose not to accept this course or, having bought into the aspiration, will fail to make the grade. The result for both groups is cultural homelessness. Clearly, the task of a pedagogy that addresses this dilemma is to address it by a critical examination of its contours, its motivations, and its consequences.

Several issues come to mind: 1. the ineluctability of the merger of masculinity with working-class identity; 2. the question of displacement and its effects on self-images; and 3. the class/gender reversals in contemporary representations in film and television, that is, the degree to which male conquest becomes the power equivalent of class difference. It is time to address these issues.

When I worked in the steel mills, the barroom was far more than a place to have a casual beer or to get drunk. It was the scene of union politics, the site of convivial relationships that were hard to sustain on the shop floor because of the noise, frequent speedups, and the ever-watchful eye of the foreman. Of course we had the john, but only for twenty minutes at a time; as the metal was heating up in furnaces, we often took a break. Sometimes, the john substituted for the barroom. Animated arguments about baseball, women, or an incident that had just occurred, usually one in which one of our fellow workers was hurt (I remember Felix who caught a hot wire in his leg). But, inevitably, the warning buzzer would interrupt our discussions— metal was nearly ready to come out and be drawn into wire.

So, the gin mill was the place where our collective identity as a community was forged and reproduced. Even when we had harsh disagreements about things that really mattered (should we stop work over a safety grievance or was Jackie Robinson a better second baseman than Billy Martin, a tinderbox of an issue in 1960), we knew that the next day we would have to pull together in the hot mill, that our disputes were in the family. We knew also that we had to fight the boss together, not only for the ordinary reasons of better pay and benefits but for our survival. The mill was a dangerous place and, for most of us, losing a limb meant losing the best-paying job we were ever likely to own. In the union shops of the 1950s and early 1960s, the job was a property right. As we used to say, the only reason you could get fired was if you punched the foreman while sober.

Steelwork was definitely male culture. As in Freud's essay on femininity, women were the mysterious "other." We did not know much about them and, apart from the incessant desire that occupied our prurient conversations, they did not enter into working lives. Women were an obscure object of our desire, but desire also reached out for a secure collective identity. For even as early as fifteen years after the war, the neighborhoods of Newark, Elizabeth, and Jersey City within which working people saw in the faces of others part of their own selves, a self that was recognized in the local grocery store, at bingo games held in the basements of the Catholic Churches which became the place where the women's community was formed, were in the process of dissolving. I remember meeting shopmates at the movies, in the neighborhood Chinese restaurant where we took the kids for dinner some Sunday evenings, in the bar on South Orange Avenue where a diemaker named John hung out (we became friends because we were both interested in music; he played the accordion professionally at Polish weddings on weekends).

I went to christenings and confirmations in the area around the plant which was located in an industrial suburb. Most of the families were of eastern and southern European backgrounds, not only Italians and Poles, although they were in the majority, but also Czechs, Russians, and Greeks. People lived around the northern New Jersey plants in wood-frame, one-family houses or in "uppers" (the second and third floors of multiple dwellings). Those of us who were veterans of neither World War II nor the Korean War did not qualify for special mortgage deals, so we rented apartments that ate about 25 percent of our monthly pay or less. However, a growing minority of my friends were moving to the middle-class suburbs where single-family housing developments were mushrooming or, more graphically, springing up like weeds. These were more modern homes often built without firm foundations even though they were constructed on landfill. They surely did not fulfill the letter of James Truslow Adam's "American Dream," but they were an acceptable facsimile until something better came along.

Suburban flight was made feasible by low-interest mortgages, but also by the federal highway program initiated by President Harry Truman and fulfilled by the Eisenhower administration. In earlier years, living fifteen or twenty miles from the plant was simply not an option because the roads were invariably local. Such a trip could take more than two hours. Now, barring traffic jams, night-shift workers could make it to work in twenty minutes. And those working days simply left home before rush hour and came back late. For many, being away from the wife and kids presented few, if any problems; male culture excluded women, and the notion that men should share child care was simply unthought in most families in those days. Certainly, many workers were left behind — blacks, Hispanics, the young, not yet able to raise a down payment or still unmarried, and older workers who had never recovered from the Depression.

White-working-class flight was engendered, in part, by the influx of southern and Caribbean blacks into large northern cities, also by the failure of federal and state lawmakers to expand the federal housing program beyond the poor. In fact, the choice of the home mortgage program was the alternative to new multiunit housing for workers. The fact is, housing for large families was simply unavailable in the cities at rents that even relatively well-paid steel and auto workers could afford. Racism was not the "cause" of white flight in the sense that individuals who harbored these attitudes decided to move to get away from blacks. Racism was the result of a combination of developments. In addition to the urban housing shortage, where virtually no new one-family moderate-income homes were constructed after the war, the era was marked by a precipitous decline in services — schools, hospitals, and amenities such as recreation and child care were in either serious disrepair or overcrowded.

In historical retrospect, the deterioration of the urban regions after the war was the result of federal and corporate policy. By the mid-sixties, center city industrial plants were closing down. In Harrison, the industrial suburb of Newark, General Motors removed its roller bearing plant to the Union County suburb, Kenilworth; General Electric closed its lamp factory in the black section of Newark. By the end of the decade, no major industrial plant remained in that city. Jersey City and Hoboken suffered similar fates; industrial expansion was still a powerful spur to economic growth, but not in the big cities. Capital and white-working-class flight, together with federal housing and highway programs and the enthusiasm of local communities, gave away the keys to the town to any corporation willing to build a plant, office building, or research facility.

The dispersion of white workers into the suburbs did not immediately destroy working-class communities, although they were considerably weakened by the late 1950s. The gin mill next to the production mill retained its pride of place. Sometimes this function was performed by a bar located in a local union hall or in a fraternal association of, say, Poles or Ukrainians. Typically, after going off shift a worker would "stop" at the bar for an hour or two before going home, even a home as far as forty miles away. There, he would play darts, shuffle board, or pool or just sit at the bar and drink and talk. Those who worked days arrived home at six o'clock (the shift ends at 3 P. M.). After supper, if there were no chores, the family might sit in front of the television set.

The television explosion of the 1950s is generally acknowledged to have changed the leisure-time activities of Americans. The simulations that film brought to theater audiences now became daily fare. The stimulation of the unconscious by imaging (the term is DiLauretis's from *Alice Doesn't Know*) consists in simulacrum of the dream work so that identities are formed through identification with the gendered characters that appear on the screen. Aural media also are powerful desiring machines, but sound is burdened with an enormous load because images must be produced by the listener. Identification can be fomented, but with difficulty. The film form invokes the stark real-life character. DiLauretis argues that women do not insert themselves into film culture, that they are absent in imagining. They cannot identify with the actual representations of women on the screen, for these women are the objects of male desire, they do not occupy subject positions from which emanate distinctive female voices. That is, there is no chance for identification unless women accept the object space to which they have been assigned.

Males identify with characters (protagonists, heroes) who are the subjects of narratives; women are objects of desire/exchange/conflicts among males and only assume distinctive character when they occupy male subject positions from which, in both comedies and drama they must inevitably fall (the Spencer Tracy, Katherine Hepburn comedies such as *Woman of the Year* and *Desk Set*, the Joan Crawford soap opera, *Mildred Pierce*, in which women who speak as male characters find that adopting these personae invites self-destruction). Male workers do find representations in film and television in the 1950s. The characters of Ralph Cramden and Ed Norton ("Honeymooners") and William Bendix's Chester Riley ("Life of Riley") are comically absurd, the situations often artificial and juvenile, but family relationships articulate with the prevalent war between the sexes, the distinctiveness of male culture, the absence of a corresponding women's community.

Cramden is a bus driver and, like many working-class men, dreams of escaping his routine, relatively low-paid job by entering a constant succession of imagined business schemes. His driving ambition for wealth is lodged entirely in the imaginary (male) fantasies that are widely shared. His wife can barely disguise contempt for these wildly improbable desires, most of which serve not to enhance the opportunity for real social mobility, but Ralph's pathetic effort to establish his dominance in the home. On the other side, Norton, a sewer worker, harbors neither illusion nor the desire to flee his job. The sewer affords him a considerable measure of autonomy, at least in comparison to factory work or bus driving. He enjoys the lack of responsibility his job entails but fervently asserts its dignified character against the constant chidings of his quixotic friend.

As with most television situation comedies, the characters have a cartoon quality; there is no room for complexity in the representations. And the stripped-down sets evoke 1930s Depression decorum rather than the postwar era. The Honeymooners have been left behind the white urban exodus; they are transhistorical working-class types. Norton is invariably dressed in a T-shirt and wears his hat indoors. Cramden dons the uniform of a bus driver, signifying the ambiguity of his situation; clearly, he is a wage laborer, but his will is that of a petty official, since genuine wealth has been foreclosed to him. Cramden displaces his frustration onto intrafamilial quarrels. His wife's (Alice) housework never counts as real work; his characteristic posture is that of an inquisitor (What have *you* done all day?). Since she rarely awards him the deference he urgently needs, given his relatively degraded social position, his usual gesture is the verbal threat of violence (against women), "One of these days...pow, right in the kisser." Alice seems bored by his remonstrations, and we, the audience, know that Ralph is simply too henpecked or, in the male vernacular, pussy-whipped to follow through.

"The Honeymooners" retains its large audience after thirty years because it displays the range of class and gender relations. Its class ideology is represented by the absence of the labor process except discursively. The family relations displace the class relations as Ralph seeks to dominate Alice, the real proletarian, who remains recalcitrant. Here we see the inner core of male fantasies: lacking the individual power to achieve the freedom wealth presumably affords, domination becomes the object of male desire. As with Hegel's master, Ralph desperately covets Alice's recognition, but is denied such pleasures, except in the last instance when, at his wits' end, Ralph demands the approbation which she must grant.

"The Honeymooners" succeeds as a tableau of the sadomasochistic version of the family romance. Ralph's infantile behavior generates Alice's maternal role even as there are no children in the household. Ralph plays master, insofar as he trumpets his breadwinner status, but also is the emotionally dependent male for whom sexuality is identical with submission. Alice is not a moral agent, only a mirror to the absurdity of male will.

Caricature notwithstanding, working-class life demanded representations in the 1950s and early 1960s. By the later years, the dispersion of working-class culture made direct representation improbable. Where the previous generation knew economic class as a regulative principle, including the real subordination of women by men, the generation of the 1960s was by comparison free floating. The universalization of postsecondary schooling (misnamed higher education then, as now) brought many working-class kids in contact with ruling- and upper-class peers. The results from the point of view of the established social structure were potentially devastating. Surely class resentments and distinctions do not disappear in youth culture, but are explicitly challenged by the effort to invent new normative principles of social relations. These relations, which held equality as their highest cultural ideal, challenge generations of difference, not only of economic power but of sexually construed cultures.

But the worker as tragic hero is a transitional figure, for the tragedy is born of the disintegration already prefigured by consumer society, especially suburbanization. Working-class culture is preeminently urban; it belongs to the industrializing era which by the late 1960s had passed. Postindustrial culture is already postmodern: it is marked by boundary crossing. While working-class culture still finds renewal on the shop floor, its residential base is dispersed. In the suburbs of major metropolitan centers, industrial workers mow their lawns alongside professionals, managers, and small-business neighbors.

By the early 1980s, Archie Bunker, the Queens, N.Y. political and social Neanderthal, had opened a gin mill. Having pushed himself up into the business-owning small middle class, Archie left his working-class roots behind, not only in his newly found proprietorship but also in his contacts. In this assimilation, he continued the tendencies of the earlier incarnation of the show; recall, the Bunker family lived in that part of New York that most resembled the suburbs. The only black family he knew owned and operated a dry cleaning business. In other ways, he rubbed shoulders with those who had more completely achieved one of the crucial elements of the American dream, a business of one's own. So it is entirely reasonable that Archie should aspire to gaining a toehold on the social ladder. With that, the Archie of that show, "Archie's Place," lasted only two seasons, then disappeared into the middle class.

From the mid-1970s, there simply are no direct representations of working-class males (much less women) in television. Representations are dispersed to beer advertisements, thirty-second images of football players hoisting their favorite brands, jostling each other in timid evocations of the ribbing characteristic of working-class bar culture, cop shows in which characteristic working-class culture is displaced and recontextualized in the station house, on the streets, the bars in which cops congregate. These are displacements, so we see only the remainders — conviviality, friendship that is overdetermined by the police buddy system, the obligatory partnership. It is in these interactions, when the partners of, say "Hill Street Blues," discuss their personal problems or their troubles with the department, that the old class solidarity bonds are permitted to come to the surface, often against the captain or even the lieutenants who are a step above the line and possess some authority. We know that the patrolmen (and some women) may rise to sergeant but are not likely to make lieutenant, much less captain. These are not educated people. Their bravery entitles them to recognition, not rank. They have their own hangouts, their personal troubles (especially with women). In contrast, officials, whatever their origins, do not congregate in barrooms; they have no sharers of their troubles because they must observe the tacit code of hierarchy. In recent films, displacement of class to the police continues, but is joined by displacement of sex (gender) relations to class as well.

Hollywood movies (*Someone to Watch Over Me, Barfly*) are marked by a conventional theme in contemporary narrative: the working-class man is powerfully attracted to an upper-class woman, disrupting not only the prohibition of interclass romance, but also the family romance. In these instances, to be working class is identified with masculinity, upper-class membership with femininity. This is exemplified in *Barfly*, the nonstory of a derelict writer who meets two women: one a derelict, apparently a renegade from upper-class life who names her profession as "drinking"; the second a publisher of a literary magazine who "discovers" the writer. The triangle is resolved by his choice of the woman barfly who, like him, lives to drink and engages in barroom brawls. Her masculinity allows him to hook up with her, to combine sex and male bonding. In contrast, his benefactor is a beautiful woman who cannot hold her liquor and, because she lives outside male lower-class culture, cannot hold him. The woman barfly engages the world like a man in other ways. She goes off with the writer's arch enemy, a bartender in his favorite hangout, because he comes to work one day with a full bottle of bourbon. Like many males, her loyalty to people is always subordinate to loyalty to pleasure. In the end, the writer admires such priorities, for his own life has been conducted according to the precept that conventional morality is for the nerds.

Someone to Watch Over Me finds a cop of plainly working-class parentage, married to a tough, feisty working-class woman; they live with their kid in a modest single-family house in Queens.

The cop is assigned to protect an upper-class woman, ensconced in a Manhattan townhouse. He is assigned the midnight shift and quickly has an affair with her, an event that disrupts his tension-filled, but stable home life. As with the young publisher of *Barfly*, the woman is attracted by the merger of class identity and masculinity and he by the reverse class/sex combination. *Someone to Watch Over Me* reenacts a crucial male working-class fantasy, to dominate a beautiful rich woman, to make the "impossible dream" real.

These films address the insufficiency of middle-class comfort for the generation of upwardly mobile working-class kids born after the war. The protagonist of *Barfly* chooses the underlife, a degraded bohemia punctuated by the struggle for male honor even in the lower depths. The cop is socialized into a conventional honorific position—the centurion—but finds it suffused with mediocrity and, most important of all, marked by repetition and continuity with the anterior generation. What is new is adventure, which can only be fulfilled by sexual indiscretion, "penetration" into the forbidden territory of the upper class. But besides the exotic, for the cop, buried in the routine tasks dictated by a bureaucracy that seems entirely beyond his power to control, sex becomes the power that can propel him out of his own real-life subordination.

It may be that the discourse of sex refers today to class issues, but it is also true that class discourse refers to gender domination. The import of the image of the working-class cop engaging in sexual relations with a woman in an entirely improbable class position is not that American society is somehow democratic; these relationships end in disaster. They are themselves sundered, but more important they wreck families, personal lives, and so forth. The significance is otherwise. Class is no barrier when upper-class women are involved. In current representations, the reverse is rarely portrayed. Femininity is not a universal signifier, the privilege is reserved for male culture.

There are, of course, no public representations of working-class culture other than the images associated with male bonding. In fact, one may read *Barfly* as a signal that one key site of class solidarity, the bar, has been declassed, or, more precisely, the lumpies are the legatees of what was once a marginalized but distinct aspect of American subcultures. And just as women are absent from media representations of social agents, they constitute no part of working-class culture. Working-class culture is almost always white and male, even in its displaced forms. The community of women is generally denied, but, as I have argued, women appear as the new proletariat insofar as maleness exercises itself as dominating power.

At first glace, *Flashdance* is an exception to the rule. A woman welder in a steel fabricating plant falls in love with the boss, himself cast in the tradition of the self-made man rather than the MBA or accountant. Here class difference is mediated by other bonds of solidarity, particularly sexuality (itself a difference and membership in the same occupational community). The film presents the "new" woman as both male and female. Yet, the relationship presupposes both her male and her female personae. Like *Barfly*, interclass sexual relations are possible only when the woman displays masculinity, which remains the privileged class position. In short, in contrast to the 1950s when a viable working-class culture, connected to powerful large-scale industry, represented America's emergence as the leading world economic power, and this work was accorded considerable status in media (*On the Waterfront*, Arthur Miller's *A View from the Bridge*, and *Saturday's Hero* are just three films of this decade), class has been displaced in two ways—first, to other signifiers of masculinity and, second, to the code violations entailed in sexual relations between working-class or declassed men and upper-class women. In this case, sex/class relations are reversed. Men achieve class parity, despite lower-class roots, with women owing to the status conferred upon masculine sexuality and its powers by society.

In *Someone to Watch Over Me* and other examples of this relationship, the absent male is a businessman. His shadow existence is owed to the obvious fact entailed by the conditions of his own success: his real marriage is to his business, not to his wife. Sexuality of the traditional sort is confined to those without sublimations, which accounts for its relatively ambiguous role in the *Barfly's* life. Writing and booze are serious competitors, but for the working-class man, neither art nor business provide the channels for the discharge of erotic energies. At the same time, sex is not really an acceptable form of power, for unlike art or business (real work) its results are horrendous from a moral point of view. The message of this film is that transgression, although possible, is not desirable. Similar to nineteenth century and early twentieth century novels (Thomas Hardy, D. H. Lawrence), love is forbidden by class difference, and when the barrier is transgressed dire consequences ensue. Yet, moral proscription aside, the sex/class/power axis in television and movies constitute a critique of the cultural ideal of consumer society that passes for the 1980s equivalent of the mobility myth. The entrepreneurial ambition which motored two generations of immigrants has disappeared from public view; the remainder is the civil service which has become the far horizon of well-being for a new working-class that can no longer count on high-paying factory jobs. The army and police force have replaced industrial labor for working-class men for whom professional options simply have never existed.

Male bonding persists in these contexts, but not the solidarity born of the mutual recognition among production workers that they share a common fate as well as a common existence. For the civil servant, existence never is identical to essence. There is always one place more in the bureaucratic hierarchy for which to strive. On this material foundation, a family could, as late as 1980, enjoy the prospect of owning a single-family home in the cop or non-commissioned-officers enclaves bordering on the suburbs. Such options are increasingly out of the question. And, because the concept of collective fate is constantly disturbed by the latest promotional examination, so is social solidarity, at least for younger officers.

The only vital life consists in dreams of power, the most vivid form of which is male sexuality. Contrasted to earlier direct representations in which sex is virtually absent from discourse, but class persists, today's movies and television code sex, class, and power interchangeably. As with earlier genres, women do not occupy subject positions, they remain the palpable objects of male desire and by this precise relation experience class reversal. In sum, the persistence of even these displaced representations of workers and their culture (Paul Schrader's *Blue Collar* [1980] may have been the last direct example) attests to the media's yearning for a source of vitality and renewal which clearly cannot be derived within ruling-class relationships, a genre that survives not in the drawing room comedy but in the old tradition of portrayals of scandal and corruption (see the Oliver Stone movie, *Wall Street*). This lack of credible ruling-class subjects occurs at a time when public confidence in business appears to be considerably higher than at any time since the Gilded Age. Yet, what excited the old public's imagination rather than admiration was the degree to which the capitalist merged with the frontiersman earlier in the century. Despite his ruthlessness, he was a romantic figure, a conqueror, a risk taker, and, above all, sexy. This figure was displaced to the underworld boss in the 1930s and 1940s, when entrepreneurship had already passed to the hijacker, the bank robber, the gambler, figures revived briefly in the 1960s.

The working class is no longer possible as mythic figure, but neither is Ivan Boesky. While politicians and investment bankers have lost any semblance of sexuality, male or otherwise, class culture survives as masculinity. What working-class culture may signify is the last hope for class equality, provided the object is a woman.

NEW PERSPECTIVES ON "MASS" CULTURE

In the last two decades, converging intellectual movements in the critical theory of education and in cultural studies have, in different ways, rejected the idea, pervasive until the 1960s, that "mass" culture was an unmitigated disaster whose outcome was nothing less than the reshaping of the human personality along the lines imposed by technological domination. In education the works of Henry Giroux, Roger Simon, and Paul Willis stand out as complementary to the arguments advanced by feminists such as Teresa DiLauretis and Ellen Willis and critics such as Robert Christgau, Simon Frith, and others who have argued that rock music, film, and other popular forms express, in different ways (generational, feminist, working class) types of social and cultural oppositions. We are at the crossroads where our thesis that schools are sites of opposition must be integrated with the critique of critical theory's dismissal of popular culture.

In the most recent past, in *Education Under Siege*, Henry Giroux and I have advanced the idea that the critique of schools was not enough, that radicals must learn to speak a language of possibility, while avoiding the illusion that a few school reforms could adequately alter the profound commitment of schools to reproduce the prevailing system of social power. Speaking a language of possibility entails speaking about the cultural experience of students as if their knowledge of rock and television and other electronically mediated popular forms was a type of reliable knowledge whose status, even though not legitimate in terms of the curriculum to which they are responsible, may be understood, at least in the classroom and among peers, as an appropriate starting point for cultural and intellectual formation. There are two ways to proceed with this project. One is to claim a rock and television aesthetic commensurate with, say, literature and classical music. A necessary corollary to this strategy is the claim that these forms embody moral and ethical values that school authorities, professional critics, and philosophers can recognize as plausible alternatives to those offered by so-called high cultural forms. This is a tricky path for it entails an explicit acceptance of the criteria that have marked high culture since the early bourgeois era, an approach already suggested, for example, by the effort of proponents to argue that jazz is "America's classical music" or the already-mentioned distinction made between "film" and "movies" which claim mass audiences. In this undertaking, the distinction between high and popular culture is recognized only as a question of audience, not an intrinsic characteristic of the work of art. Thus placing pop art in a museum marks it off from its more commercial representations. Or, the difference in the minimalism of Glass and Reich from that of punk rock is played out largely in the presentation of the former in the concert hall while the latter plays in clubs and large sports stadiums and sells records in shops designed exclusively for the pop market. The first perspective also challenges the curriculum to make a place for popular culture, if it proves that the work merits consideration as legitimate knowledge.

This approach is consistent with the dominant doctrine, rarely practiced in schools, of pluralism. It would not deny the validity of literature of film, or what is called classical music, but would demand that the repertoire of acceptable cultural objects be expanded. Further, it might claim that beginning from student experience, validating what students already know, is just good pedagogy that can influence the process of language acquisition, written expression, in short, the learnings that are currently grouped under the rubric of literacy. This is, of course, an expression of "new realism" that increasingly characterizes left politics in an era when cultural radicalism is in retreat. The question posed by this strategy is whether its success undermines the radical content of the cultural project itself by facilitating its integration into the prevailing curriculum.

Obviously, the second perspective would insist that the popular forms possess significance lacking in contemporary high art which, it can be easily shown, survives primarily as a weapon of distinction, part of the apparatus which maintains class and generational differences. The second strategy is to argue for the historicity of high culture as an avant-garde—those who propose through their art a utopian future—to be located chiefly, even if not exclusively, in such expressions as can be identified in popular culture. It would have to demonstrate that popular expressions propose a new vision of the future as well as a different critique of the present, whether coded or not. And the fundamental issue is surely pleasure, for if rock music can be delineated from other forms it is precisely its evocation of pleasure as a mode of life that moves its detractors to the lengths of Allan Bloom. Bloom castigates rock and roll for its suggestion of sexual intercourse as if this were an aesthetic crime. Presumably the representation of sexuality in art must remain a delicate matter, best exemplified, one supposes, by the muffled repressed invocations of Victorian literature, a Henry James perhaps, or even better Gustave Flaubert. In any case, the claim that youth culture possesses a radical alternative aesthetic of pleasure spills over to the critique of the schools as institutions of deprivation and, equally important, constitutes a harsh critique of the workworld as necessarily opposed to the kind of life that rock dreams articulate. Cultural radicalism has absolutely no chance of being accepted, even on pluralist grounds, in the present conjuncture. It would not legitimate its ideology by reference to accepted educational norms. On the contrary, it would propose a new relationship between work and play that would posit their necessary integration rather than opposition, and opposition, which in the current arrangements, ineluctably entail the subordination of the latter.

Clearly, either regime would integrate writing and reading with popular knowledge. But it would by necessity break the line between critique and practice. A curriculum in popular cultural studies would be required to include at its center video and music production and performance. Students would make videos that expressed their own ideas—writing the scripts, producing the documentaries, learning how to write and perform the music, and so forth. This departure from traditional humanities and cultural studies programs at the secondary and postsecondary levels is crucial if the privileged place of science over technique, of criticism over production, of intellectual over manual labor is to be overcome.

Conclusion

SCHOOLING, POPULAR CULTURE, AND A PEDAGOGY OF POSSIBILITY

Henry A. Giroux and Roger I. Simon

♦ Recent educational debate in North America and England has focused primarily on two related issues. On the one hand, educational reform has been linked to the imperatives of big business. Schools are fashioned as training grounds for different sectors of the workforce and play a major role in providing the knowledge and occupational skills necessary for domestic production and expansion capital abroad. This view links schooling to the demands of a technocratic and specialized literacy. Its offensive is less ideological than it is technicist and instrumental in nature. On the other hand, this decade has witnessed the increasing rise of the culturalist wing of the far Right, especially in the United States. The political impetus for this ideological detour in the conservative offensive has been legitimated and sustained in the United States largely because of the presence of President Reagan's former secretary of education, William Bennett. Bennett has broadened the conservative's definition of schooling by reaffirming its primacy as a guardian of Western Civilization. Reiterating the call for excellence, Bennett has attempted to promote a nineteenth-century brand of elitism through an appeal to a narrow and unitary definition of classical, Western tradition while simultaneously arguing for a pedagogy unencumbered by the "messy" concerns of equity, social justice, or the need for a critical citizenry. Bennett's redefinition of the purpose of education and the role that teachers might play within its restricted notion of academic achievement has set the stage for a number of ideological assaults against liberal and radical views of schooling. In this refurbished conservative discourse, the scorned culprits are modernity, democracy, and difference. Classical Western traditions are defended against a host of enemies, including the alleged relativism running rampant in the various academic disciplines in the universities; in the social protest movements of students, who appear to threaten the various forms of authority that constitute the social order; in the increasing cultural and ethnic diversity of the United States, which threatens the dominant culture's hegemonic and patriarchical claim to universality; and in the expanding sphere of popular culture, which is viewed as a tasteless and dangerous threat to the notions of civility and order.

Although these positions defend various aspects of the conservative agenda for schooling and manifest themselves in different ways in various Western countries, they share a common ideological and political thread. They view schools as a particular way of life organized to produce and legitimate either the economic and political interests of business elites or the privileged cultural capital of ruling-class groups. More importantly, both positions represent an attack on the notion of culture as a public sphere in which the basic principles and practices of democracy are learned amid struggle, difference, and dialogue. Similarly, both positions legitimate forms of pedagogy that deny the voices, experiences, and histories through which students give meaning to the world and in doing so often reduce learning to the dynamics of transmission and imposition.

We want to intervene in this debate by arguing for schools as sites of struggle and for pedagogy as a form of cultural politics. In both cases, we want to argue for schools as social forms that expand human capacities in order to enable people to intervene in the formation of their own subjectivities and to be able exercise power in the interest of transforming the ideological and material conditions of domination into social practices which promote social empowerment and demonstrate democratic possibilities. We want to argue for a critical pedagogy that considers how the symbolic and material transactions of the everyday shape the meaning and ethical substance people give to their experiences and voices. This is not a call for a unifying ideology by which to construct a critical pedagogy; it is a call for a politics of difference and empowerment as the basis for a developing a critical pedagogy through and for the voices of those who are often silenced. This is a pedagogy that refuses detachment, one that understands how multiple forms of power and experience structure and position different groups in sets of relations that must always be questioned as part of a larger project of extending and improving human capabilities; for a pedagogy that recognizes that teaching and learning represent different aspects of how meaning is produced through the construction of forms of power, experiences, identities that also have wider political and cultural significance.

With these issues in mind, we want to emphasize the importance of critical pedagogy by analyzing its potentially transformative relations within the sphere of popular culture. In our view, popular culture represents a significant pedagogical site that raises important questions about the relevance of everyday life, student voice, and the investments of meaning and pleasure that structure and anchor the why and how of learning.

At first glance, the relationship between popular culture and classroom pedagogy may seem remote. Popular culture is organized around the investments of pleasure and fun, while pedagogy is defined largely in instrumental terms. Popular culture is located in the terrain of the everyday, while pedagogy generally legitimates and transmits the language, codes, and values of the dominant culture. Popular culture is appropriated by students and is a major source of knowledge for authorizing their voices and experiences, even as pedagogy authorizes the voices of the adult world of teachers and school administrators.

Yet, there is a fundamental similarity between popular culture and pedagogy that needs to be articulated. Both exist as subordinate discourses (Grossberg 1986). For both liberals and radicals, pedagogy is often theorized as what is left after curriculum content is determined. It is what follows the selection of ideologically correct content, its legitimacy rooted in whether or not it represents the proper teaching style. In the dominant discourse, pedagogy is simply the measurable, accountable methodology used to transmit course content. It is not a mutually determining element in the construction of knowledge and learning; it is an afterthought reduced to the status of the technical and the instrumental. In a similar mode, in spite of the work that has been done in the area of cultural studies in the last decade, popular culture is still largely defined in the dominant discourse as the cultural residue which remains when high culture is subtracted from the overall totality of cultural practices; it is the trivial and the insignificant of everyday life, a form of popular taste often deemed unworthy of either academic legitimation or high social affirmation.

These differences and similarities point to a theory of schooling and culture that devalues pedagogy as a form of cultural production and ignores popular culture as a social practice deeply implicated not only in various forms of domination but also in the construction of active resistance and struggle. Needless to say, while popular culture is generally ignored in the schools, it is not insignificant in shaping how students view themselves and their own relations to various forms of pedagogy and learning. In fact, it is precisely in the relationship between pedagogy and popular culture that the important understanding arises of making the pedagogical more political and the political more pedagogical. It is precisely this dangerous absence regarding the relationship between pedagogy and popular culture that needs to be made theoretically visible and pedagogically operative in the language of schooling. Rather than being marginalized and rendered insignificant in the discourse of schooling, popular culture and pedagogy represent important terrains of cultural struggle which offer both subversive discourses and important theoretical elements through which it becomes possible to rethink schooling as a viable and important form of cultural politics.

PEDAGOGY AND THE PRODUCTION OF KNOWLEDGE

Pedagogy is a deliberate attempt to influence how and what knowledge and identities are produced within and among particular sets of social relations. It can be understood as a practice through which people are incited to acquire a particular moral character. As both a political and practical activity it attempts to influence the occurrence and qualities of experiences. When one practices pedagogy one acts with the intent of creating experiences that will organize and disorganize a variety of understandings of our natural and social world in particular ways. What we are emphasizing here is that pedagogy is a concept that draws attention to the processes through which knowledge is produced.

> It enables us...to ask under what conditions and through what means we "come to know." How one teaches is therefore of central interest but, through the prism of pedagogy, it becomes inseparable from what is being taught and, crucially, how one learns....What pedagogy addresses is the process of production and exchange in this cycle, the transformation of consciousness that takes place in the interaction of three agencies—the teacher, the learner, and the knowledge they produce together. (Lusted 1986: 3)

Such an emphasis does not at all diminish pedagogy's concern with "what is to be done?" As a complex and extensive term, pedagogy's concern includes the integration in practice of particular curriculum content and design, classroom strategies and techniques, a time and space for the practice of those strategies and techniques, and evaluation purposes and methods. All of these aspects of educational practice come together in the reality of the classroom.

But the discourse of pedagogy centers something more. It stresses that the realities of what happens in classrooms reveal how a teacher's work within an institutional context specifies a particular version of what knowledge is of most worth, in what direction we should desire, what it means to know something, and how we might construct representations of ourselves, others, and our physical and social environment. In other words, pedagogy is simultaneously about the practices students and teachers might engage in together *and* the cultural politics such practices support. In this sense, to propose a pedagogy is to construct a political vision.

For this book, we have invited a number of contributors to explore the relation between aspects of what we have come to refer as "critical pedagogy" and the manifold characteristics of popular culture. The education organized by a critical pedagogy is one that must raise questions of how we can work for the reconstruction of social imagination in the service of human freedom. What notions of knowing and what forms of learning are required by such a project? Required is an education rooted in a view of human freedom as the understanding of necessity and the transformation of necessity. We need a pedagogy whose standards and achievement objectives are determined in relation to goals of critique and the enhancement of human capacities and social possibilities. This means that teaching and learning must be linked to the goals of educating students: to understand why things are the way they are and how they got to be that way; to appropriate critically forms of knowledge that exist outside of their immediate experience; to make the familiar strange and the strange familiar (Clifford 1981; Clifford and Marcus 1986; McLaren 1986; McLaren 1989); to take risks and struggle with ongoing relations of power from within a life-affirming moral culture; and to envisage a world which is "not yet" in order to enhance the conditions for improving the grounds upon which life is lived (Simon 1987; Giroux 1988).

EDUCATION AND THE POPULAR

The development of cultural studies in the last two decades has produced an intense interest in the concept of popular culture and, correspondingly, a number of important efforts to theorize the idea of the popular. Given our specific concern with popular culture and its relation to pedagogy, it is important to recognize that well over one hundred years ago those who controlled the developing agenda of state schooling were implicitly, if not explicitly, theorizing a notion of the popular that has dominated the practice of schooling ever since.

At the dawn of Canadian Confederation (1860–1875), Egerton Ryerson, a social architect and then head of Ontario's emerging public school system, was writing and speaking against a particular form of "the popular." Addressing himself to educators, he warned against the "trashy and positively unwholesome literature which is so widely extended throughout the country in the shape of…novelette papers" (Ryerson 1868: 72). He was convinced that reading such material would help undercut "our [Canada's] connection with the mother country" and that officials should be intercepting at the U.S.-Canadian border all "obscene" and "filthy" publications "now so abundant in the States." Ryerson thought that "persons who read little or nothing besides the trashy novels of the day would do better not to read at all." Yet he admitted "the most popular and best thumbed works in any of our common reading-rooms are invariably those which are the most worthless — we might say the most dangerous" (Ryerson 1870: 53).

What Ryerson was talking about was not material analogous to contemporary pornography. He was referring to relatively inexpensive publications of short stories and novels filled with local vernacular expressions and "republican ideas." It was in a context such as this that, for instance, Mark

Twain's *Tom Sawyer* provoked vilification (Morgan 1987). What is at issue in positions such as Ryerson's is not simply an attempt at aesthetic definition, a matter, for instance, of articulating the distinguishing features between a "high" and "low" or "popular" culture. Rather, given the current control over the social field by individuals who have sentiments similar to Ryerson's, what is more fundamentally at issue is which set of cultural forms will be acknowledged as the legitimate substance of state-provided schooling. How will state schooling be used as an agency of moral regulation. The issue here is very basic; it is a matter of what vision of future social relations a public school system will support. Such visions have always been defined by a few for the many. Examining what has been excluded as well as required in official curricula clearly reveals, in country after country, that such decisions have been dialectically structured within inequitable and unjust relationships. Indeed, Ryerson's invective against the popular was asserted from the assumption of a superiority and natural dominance he associated with his class, gender, and race.

The popular has been consistently seen by educators as potentially disruptive of existing circuits of power, as both threat and profane desire, subversive in its capacity to reconstruct the investments of meaning and desire and dangerous in its potential to provide a glimpse of social practices and popular forms that affirm both difference and different ways of life (Rockhill 1987). The year 1988 is no exception. Allan Bloom, for example, in his best-selling book in the United States, *The Closing of the American Mind*, argues that popular culture, especially rock and roll, has resulted in the atrophy of both nerve and intelligence in American youth. Rock and roll and, more generally, popular culture represent in Bloom's mind barbaric appeals to sexual desire. Not to be undone by this insight, Bloom further argues that since "Young people know that rock has the beat of sexual intercourse" (Bloom 1987: 73), popular culture is simply synonymous for turning "life…into a nonstop, commercially prepackaged masturbational fantasy" (p. 75). Of course, Bloom's sentiments have been shaped by what he perceives as indices of a serious moral and intellectual decline among American youth: the challenge to authority formed from the student movements of the 1960s and the leveling ideology of democratic reform characteristic of the discourse of radical intellectuals. In effect, what one is offered in Bloom's book are the unsupported authoritarian ravings that appear to emulate the very convulsions he suggests characterize the popular forms he attacks. He writes:

> The inevitable corollary of such sexual interest is rebellion against the parental authority that represses it. Selfishness thus becomes indignation and then transforms itself into morality. The sexual revolution must overthrow all the forces of domination, the enemies of nature and happiness. From love comes hate, masquerading as social reform. A worldview is balanced on the sexual fulcrum. What were once unconscious or half-conscious childish resent-

ments become the new Scripture. And then comes the longing for the classless, prejudice-free, conflictless, universal society that necessarily results from liberated consciousness—"We Are the World," a pubescent version of *Alle Menschen werden Bruder*, the fulfillment of which has been inhibited by the political equivalents of Mom and Dad. These are the three great lyrical themes: sex, hate, and a smarmy, hypocritical version of brotherly love. Such polluted sources issue in a muddy stream where only monsters can swim. (p. 74)

The monsters who inhabit this terrain are contemporary youth, subordinate groups, and all those others who refuse to take seriously the canonical status of the Great Books that embody Bloom's revered notion of Western Civilization. Those more specifically responsible for this version of contemporary madness are the Left, feminists, Marxists, and anyone who uses a Walkman radio. Bloom's discourse is based on the myth of decline, and his attack on popular culture is inextricably linked to the call for the restoration of a so-called lost classical heritage. Rather than a sustained attack on popular culture, this is an all-encompassing discourse of totalitarianism parading behind a veil of cultural restoration. Its enemies are democracy, utopianism, and the unrealized political possibilities contained in the cultures of "the other," those who are poor, black, female, and share the common experience of powerlessness. Its goal is a form of education that presupposes moral and social regulation in which the voice of tradition provides the ideological legitimation for a ministry of culture. Its echo is to be found in Hitler's Germany and Mussolini's Italy; its pedagogy is as profoundly reactionary as its ideology and can be summed up simply in these terms: transmission and imposition.

In mentioning Ryerson and Bloom, we are stressing the rather straightforward point that, historically, state-regulated forms of schooling have viewed popular culture as marginal and dangerous terrain, something to be inoculated against, though occasionally explored for the incidental motivational ploy that might enhance student interest in a particular lesson or subject. In other words, educators have traditionally viewed popular culture as those knowledges and pleasures distinguished from, properly subordinate to, and at times co-optable by, the agenda of schooling. As will become apparent, we contend this notion of popular culture must be rethought. However, if we are particularly interested in the possible relationships between pedagogy and popular culture, this traditional view cannot be completely dismissed. What we think must be preserved is the centrality of teachers' work. That is, useful notions of popular culture must be articulated to a particular notion of pedagogy.

PEDAGOGICAL RELEVANCE OF POPULAR CULTURE

Our interest is not in aesthetic or formal qualities of popular cultures. Nor are we particularly concerned with the way in which various popular forms might be codified into subjects or themes for study in cultural studies programs. Rather we begin with more fundamental questions, those, for instance, that are raised by teachers: What relationship do my students see between the work we do in class and the lives they live outside of class? Is it possible to incorporate aspects of students' lived culture into the work of schooling without simply confirming what they already know? Can this be done without trivializing the objects and relationships important to students? And can it be done without singling out particular groups of students as marginal, exotic, as "others" within a hegemonic culture?

We have to assume that pedagogy never begins on empty ground. A good starting point would be to consider popular culture as that terrain of images, knowledge forms, and affective investments which define the ground on which one's voice becomes possible within a pedagogical encounter (Giroux 1988). In stating this it is apparent that when we consider the relationship between popular culture and pedagogy, we have a particular form of teaching and learning in mind, the specifics of which we shall elaborate below. Rethinking the notion of the popular is a difficult and hazardous task. Briefly, we wish to share our sense of some of these difficulties.

Popular cultural practices display a wide variety of differences, differences in part organized by the struggles inherent in existing gender, class, racial, ethnic, age, and regional relations. As long as such differences are used to establish and maintain disadvantage and human suffering, we need in any discussion of pedagogy and popular culture to register the notion of difference clearly and loudly. Our preference, then, is to eliminate the singular and always speak about popular cultural *practices*. It is also important to stress that we view such practices as lived processes, as part of the way in which everyday life is experienced and responded to differently by different groups. However, there is a danger here of reducing particular students to simple reflections of some putative characteristics of group membership. This is a path of classism, sexism, and racism, Yet, it is equally objectionable to avoid consideration of the social construction and regulation of both knowledge and desire.

We think it is important to retheorize the term "mass culture" in any analysis of popular culture. The agenda is not to simply assert the existence of homogenization and domination of everyday life. We do not wish to conflate those forms which are mass-produced and distributed as products (toys, books, films, records, television programs) with popular culture. Of course, we are interested in those forms as they both offer and give shape to (but not mechanically impose) the practices which organize and regulate acceptable styles and images of social activity and individual and collective identity. However, we think it is a mistake to reduce the discussion of popular cultures to a discussion of products. If we want to sustain the notion of popular culture as a terrain of possibilities, not just of threat and profane desire, then we require other ways of conceptualizing the term. One alternative consistent with our emphasis on popular cultural practices is to consider commodities in their circuits of distribution, focusing on the commodity not as text but as event. This means considering both the structured occasion of engaging a commodity and the ways in which a product is employed or taken up (Radway 1984).

In making this suggestion we are stressing that popular cultures are constituted not just by commodity forms but by practices which reflect a creative and sometimes innovative capacity of people. Popular cultures may contain aspects of a collective imagination which make it possible for people to surpass received knowledge and tradition. In this sense, popular cultures may inform aspects of a counterdiscourse which help to organize struggles against relations of domination. As Tony Bennett has written:

> A cultural practice does not carry its politics with it, as if written upon its brow for ever and a day; rather, its political functioning depends on the network of social and ideological relations in which it is inscribed as a consequence of the ways in which, in a particular conjuncture, it is articulated to other practices. (1986 p. xvi)

This notion was recently illustrated for us in an essay written by a teacher participating in a master of education course on the relation of pedagogy and popular culture. In this paper she reflected on her fondness for the persona of Marilyn Monroe as expressed in both Monroe's films and public imagery (Rowe 1987). On the one hand, a given popular cultural practice — the event of watching Monroe's movies — may include narratives which implicate knowledge and pleasure in existing forms of domination (e.g. patriarchy). At the same time such forms can be an acknowledgment of the nondeterministic subjective side of social relations in which human beings are characterized by an ideal or imaginary life, where will is cultivated, dreams dreamt, and categories developed. Rowe illustrated how, for a young girl growing up amid the patriarchal relations of a traditional rural farm family, such forms can provide a type of counterdiscourse which is, in part, a promise of possibility.

Not to recognize this is to fail to understand that our material lives can never adequately reflect our imaginary lives and that it is imagination itself which fuels our desire and provides the energy to reject relations of domination and embrace the promise of possibility (Fitting 1987).

This view is not naively romantic. We cannot suppress those aspects of popular cultures that we may see as regressive; rather, we must face them for what they are and attempt to move beyond them. Fascism was and still is viable as a particular practice of popular culture. We must not forget there will always be a moral project associated with particular cultural practices, and we need to understand and assess the relation of such practices to the commitments we hold as educators and citizens. It is important to re-emphasize popular culture as a terrain of struggle infused with practices that are both pedagogical and political. Since consent has to be won for popular forms to be integrated into the dominant culture, popular culture is never free from the ideologies and practices of pedagogy. Similarly, popular forms have to be renegotiated and represented in order to appropriate them in the service of self- and social empowerment. This suggests a critical pedagogy disrupting the unity of popular culture in order to appropriate those elements which enable the voice of dissent while simultaneously challenging the lived experiences and social relations of domination and exploitation. Adam Mills and Phil Rice capture the complexity of these issues and are worth quoting at length:

> "[P]opular culture is always a threat": by always occupying the subordinate, illegitimate pole in the field of cultural relations the values embodied in the practices and representations there are antithetical to, what are by definition, the minority values of "elite" cultures. Of necessity those discourses and forms which originate in the dominant cultural institutions, as Stuart Hall suggests, must activate the "structural contradiction which arises whenever a dominant culture seeks to incorporate" and include, within its boundaries, the people. They must raise, in other words, even if it is only an attempt to neutralize, the spectre of oppression and subordination. That certain forms are popular must then require of analysis a recognition both of the means by which consent is won for those dominant discourses, and the way in which those discourses, by presenting themselves as popular, re-present yet con-nect with the lived practices and experience of subordinate social classes. This suggests that the popular is a site of political and ideological struggle, first and foremost over the formation of what is given as "popular," and beyond that over the formation of "the people." But more than this, it suggests that cultural forms can no longer be regarded as coherent, expressive unities, or even that popular forms are no more than one-dimensional commodities functioning as standardized and stupefying cultural narcotics for the masses. What is implied is that cultural forms comprise a contradictory and uneven balance of elements, both dominant and subordinate—those which connect with "popular" social life, and those dominant elements which attempt to close or constrain alternative meanings and which attempt to mute the voice of dissent. (1982: 24–25)

A pedagogy which engages popular culture in order to affirm rather than mute the voice of student is not without its difficulties. Michel Foucault, in the first volume of *The History of Sexuality*, comments on "the pleasure of analysis," the pleasure of discovering and exposing the secrets of human pleasure. The teacher engaged in a pedagogy which requires some articula-tion of knowledge forms and pleasures integral to students' daily life is walking a dangerous road. Too easily, perhaps, encouraging student voice can become a form of voyeurism or satisfy a form of ego-expansionism constituted on the pleasures of understanding those who appear as Other to us. This is why we must be clear on the nature of the pedagogy we pursue.

Popular culture and social difference can be taken up by educators either as a pleasurable form of knowledge/power which allows for more effective individualization and administration of forms of physical and moral regulation, or such practices can be understood as the terrain on which we meet our students in a pedagogical encounter informed by a project of possibility that enables rather than disables human imagination and capacities in the service of individual joy, collective prosperity, and social justice. Dick Hebdige (1982) warns us when he reports the words of a young member of a subculture he was studying: "You really hate an adult to understand you. That's the only thing you've got over them, the fact that you can mystify and worry them" (p. 167). Contemporary youths have cause to be wary of giving up their anonymity, they have reason to be concerned about making their private and lived voices the object of public and pedagogical scrutiny.

There is yet one more caution to raise. We think it important to question the notion of what it means to put popular cultural practices into play in the context of a pedagogical encounter. Does it mean to make such practices topical as curriculum content, to put such practices up for discussion? Would doing so not fundamentally change their character? Iain Chambers has written quite explicitly about this question, and his admonition should be pondered:

> High culture, with its cultivated tastes and formally imparted knowledge, calls for particular moments of concentration, separated out from the run of daily life. Popular culture, meanwhile, mobilizes the tactile, the incidental, the transitory, the visceral....It does not undertake an abstract aesthetic research amongst already privileged objects of cultural attention, but invokes mobile orders of sense, taste, and desire. Popular culture is not appropriated through the apparatus of contemplation but, as Walter Benjamin put it, through "distracted reception."...To attempt to explain fully...would be to pull back [popular culture] under the contemplative stare, to adopt the authority of the patronizing academic mind that seeks to explain an experience that is rarely his or hers. A role as Barthes has said that "makes every speaker a kind of policeman."...The vanity of such a presumed knowledge runs against the grain of the popular epistemology I have tried to suggest: an informal knowledge of the everyday, based on the sensory, the immediate, the concrete, the pleasurable. These are areas that formal knowledge and its culture continually repress. (1985: 5)

THE PRACTICE OF CRITICAL PEDAGOGY

The issue is: How does one make popular culture an object of pedagogical analysis without undermining its privileged appropriation as a form of resistance? How can popular culture become part of a critical pedagogy that does not ultimately function to police its content and forms?

A pedagogy which takes popular culture as an object of study must recognize that all educational work is at root contextual and conditional. Such a pedagogy can only be discussed from within a particular point of practice, from within a specific time and place and from within a particular theme. This points to a larger issue concerning the nature of critical pedagogy itself: doing critical pedagogy is a strategic, practical task, not a scientific one. It arises not against a background of psychological, sociological, or anthropological universals (as does much educational theory related to pedagogy), but from such questions such as: How is human possibility being diminished here?

We are deliberately offering an expanded and politicized notion of pedagogy, one that recognizes its place in multiple forms of cultural production, not just in those sites which have come to be labeled "schools." Any practice which intentionally tries to influence the production of meaning is a pedagogical practice. This includes aspects of parenting, filmmaking, theological work, social work, architecture, law, health care, and advertising. These are all forms of cultural work. There are possibilities for pedagogy in any site: schools, families, churches, community associations, labor organizations, businesses, local media. All work in such sites must begin with naming and problematizing the social relations, experiences, and ideologies constructed through popular forms that directly operate within such sites, as well as those that emerge elsewhere but exercise an influence on those who work within them. Similarly, all work in such sites has important connections as a form of political activity, and a good part of the political work of pedagogy includes the articulation of practices not only within sites but also across them. Indeed, one of our long-term tasks as educators must be to define a framework that is helpful in articulating what critical pedagogies would be possible in a variety of sites of cultural work. This point is essential. The practical efficacy of our own commitment rests with the possibility of constructing an alliance of different forms of cultural work within a project of possibility.

In what follows we want to bring our discussion to bear more directly on classroom reality by presenting a list of problems raised by students and a diverse group of educators (elementary and secondary school teachers, university professors, literacy workers, health care professionals, artists, and writers) in the process of sharing their own cultural work as well as their readings of various articles and books. In many ways, the questions and the issues they raise make clear that the journey from theory to pedagogical possibility is rarely easy or straightforward. At the same time, these problems suggest new and alternative directions for pedagogy as a form of cultural politics supportive of a project of hope and possibility. Such problems are symptomatic of the fact that a critical pedagogy is never finished; its conditions of existence and possibility always remain in flux as part of its attempt to address that which is not yet, that which is still possible and worth fighting for.

CURRICULUM PRACTICE

Of course, a critical pedagogy would be sensitive to forms of curriculum materials that might be implicated in the reproduction of existing unjust and inequitable social relations (e.g. sexism, racism, classism, heterosexism). But just what does this sensitivity imply? Does it lead to a legitimate form of censorship of material? The other side of censorship is the exclusionary choice we all make as to what set of materials we will use in our teaching during any particular period of time. What forms of authority can be invoked to make such choices? How should we make such choices? Can we employ reactionary material in the service of a progressive pedagogy? If one argues that we should include materials that, although reactionary, are integral to the dominant mythos of the community and hence ripe for critical analysis, in what ways would the material chosen for use be similar or different in the southern United States, the northern United States, in English Canada, in French Canada, in England, in Australia? What balance and integration should be given to the interrogation of global and regional social cultural forms?

Critical pedagogy always strives to incorporate student experience as official curriculum content. While articulating such experience can be both empowering and a form of critique against relations that silence, such experience is not an unproblematic form of knowledge. How can one avoid the conservatism inherent in simply celebrating personal experience and confirming what people already know? In other words, how can we acknowledge previous experience as legitimate content and challenge it at the same time (Giroux 1988)? How do we affirm student voices while simultaneously encouraging the interrogation of such voices (Giroux 1986).

Popular memories and "subjugated knowledges" (Foucault 1980a) are often discussed as useful forms of critique of dominant ideologies. How can one draw on such knowledges in one's pedagogy (Giroux 1988)? Since, as we have suggested earlier, this means working with the knowledge embedded in the forms of sociality, communities of discourse, and popular forms students invest with meaning, what should be done to avoid making students who live outside of dominant and ruling forms feel that they are being singled out as the marginal Other when we take seriously the knowledge organized within the terms of their lives? Furthermore, how do we confront forms of resistance by students to what they perceive as an invasion by the official discourse of the school into private and nonschool areas of their lives?

Cultural Politics, Social Differences, and Practice

In planning and enacting a pedagogy whose central purpose is directed toward enhancing human possibility and the establishment of a just and caring community, how do we know what we are doing is ethically and politically right? How can we keep from slipping from a vision of human possibility into a totalizing dogma?

Many teachers want to help students identify, comprehend, and produce useful knowledge, but what constitutes useful knowledge? Is it the same for all students no matter what their gender, class, race, ethnicity, age, or geographic region? If not, then how can we cope intellectually, emotionally, and practically with such diversity and social difference? What if our view of useful knowledge differs from what students and their families think? What should happen to our teacher's vision of education? How far does one go in doing critical pedagogy if people are not interested in our agenda or see it as suppressing theirs? Do democratic forms of curriculum making ensure a critical pedagogy?

What can or should we know about the basis of the interest or noninterest of students to the topics and materials of our pedagogy? How can such knowledge make a difference to our practice? What would it mean to understand ignorance as a dynamic repression of information (Simon 1984)? Is there a form of ignorance that is produced as a defense against hopelessness?

What does it mean to work with students in different class, race and gender positions with regard to privilege? Why would those whose interests are served through forms of oppression want to change the situation? Is the structural conflict implied by the previous question inevitable in our present society? Are there not issues and values that could mobilize broad interest in social transformation (e.g., ecology, peace, health)?

Guarding Against Hopelessness

Sometimes, when students and teachers engage in a critique of existing social practices or forms of knowledge, a feeling of powerlessness comes over the group. Doing critical pedagogy can turn an educational setting into a council of despair. How can we guard against the production of hopelessness when taking up an agenda of critique and social analysis? Given all the limitations of teaching and schooling, how can we effectively empower people (Aronowitz and Giroux 1985; Simon 1987; McLaren 1986)?

Working with students to make clear the social contradictions we all live is an important aspect of critical pedagogical practice (Simon 1984). However, will not raising contradictions in student's lives simply threaten them (Williamson 1981–1982)? Will not pointing to social contradictions lead to cynicism and despair? Furthermore, if the value of understanding ideology is to stress that what is often taken as natural and inevitable is historically constructed and morally regulated, will not ideology critique destabilize identity and paralyze action? If we start questioning the givens of everyday life, won't this simply be overwhelming?

The Work of Teaching

How can we understand the constraining effects of the administrative and economic contexts within which we work? How should one take into account the realities of state regulation and the limitations imposed by a corporate economy? Should these always be seen as limits?

For those of us who work within public education, why should a teacher act in a way that might be contrary to school board policy or directive? When would a teacher be justified in doing so? What would be the consequences? Should teachers be accountable to specific groups or an organized public sphere? In practice, how would/should this be done?

Given that critical pedagogy requires a substantial personal investment of time and energy, does it also require the near abandonment of a teacher's private life? How can one cope with the moments of depression and emotional disruption that come from a continual concern with the extent of injustice and violence in the world? How can we develop forms of collegial association that might support our efforts?

CONCLUSION

These questions should not suggest that they they have not been addressed either historically or in contemporary forms of social and educational theory. In fact, much of our own work has developed in response to many of the issues and questions we have presented above. What we want to re-emphasize is the openness and specificity, as well as the politics and ethics, at work in constantly reconstructing and addressing similar questions that emerge at different times from diverse voices under widely differing educational contexts. The notion of critical pedagogy begins with a degree of indignation, a vision of possibility, and an uncertainty; it demands that we constantly rethink and renew the work we have done as part of a wider theory of schooling as a form of cultural politics. Defining the connections between popular culture and critical pedagogy is only one part of this ongoing task, and our introductory comments on this issue have attempted to sketch our view of the work that lies ahead. We believe that the chapters in this book have contributed to this effort. We will have been successful if we have stimulated the search for new ways of thinking about the notion of popular culture and specifying its relation to a pedagogy of possibility.

NOTE

A version of this chapter first appeared in the *Journal of Education* 170(1): 9–26.

REFERENCES

Aronowitz, Stanley, and Henry A. Giroux
   (1985)   *Education Under Seige*. South Hadley, Mass.: Bergin & Garvey.
Bennett, Tony
   (1986)   "Popular Culture and the Turn to Gramsci." In Bennett, Mercer, and

Woolacott, eds. *Popular Cultural and Social Relations* London: Open University Press.

Bloom, Allan
(1987)   *The Closing of the American Mind.* New York: Simon & Schuster.

Chambers, Iain
(1985)   "Popular Culture, Popular Knowledge." *One Two Three Four: A Rock and Roll Quarterly* 1–8.

Clifford, James
(1981)   "On Ethnographic Surrealism." *Comparative Studies in Society and History*, No. 18: 539–64.

Clifford, James, and George E. Marcus, eds.
(1986)   *Writing Culture: The Poetics and Politics of Ethnography.* Berkeley: University of California Press.

Corrigan, Philip
(1987)   "In/Forming Schooling." In David W. Livingstone, ed. *Critical Pedagogy and Cultural Power.* South Hadley, Mass.: Bergin & Garvey.

Fitting, Peter
(1987)   "The Decline of the Feminist Utopian Novel." *Border/Lines*, No. 7/8 (Spring-Summer): 17–19.

Foucault, Michel
(1980a)   "Two Lectures." In *Knowledge/Power.* Colin Gordon, trans. New York: Pantheon.
(1980b)   *History of Sexuality.* vol. 1. *An Introduction.* New York: Vintage.

Giroux, Henry A.
(1988)   *Schooling and the Struggle for Public Life.* Minneapolis: University of Minnesota Press.

Grossberg, Lawrence
(1986)   "Teaching the Popular." In Cary Nelson, ed. *Theory in the Classroom.* Urbana: University of Illinois Press.

Hall, Stuart
(1981)   "Notes on Deconstructing 'the Popular'." In Raphael Samuel, ed. *People's History and Socialist Theory.* London: Routledge & Kegan Paul.

Hebdige, Richard
(1979)   *Subculture: The Meaning of Style.* New York: Methuen.

Lewis, Magda, and Roger I. Simon.
(1986)   "A Discourse Not Intended for Her: Learning and Teaching Within Patriarchy." *Harvard Educational Review* 56 (4):457–72.

Lowy, Michael
(1976)   "Interview with Ernst Bloch." *New German Critique* 9 (Fall): 48–69.

Lusted, David
(1986)   "Introduction: Why Pedagogy?" *Screen* 27 (5): 2–14.

McLaren, Peter
(1989)   *Life in Schools.* New York: Longman.
(1986)   *Schooling as a Ritual Performance: Toward a Political Economy of Educational Symbols and Gestures.* New York: Routledge & Kegan Paul.

Mills, Adam, and Phil Rice
(1982)   "Quizzing the Popular," *Screen Education* No. 41 (Winter/Spring): 15–25.

Morgan, Robert
  (1987)   "English Studies as Cultural Production in Ontario, 1860–1920." Ph.D.
            diss. Ontario Institute for Studies in Education.

Radway, Janice
  (1984)   *Reading the Romance: Women, Patriarchy, and Popular Literature.*
            Chapel Hill: University of North Carolina Press.

Rockhill, Kathleen
  (1987)   "Literacy as Threat/Desire: Longing to be Somebody." Unpublished
            paper, Ontario Institute for Studies in Education.

Rowe, Ella
  (1987)   "Desire and Popular Culture: The Ego Ideal and Its Influence in the
            Production of Subjectivity." Unpublished paper, Ontario Institute for
            Studies in Education.

Ryerson, Egerton
  (1870)   "The General Absence of Good Breeding." *The Hamilton Spectator* 29:
            53.
  (1868)   "Summary of a Speech at the Ontario Literary Society." (Ontario,
            Canada) *Journal of Education* 21: 72.

Sartre, Jean-Paul
  (1963)   *Search for a Method.* New York: Knopf.

Simon, Roger I.
  (1987)   "Empowerment as a Pedagogy of Possibility." *Language Arts* 64
            (4):370–81.
  (1984)   "Signposts for a Critical Pedagogy: A Review of Henry A. Giroux's
            Theory and Resistance in Education." *Educational Theory* 34 (4):
            379–88.

Williamson, Judith
  (1981–82) "How Does Girl Number 20 Understand Ideology?" *Screen Education*
            No. 40 (Autumn/Winter): 80–87.

CONTRIBUTORS

Stanley Aronowitz is Professor of Sociology in the Graduate School, City University of New York. His books include *False Promises, Working Class Hero, Education Under Siege* (with Henry Giroux), and *Science as Power.*

R. W. Connell is Professor of Sociology at Macquarie University, Australia. His books include *Teacher's Work, Gender & Power: Society, the Person and Sexual Politics*, and *Staking A Claim: Feminism, Bureaucracy, and the State* (forthcoming).

Philip Corrigan is a professor in the Department of Sociology of Education at the Ontario Institute for Studies in Education. His most recent book is *The Great Arch: English State Formation as Cultural Revolution.*

Elizabeth Ellsworth is an assistant professor in the Departments of Curriculum and Instruction and Women's Studies, University of Wisconsin-Madison. She is one of the co-authors of *Becoming Feminine: The Politics of Popular Culture.*

Henry A. Giroux is Professor of Education and Renowned Scholar-in-Residence at Miami University, Ohio. His books include *Ideology, Culture and the Process of Schooling, Theory and Resistance in Education, Education Under Siege* (with Stanley Aronowitz), *Teachers as Intellectuals*, and *Schooling and the Struggle for Public Life.*

Lawrence Grossberg is an associate professor at the University of Illinois at Urbana-Champaign, with appointments in Speech Communication, Communications Research, and the Unit for Criticism and Interpretive Theory. He is the co-editor of *Marxism and the Interpretation of Culture.*

Peter McLaren is an associate professor in the School of Education and Allied Professions at Miami University, Ohio. He is the author of *Cries from the Corridor, Schooling as a Ritual Performance*, and *Life in Schools.*

Roger I. Simon is an associate professor in the Department of Curriculum at the Ontario Institute for Studies in Education. His major professional interests include teaching, research, and curriculum writing in the areas of critical pedagogy and cultural studies. His forthcoming book in *Teaching Against the Grain.*

Paul Smith earned a Ph.D. from the University of Kent at Canterbury (1981) and now teaches in the Literary and Cultural Studies Program at Carnegie Mellon University. He is the author of *Pound Revised* and *Discerning the Subject* and editor, with Alice Jardine, of *Men in Feminism.*

Richard Smith is Professor and Head of the Department of Social and Cultural Studies in Education, Majes Cook University, Townsville, Queensland, Australia. He has numerous publications in the areas of cultural studies, the sociology of education, and critical pedagogy.

Mimi White is an associate professor in the Department of Radio/Television/Film at Northwestern University. She writes extensively in the field of popular culture and cultural studies.

Paul Willis is currently a Visiting Professor at Wolverhampton Polytechnic, England, and is a freelance writer and researcher on youth and culture. His published books include *Profane Culture, Learning to Labor*, and *The Youth Review.*

INDEX